Came Men on Horses

Came Men on Horses

The Conquistador Expeditions of
Francisco Vázquez de Coronado and Don Juan de Oñate

Stan Hoig

UNIVERSITY PRESS OF COLORADO
Boulder

© 2013 by University Press of Colorado

Published by University Press of Colorado
5589 Arapahoe Avenue, Suite 206C
Boulder, Colorado 80303

 The University Press of Colorado is a proud member of
the Association of American University Presses.

The University Press of Colorado is a cooperative publishing enterprise supported, in part,
by Adams State University, Colorado State University, Fort Lewis College, Metropolitan
State University of Denver, Regis University, University of Colorado, University of Northern
Colorado, Utah State University, and Western State Colorado University.

∞ This paper meets the requirements of the ANSI/NISO Z39.48-1992 (Permanence of Paper).

Library of Congress Cataloging-in-Publication Data

Hoig, Stan.
  Came men on horses : the conquistador expeditions of Francisco Vázquez de Coronado and
Don Juan de Oñate / Stan Hoig.
    p. cm.
  Includes bibliographical references and index.
  ISBN 978-1-60732-194-1 (hardcover : alk. paper) — ISBN 978-1-60732-206-1 (ebook)
  1. Coronado, Francisco Vásquez de, 1510–1554. 2. Oñate, Juan de, 1549?–1624 3. Southwest,
New—Discovery and exploration—Spanish. 4. Southwest, New—History—To 1848. I. Title.
  E125.V3H65 2012
  979'.010922—dc23
                                    2012033613

Design by Daniel Pratt

22   21   20   19   18   17   16   15   14   13   10 9 8 7 6 5 4 3 2 1

Contents

CONTENTS

Illustrations

Preface

As do most historical studies, this work stands on the shoulders of many people: event participants, witnesses, historians, and writers, past and current. Most significant, of course, are those Spaniards who during the Era of the Conquistador wrote, reported, or testified about their experiences. I have taken their words as though they were spoken directly to and for us today, rejecting any notion that they hold any less value because of their antiquity. At the same time, however, I have considered any potential contamination of their truth stemming from societal or personal attitudes of the ages.

Yet it is important to be clear. While the heroic efforts of the conquistador in his discovery of the American world are fully appreciated, the actions and events dealt with here are measured by today's moral standards that accept and appreciate the humanity of America's native occupants.

We are most fortunate that Spain was such a highly literate nation as to amass a quantity and quality of written record that gives testimony to the conquistador. But no study of the Spanish conquistador can be other than humbly grateful to those modern scholars who have gone to archives in the United States, Mexico, Spain, and elsewhere to read the difficult, quill-produced cursive of the many Spanish documents, translate them into English, annotate them, and have them published for others to study and make use of.

Among those who have rendered valuable translations and narratives are George Parker Winship with *The Coronado Expedition, 1540–1542* (1964) and George P. Hammond and Agapito Rey with *Narratives of the Coronado Expedition, 1540–1542* (1940), as well as *Don Juan de Oñate, Colonizer of New Mexico, 1595–1608* (1953). These works provide both the original Spanish documents and their translations into English. Though the narratives that accompany these translations are outdated in some respects, these sources were important in the preparation of this book.

History of Central America by Hubert Howe Bancroft and *Coronado, Knight of Pueblos and Plains* by Herbert E. Bolton helped awaken American readers to the day of the conquistador and his role in the history of the United States, Mexico, and North America in general. These sources provided a primary introduction to this study of the two conquistador expeditions.

The prodigious scholarly production *Documents of the Coronado Expedition, 1539–1542* (2005), edited, translated, and annotated by Richard and Shirley Cushing Flint, however, was chosen over previous Coronado translations in the main. This work extensively updates the earlier studies and contains valuable documents and notes not found otherwise.

I have, however, provided citation references for all three of the major Coronado translations listed here where possible. There are variations of interpretation among the three, and at times the innuendos of meaning can be significant in determining precisely what the Spanish author actually wished to convey.

The debt this book owes to these studies makes it seem particularly less than grateful to argue with historical conclusions made by those translators and authors. The privilege of my doing so, however, is an inherent value of their scholarly efforts and an absolute necessity in sorting out the truth of history. Still, I bow respectfully not only to their invaluable work but to their intellectual thought as well.

PREFACE

I express my thanks to Paula Aguilar, Teresa Neely, and Nancy Brown-Martinez of the Center for Southwest Research at the University of New Mexico for their research assistance. And once again I must give great credit and extend sincere appreciation to my wife, Pat Corbell Hoig, whose reading, editing, and consultation contributed much to this book.

STAN HOIG, PhD

Came Men on Horses

Introduction

For Riches Yet Unfound

There might still be large treasures which the Aztecs had hidden to spite their foes . . . The search continued: houses were again ransacked, gardens upturned, cellars and passages examined, and graves were opened and the lake was dragged.

Bancroft[1]

It may seem curious to debate the question of what brought the Spanish conquistador to North America. Those who have read early accounts of the conquistador would likely answer the question in a single word—"gold." Authoritative studies such as *Rivers of Gold* (2003), by the accomplished British scholar Hugh Thomas, provide solid evidence of the impetus gold gave to Spanish exploration from the famous first voyage of Columbus forward.

Other reputable historians today dispute this, however. They charge that historians and popular writers of the past have wrongly portrayed the conquistadors as so single-minded in their search for gold as to be "lustful." As an example, they point to the way journalist Paul Wellman described the conquistadors in his 1954 book *Glory, God, and Gold*. "Every Spaniard," Wellman wrote, "would plunge his arms elbow-deep in gold ingots before he returned."[2]

Wellman's description was an improbable exaggeration designed to emphasize a point and was not intended to be taken as a literal fact. Indeed, it may be difficult to prove that conquistador leaders or their expedition members were inordinately "lustful" in their search for gold. It is also difficult to prove that they weren't.

Hernando Cortés, the most prominent of the conquistadors—who knew if anyone did—once spoke about the matter to the Aztec leader Montezuma. "The Spaniards," Cortés confessed, employing his own improbable exaggeration, "had a disease of the heart that only gold could cure."[3] Bartolomé de las Casas, the censorious Catholic clergyman, declared more directly: "Their [the conquistadors'] whole end was to acquire gold and riches in the shortest time so that they might rise to lofty positions out of all proportion to their wealth."[4] "For Spaniards," current historian David J. Weber concurs, "the accumulation of gold and silver was not merely a means to an end, but an end in itself."[5]

All of the European nations in the sixteenth century, in fact, were desperate for gold. Spanish author Jean Descola addressed this matter: "Europe lacked gold. What was looted from Turkish coffers, the few nuggets brought back from Africa by Portuguese explorers, and the melting down of gold plate had increased the reserves of metal very little . . . Localized for a long time to the land routes of Oriental caravans and the sea routes along the African coasts, the battle for gold was soon to spread to the Dark Sea. Where could gold be found, indeed, if not in the Indies?"[6] It is entirely true, however, that past literature in America was prone to emphasize the conquistadors' desire to find gold to the exclusion of other significant goals. Earlier scholars and writers had good cause to be one-sided on this issue, given the enormous witness by sixteenth-century literature and art to the extent the early conquistadors would go to obtain gold.

The essential fact is that obtaining gold abetted all other ambitions of Spanish conquest. In many instances, and this was true of both Coronado and Oñate, gold was not the ultimate objective of a conquistador expedition. The hope of finding it, however, was the principal avenue of achieving other objectives. But on a personal level, there can be little doubt that such hope excited the passions of those who enlisted in conquistador expeditions.

Further, what is missing from this argument over the importance of gold is recognition of the difference between the first generation of conquistadors that flourished during the early sixteenth century and the ensuing second- and third-generation conquistadors such as Coronado and Oñate. In *No Settlement, No Conquest,* Richard Flint lists 132 major Spanish-led expeditions.[7] The Conquistador Period lasted essentially from Columbus in 1492 past Oñate in 1598, providing more than a full century in which generations, and world conditions with them, changed.

These first expeditions embarked from Europe largely to explore, discover, and conquer land and seek gold but not principally to colonize or Christianize. In the main, the head conquistadors were out to find wealth and conquer territory for Spain and to gain fame and position for themselves, and they suffered little restraint from the state or the church as to how they got them. In addition to discovering an entirely new land mass on the earth that humankind knew, through his exploitations Columbus also excited the European world to the potency of a new land rich with gold.

While Spanish conquistadors of ensuing generations were likewise contaminated by exotic myths of lost riches, their missions were conducted largely as colonizing efforts. Discovered wealth was essential to that purpose. Well-positioned members looked to obtain grants for estates among the Indians (called *encomiendas*), while others hoped to improve their fortunes in the new colony through their occupational skills and trades. At the same time, they, too, fantasized about finding "lost cities of gold."

The earlier conquistadors had gained a wide reputation for cruelty and brutality that had been labeled the "black legend." In April 1549, following a vigorous debate regarding Spanish morality between las Casas and Spanish humanist Juan Ginés de Sepúlveda, the king mandated a new set of rules for conquistador expeditions.[8]

By edict, conquistadors were to act more humanely than their predecessors had toward American natives. Such edicts, however, were far removed from the fields of contest in the Americas. The later expeditions did improve some on past conquistador behavior toward native people, but both the Coronado and Oñate Expeditions featured their own excesses.

Other factors, of course, motivated all of the conquistadors. Columbus's discovery of America had opened great vistas of curiosity that were irresistible to adventurous men. A mysterious New World of unlimited wonders and potentially unlimited wealth awaited discovery and exploitation. Spaniards of both generations were similarly affected. Most of them nourished a fierce zeal to serve the Spanish Crown and to advance its empire and, yes, Christianity but also to advance the world presence of the Catholic Church through the process of discovery, conquest, and colonization.

The answer, therefore, to the question of what brought the conquistadors to America—and to North America in particular—was a mixture of motives. But evidence clearly indicates that, for the most part, conquistadors chose gold and empire over godly pursuits.

In 2003 Penn State professor Matthew Restall published his revealing *Seven Myths of the Spanish Conquest* regarding misconceptions of the historical image of the Spanish conquistadors. The erroneous views he points to are those that evolved from early literary accounts in both formal histories and popular writings. They can rightly be classed as "literary myths." In contrast, myths referred to in this study are those of Old World origin that came from Europe to America, as well as those generated by Indians in the New World to act upon the conquistador period of discovery. Here they will be called "gossip myths."

Restall appropriately reveals several erroneous views of the conquistador that have developed over time in today's United States: the misleading view that expeditions were sponsored and soldiered by the state, the false mystique regarding the conquistador leaders' exceptional military experience and ability, and the validity of the Spanish "requirement" for Indian submission. On one point, however, Restall stands to be challenged. In making his argument regarding the role of gold in conquistador quests, he cites the instance of Francisco Pizarro in Peru: "The 'most important thing' to Pizarro was not gold, but the governorship [of Peru]. However, he needed to find gold in order for there to be a governorship worth having. *Put in the larger context, Spaniards had no interest at all in the metal per se*, any more than we treasure credit cards as objects" (emphasis added).[9]

Because the Spanish hunger for gold is so blatantly clear, both in official Spanish records and in literature of the day, the conclusion drawn in this statement requires further consideration. During the sixteenth century, as it had been for the Roman Empire and others before, gold was a dominating concern of kings and queens (e.g., Isabella of Spain), as well as of the men they sent afar to search out the New World. It was a craving that infested the European world. The day of the Spanish conquistador featured a predominant mind-set on gold, even as American society today is fixated on sex or automobiles.[10]

Throughout world history, gold has been the base value item upon which empires were built and by which nations functioned. Indeed, gold may have served the purpose of obtaining the governorship for Pizarro, but that was not its sole attribute. To most people of that day, gold held much of the intrinsic quality of jewels. The metal, precious in the arena of trade, gleamed and sparkled, and it could be used to adorn other things. Significantly, its presence gave off the aura of wealth and social distinction.

From the advent of early civilizations, the metal has been coveted not only for trade purposes but also for its inherent beauty as adornment, whether for household dressings; armament such as helmets, sword hilts, and spurs; the trappings of horse gear; or other objects where the glittering metal added a special allure and beauty. Gold not only "held" wealth; it "symbolized" such.

It is not by happenstance, therefore, that gold was the ultimate promise of many myths. By the time the Spanish began exploring the New World, the desire for gold, inflamed by the ultimate promise of mythical lost cities where gold abounded freely, was a foremost impulse of adventurous men.

In the main, Restall's statement makes the same error in reverse that earlier historians committed in disregarding other motives for wanting gold. It is equally fallacious to deny gold in favor of other conquistador motivations.

Spaniards of the sixteenth century were heirs to a heroic generation that had just driven the Islamic Moors from Spain. Their great victory at Granada came in 1492, the same year Columbus discovered America. Inspired Spaniards set forth with national and religious fervor to explore and conquer the New World. For them, and for the generation that followed, the call of Spanish heraldry was a potent force that impelled men forth to seek *hidalgo*, *caballero*, or even *adelantado* (governorship) status and position.

It was a general assumption that conquistador parties would conduct military conquests of Indian settlements and confiscate any accumulated wealth they might find. But conquistador ventures were not state-supported, with either money or soldiers. As privately financed ventures, conquistador expeditions required the recruitment of members. Men to win the conquest and others to colonize with their women or entire families were enticed to enlist in expeditions largely through the promise of sharing in the rewards.

Once a settlement was subdued, a system known as the *encomienda* (or *repartimento*) grant (a grant of authority) was instituted. Under this mandate, certain Spaniards of position were given the right to lord over a community of native people. The *encomendero* could then demand of the natives "tributes" in terms of labor or material wealth. In turn, the Spanish overlord was required to provide military protection for his charges and see to their indoctrination in the Christian religion by friars of the Catholic Church.

The practice of *encomienda*, which had been brought to the New World by Columbus, fit well with the purposes of both the Crown and the church. Though certain aspects were different, the *encomienda* functioned much the same as the American plantation in keeping a body of people in servitude to the financial advantage of an overlord and a dominant race at large. The system, which for many years featured abject slavery, served the cause of Spanish colonization well, with little cost to the Crown.

While *encomiendas* promised the reward of tributes, they were only one way expeditionary rewards were won. The first and most enticing reward was the discovery prize. Under Spanish law, it was fixed that when discoveries of great wealth occurred, as with Cortés in Mexico and Pizarro in Peru, the discovering party would reap four-fifths of the prize and the state one-fifth.[11]

Discovery prizes had to be divided among the conquistador party. Sometimes this was done on a service basis, such as rewarding the horsemen more than the footmen in the expedition. Generally, the expedition commander chose whatever method pleased him—which was whatever he could get away with. There was no official rule for dividing the four-fifths of the looted prize among a conquistador party. It was achieved by various methods, including status of rank. The conquistador leader and his principal lieutenants always took their share first.[12]

Cortés had recruited his Spanish fighting men on the promise of potential reward once victory was achieved. Assembling his force to make the divide, he first put aside the government's royal fifth and gave another fifth to himself as captain general. He then set apart other large sums to cover costs of his fleet, for personnel horses killed during his conquest, and to reward the *procuradores* in Spain. After all this he gave special shares to the priests who had accompanied his army, to his captains, and to archers and men with firearms and crossbows. The lesser rank-and-file members of his expedition received far smaller shares. When his looted treasures ran out, Cortés turned to *encomiendas* as a way of rewarding followers.[13]

Certain expedition members' hope to obtain *encomiendas* did not preclude the pervasive hope of everyone on a given expedition to find the lost treasures repeatedly promised by prevailing myths. *Encomiendas* and gold were not mutually exclusive goals. Sometimes they were so interrelated, in fact, that it becomes difficult to determine which was primary and which was secondary. Coronado scholar Richard Flint speaks to this essential relationship in *Great Cruelties Have Been Reported*: "The ultimate aim of most members of the [Coronado] expedition was enrichment from precious metals. They were expecting, however, that those precious metals would already be exploited by a sophisticated native population. Tribute and encomienda were the means the expedition had for tapping into that expected wealth."[14] From this, the question arises: was taking forced tributes from impoverished natives through the *encomienda* any less "lustful" than looting the coffers of a tribal sachem?

Throughout history, the much desired yellow metal has been a prime medium of exchange, an exalted symbol of material value by which other wants of life can be obtained. At times it became even more, a mind- and soul-consuming craving in itself. Such historic moments include the gold rushes to California in 1849, to Colorado in 1859, and to Alaska in 1898—all of which are known instances in which the desire to find gold mounted to the level of mass obsession. Why should we think that the conquistadors, having often heard the exalted tales—both fictional-based and real—of golden treasures in the New World, were an exception to such human compulsions? Evidence of an impelling desire specifically to find golden wealth is replete throughout the records of Spanish conquest.

Both Coronado and Oñate were men of wealth even before they set forth on their quests, and both saw the achievement of conquistador status as a steppingstone to a governorship in Nueva Mexico. But, as with Pizarro, finding new wealth was an absolute necessity for maintaining a new Spanish province. The immediate hope was to find that wealth pre-accumulated by some Indian leader. But if not, there was always the potential of gathering it, as in the Indies, through gold or silver from mines worked by Indian labor.

Flint observes that "the Coronado expedition was decidedly not a prospecting and mining endeavor."[15] Expedition members, he notes, took with them very little of the equipment or tools required to mine, conduct assays, or work gold. Expedition members' mining experience was scarce or nonexistent. Many were artisans of various practices, and others had no interest whatever in digging for metals or gems. But still, this does not say that they had no passion for discovering a fabulous booty of gold as promised by the prevailing myth of lost cities of gold.

The Oñate Expedition, on the other hand, did look to mining prospects if the need arose. Juan de Oñate y Salazar and the Zaldívar brothers, Juan and Vicente, who were officers in his expedition, had long operated silver mines in Mexico prior to marching north. Records of Oñate's expedition reveal that its baggage included mining and assay needs such as quicksilver.[16] Members of the expedition, however, marched north with exalted dreams of discovering great stores of wealth already accumulated, as in Mexico City and Peru. They, too, looked with great hopes to the mythical promise of Quivira.

Nothing better illustrates the Coronado Expedition's fervor to find gold than the instance of Bigotes, the friendly and helpful Cicuye (Pecos Pueblo) warrior who was held in captivity. He was dragged about in an iron collar and suffered having dogs set on him while manacled, all because Coronado and his captain, Hernando de Alvarado, suspected (almost surely erroneously) that Bigotes possessed a gold bracelet.[17]

The two men were fully determined—no matter the moral cost—to do anything to anyone to obtain the bracelet. Whether they had in mind the reward of *encomiendas* or of a potential city of gold is anybody's guess, but both spoke to the same intense purpose of obtaining great wealth.

The Indian slave Jusepe told Juan de Oñate that the fugitive expeditionary captains Francisco Leyva de Bonilla and Antonio Gutiérrez de Humaña had been "lured forth by extravagant tales [myths] of gold which abounded in the many towns in those regions [of northern Mexico]."[18]

In his *History of New Mexico*, essentially a personal account of the Oñate Expedition, Captain Gaspar de Villagrá, a prominent member of the expedition, wrote of the exasperation that existed when they did not find riches. "Because they did not stumble over bars of gold and silver immediately," Villagrá observed scornfully of the colonists, "they cursed the barren land and cried out bitterly against those who had led them into such a wilderness."[19] This testimony to the Spaniards' passion to find riches in the Americas—even six decades after Coronado—was again expressed by Rodrigo del Rio de Losa, Knight of the Order of Santiago and former governor of Nueva Galicia, who wrote in 1602, "We may well believe that there are people [in Tierra Nueva] who bear a metal crown like our kings, there are walled houses of five, six, or seven storeys [*sic*] and silver and gold as in other lands and in the Indies. For the greed of these riches, we Spaniards came to these parts, which is the main bait that attracts us here."[20]

The Coronado and Oñate Expeditions from deep in present Mexico to the American Southwest were elaborate *entradas* (excursions) from Spanish-controlled New Spain (Nueva España as of 1518) to Tierra Nueva (North America), the wilderness lands to the north. The first was conducted by Francisco Vázquez de Coronado in 1541 and the second sixty years later by Don Juan de Oñate in 1601.

Though neither expedition discovered a golden city, these ventures from Mexico and their expeditionary searches in New Mexico, to the West Coast, and eastward onto the Central Plains awakened recorded history of the southwestern United States as it existed prior to European influence. The two expeditions are at the very beginning of our national experience.

Interestingly, the "grand reward" of the golden myth was always just beyond reach. If not found on one of the Antilles Islands, then perhaps on the America mainland; if not in the Brazilian jungle or the mountains of northwest Mexico, then at Cibola; if not at Cibola, then at Quivira. But even when no city of gold was found on the plains of Kansas, some members of the Coronado and Oñate Expeditions felt they had simply not searched far enough. Surely they would find gold, some thought, if only they would push on to Harahey or Enchuche.

ABBREVIATION KEY

H/R-*DJO* = Hammond and Rey, eds., *Don Juan de Oñate*

NOTES

1. Bancroft, *History of Mexico* 2: 2, 4.

2. Wellman, *Glory, God, and Gold*, 18.

3. Weber, *Spanish Frontier*, 23; Flint, *No Settlement, No Conquest*, 36–38.

4. Bartolomé de las Casas, *Brevísima relación de las destrucción de las Indias* (abridged edition of the *Biblioteca encyclopédica popular*, 77 [Madrid: Fundación Universitaria Española, 1977]), paragraph 16; cited in Leonard, *Books of the Brave*, 1.

5. Weber, *Spanish Frontier*, 23.

6. Descola, *Les Conquistadors*, 10.

7. Flint, *No Settlement, No Conquest*, 261–266.

8. Hemming, *The Search for El Dorado*, 138–139.

9. Restall, *Seven Myths of the Spanish Conquest*, 22. Richard Flint concludes as well that: "*The [Coronado] expedition was not in a literal* [i.e., actual or real] *sense looking for gold*" (emphasis added). Flint, "What They Never Told You," *Kiva: The Journal of Southwestern Archaeology and History* 71, no. 2 (Winter 2005): 204; Flint, *No Settlement, No Conquest*, xv.

10. Though seldom mentioned by historians, the pleasures of native women also ranked high as a prize of conquistador conquest. But gold and other treasure was often the prize that inspired expedition members.

11. Cortés's royal four-fifths was described as consisting of 32,400 and odd *pesos de oro*, or melted gold; 100,000 ducas' worth of unbroken jewels, feathers, and similar items; and 1,000 or more *marcos* of silver. Bancroft, *History of Mexico* 1: 343n31.

12. Ibid., 343. Many of the jewels and much of the gold, including that belonging to the king, were lost during the Spaniards' desperate retreat from Mexico City in June 1520. Some of Cortés's men were drowned by the weight of the gold they carried, while others threw their treasure into the lake they were crossing in an attempt to survive the battle. Aztec Indians came later, many believed, and dragged the lost fortune from the lake. Ibid., 475–477, 483.

13. Thomas, *Rivers of Gold*, 490.

14. Flint, *Great Cruelties*, 540.

15. Flint, "What They Never Told You," 208–209.

16. "Ulloa Inspection," H/R-*DJO* 1: 136: "Salazar Inspection," ibid., 225.

17. In *No Settlement, No Conquest*, 137–138, Flint calls attention to Coronado's denial that he ordered that the dogs be set onto Bigotes.

18. Villagrá, *A History of New Mexico*, 58–59.

19. Flint, *No Settlement, No Conquest*, 148.

20. "Rio de Losa to Viceroy," H/R-*DJO* 2: 764.

Part 1

The Coronado Expedition

Today, archaeologists are scouring historic sites in the Southwest and Central Plains searching for clues to the drama of our Indian past and the conquistador era. Ever so gradually, more and more revelations are coming to light. It is with the discovery of an outline of a prehistoric Indian pit house, a piece of chain mail, a rusted knife blade, or a copper arrowhead once employed by a Spanish crossbow that more truths about the past emerge.

But we have been rewarded in another very significant way. The Spanish were the first Europeans known to enter the American Southwest. As it emerged into a world power, the Spanish Empire of the fifteenth through seventeenth centuries featured literate men and written works. Reports, narratives, letters, testimonies, and other writings left behind from their era of exploration and discovery provide the details of the Spaniards' adventures in America.

We can almost imagine that the persons who penned these historical documents blew the ink on them dry and handed them to us to read—except that would be slighting the scholars who uncovered them yellowed with the ages from distant archives, poured over their antique script, and translated them for further study.

Through these documents we discover that within the gilded romance of the Spanish conquistador lies embedded not only bravery and resolve but some other less admirable traits as well. America's history of record begins here.

1

Of Myths and Men

The inhabitants [of Topira] wear gold, emeralds, and other precious stones and serve [meals] on silver and gold, [with] which they cover their houses. The principales wear heavy, well-worked chains of gold around their necks.

Coronado's Myth[1]

When the Spanish conquistadors came to America to conduct their conquests for the Spanish Empire, they were inspired and guided to an indefinable but significant extent by popular myths that featured fabulous cities of golden wealth or other worldly rewards. Because the ethic of recorded history requires tangible, provable fact, the concrete influence of elusive, popularly propagated myths has generally been slighted. Conversely, however, few historical studies, especially nationalistic ones, avoid dependence to some degree on mythical input relative to either events or personalities.

It may seem spurious to give myths such strong responsibility in as important an event as exploration of the New World. But, in truth, these societal delusions played an influential role throughout the period of Spanish exploration of the Americas. Their tangible effect is difficult to deny. Many were born as infectious Old World mythologies that, fostered by fanciful delusion, flowed through folk legend and early literature from the Old World westward through Europe and on to the Antilles (the West Indies). From there they were carried onward to the American continents by aspiring conquistadors. Throughout the period of Spanish discovery, myths influenced the actions of policy-makers, conquistador leaders, and expeditionary aspirants alike.

In his study of the sixteenth-century Spanish conquest, *Books of the Brave*, Irving Albert Leonard tells how these ancient legends were spread by the development of printing and the production of romantic novels. Rumor-filled travel histories provided by the Italian Marco Polo, Englishman Sir John Mandeville, and Spaniard Pedro Tafur were read avidly by those who could do so.[2]

The seeds for many of the enduring fantasies of New World explorations took root during the Moorish-Muslim invasion of the Iberian Peninsula in the early eighth century. A Portuguese archbishop was said to have fled by ship out into the little sailed and scantly explored Atlantic Ocean. He was joined by six other bishops and their Christian followers with all their goods and livestock, disappearing from the known world of Europe.[3]

Over time, a legend—a very potent one—developed, taking in part from Plato that the bishops had established "seven cities" on an island called Antilia. The idea that the lost cities were resplendent with gold developed mysteriously over the years. Occasional sightings of the fabled island were reported by ocean navigators who may have long been at sea:

> Plato spoke of the mysterious civilization of Atlantis and the island
> of Antilia, or the Seven Cities, located beyond the Pillars of Hercules.
> These accounts wound their way through Western Civilization,
> accumulating other ancient myths such as lands inhabited by Amazons,
> valiant women warriors who cut off their left breasts in order to use bow
> and arrow, lands of gold and jewels, fountains of youth, and Christian
> communities isolated from the rest of Christendom.[4]

These fanciful myths of antiquity spread to Spain and Portugal, where they flourished. Spain in particular, with its background of Christian versus Muslim wars, became steeped in a tradition of mythology befitting its age of knighthood and chivalry. These traditions "had most of the ancient myths enveloped with a patina of historical fact."[5] Thence from Europe the legends were carried across the Atlantic Ocean to the Americas by a generation of determined adventurers.

Spanish explorers were not alone in hearing the legends of golden cities. The English explorer John Cabot, on his 1497 voyage to Newfoundland, thought he had discovered the "isles of Brazil and the Seven Cities of Antilia."[6]

Myth creation, however, did not end with Old World concoctions. A curious phenomenon developed in the New World of the Americas. With far more intellect than has been recognized, the Indian natives played upon the avaricious invaders with their own fanciful variations of cities of gold, beautiful women, and promises of eternal youth. It is not known whether the Indian tales were adaptations of the myths they had heard from the Spaniards or were simply fantasies extended from passions the conquistadors exhibited. Some authors have suggested that at times American Indians concocted their own tales of wondrous rewards to be found simply to amuse themselves with the myth-cultivated Europeans. At other times, apparently, a more sinister motive was involved—the Indians were cleverly inveigling their unwanted guests into going elsewhere.

But always there existed the troublesome barrier of language. The Spaniards had to depend on native translators, and the nuance of meaning was often lost. Hand signs were fallible. The myth-influenced Spaniards often pointed to some gold or gold-colored object to obtain verification of the metal elsewhere. They then read more into native replies than was there and enlarged upon them to match their own aspirations.

Skeptics of today should understand that, for the human intellect of the early centuries, much of world existence was yet unknown. Under such conditions, imaginations were much freer to conceive fantasies now seen as improbable or impossible. Of the conquistador, Leonard wrote, "The marvelous exploits and fantastic accounts of persons and places thus brought to the eyes and ears of the conquerors now encamped in the midst of an unknown continent could not fail to stimulate their already fevered imaginations and easily prepared their minds to accept avidly the wildest rumors of riches which were forever luring them on."[7]

The advent of the Turks conquering Constantinople in 1453 had cut Europe off from the silks and spices obtained in trade with China, Japan, and India. This led Spain to look for another route of Far East trade by way of the Atlantic and gave Queen Isabella reason to support the voyage of Christopher Columbus. In addition, Spain badly needed gold, and Columbus was eager to find it for her. He had, after all, read Marco Polo's story of an island (probably Japan) where temples and palaces were roofed

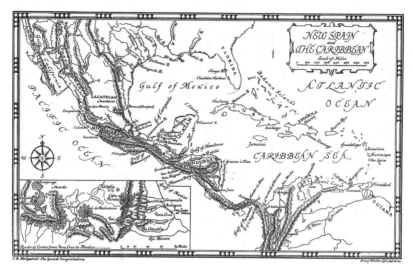

FIGURE 1.1. *Map of New Spain and the Caribbean (antique map)*

with gold. One historian observed: "With the Moors prostrate [defeated in the 1492 conquest of Granada], the Queen was looking outward toward empire, and perhaps this persistent man from Italy could bring her the gold of the Orient."[8] She sold her own jewels to finance Columbus's voyage. Who is to say that the queen herself had not become enraptured by rumors of golden cities on isles out in the sea?

Columbus's momentous quest the same year as the Granada victory led to Spain's Age of Discovery and Extension of Empire. The Spanish conquistadors, enlivened by the ancestral victories over the Moors, were driven forth by religious and military history. They were infused with the fierce belief that their cause was that of God but that it was also to discover and conquer myth-proclaimed riches.[9]

The idea of the existence of a city of gold somewhere beyond the ports of the Mediterranean and the shores of Eastern Europe excited the hopes of sailors and voyagers of Columbus's day (see figure 1.1). Such notions spread across the Atlantic to the New World of the Americas, becoming infused with native lore. Emboldening the minds of ambitious men in New Spain (essentially Central America), the fantasies sent them northward to the unexplored lands beyond.

Mythical illusions were aboard when Columbus set out on his first historic voyage. At one point he and his crew thought they had sighted the Isle of Antilia. They rejoiced heartily, only to find later that what they had seen was just a cloud bank on the horizon.[10]

The "Lost City of Gold" myth abetted all other goals. Always there were gilded promises of great personal benefit offered by the myths. Many of the paths through New World history, where personal ambition mixed potently with national purpose, were fatefully linked to mystic stories promising undiscovered meccas of enormous treasure that awaited their finder.

At the same time, when hearing native stories of fantastic riches, solemnly sworn to, conquistadors faced a crucial decision. If they went in search of a supposed "city of gold," it could prove to be a hoax. On the other hand, if they did not attempt the search and someone else did and found such a city, the failure of not searching would be monumental. In part, conquistadors aspired to make their quest, and in part they had little choice but to do so.

The myths of golden cities were bolstered greatly by New World discoveries that gave added support to potential cornucopias of riches. The bonanzas of accumulated wealth discovered by Hernando Cortés in Mexico and Francisco Pizarro in Peru convinced others ever more firmly that more treasure troves surely awaited discovery in the yet-unseen corners of the Americas. Who knew what other rich Aztec- or Inca-like civilizations were flourishing in the mysterious lands north of New Spain?

When Cortés displayed his Mexican treasures in Europe, even the most ardent doubters were impressed by the dazzling booty. Such riches, which bespoke the promise of others, were highly compelling for ambitious men of New Spain. Often these men hearkened to status in Spanish nobility and yearned for the title of a caballero or hidalgo through service as a knight errant. They readily turned their wants for wealth and position to the enticing tales of "seven golden cities" they heard from native occupants of New Spain.

The entrancing numeral "seven" had long been a dominant factor in Old World mythology. It is a revealing fact of history that the number was repeated time and again in myths during the conquistadors' advance northward from the region of today's Mexico City. The number was a magical element of the Antilia myth as well as the myth of the Seven Caves of Aztlán, a supposed site in the north from which the Mexica-Aztecs had migrated. And there were other instances.[11]

At Quito, Ecuador, in 1541, natives laced the minds of the conquering Spaniards with tales of a shadowy Indian leader named El Dorado,

FIGURE 1.2. *The El Dorado legend: El Dorado being powdered with gold*

who was so rich that he powdered himself with gold dust before taking his morning dip in a lake of pure water (figure 1.2). Supposedly, this Indian "king" dressed himself totally in gold on festive occasions.[12] Eventually, the story evolved from simply that of a resplendent monarch into a land overflowing with precious stones and golden objects.

Some early accounts tell of a religious ceremony the Musca Indians conducted on a sacred lake that some called Lake El Dorado. This scenario found substance in a "golden raft" artifact discovered on the shoreline of today's Lake Siecha in Columbia (figure 1.3). On the raft were figures in gold of what appear to be a priest and four attendants. Two small tubes held by the priest are thought to represent human heads being offered as trophies to the lake diety.[13]

Other accounts placed the lake elsewhere. The Spaniard Gonzalo Pizarro heard such stories and Indian tales. He had been witness to the enormous gold and silver ransom the Incas had paid his half-brother Francisco Pizarro on behalf of their foredoomed king Atahualpa. Gonzalo frothed to conduct an expedition eastward across the Andes Mountains from present Ecuador in search of the wealthy-beyond-imagination El Dorado.

FIGURE 1.3. *The golden raft*

Gonzalo and his men whacked their way eastward through the Brazilian jungles until the expedition was torn apart by disease, starvation, and Indian attacks. In desperation, Gonzalo sent his nephew, Lieutenant Francisco de Orleana, ahead down the stream they had been following to find food. But Orleana did not return. Instead, he followed the demanding current downstream and became famous as the first man to navigate the entire length of the river now known as the Amazon.[14]

In relating the Orleana journey, Friar Gaspar de Carvajal, who chronicled the trip, told of an occasion when the party was attacked by a band of fierce female warriors. He described the women as "white and tall, and they have long braided hair wound about their heads; they are robust and go about naked, their privy parts covered. With bows and arrows in hand they do as much fighting as ten Indian men."[15]

FIGURE 1.4. *The landing of Columbus—frontispiece in* Journal of First Voyage to America

This was a significant revelation—and inspiration—for many Europeans, who connected it to the ancient myth of the "Amazon women of war" known prominently in Greek and Roman mythology. In 1493, slightly clad Amazon women were visualized with a New World presence in the woodcut illustration in the publication of Columbus's journal (figure 1.4).[16] The image of naked native women with unclothed breasts, though scarcely admitted to in solemn studies, had timeless appeal in New World discovery as well.

Even when Cortés set out from Cuba for Yucatan in 1519, he was instructed, among other objectives, to find out "where and in what direction are the Amazons, who are nearby, according to the Indians whom you are taking with you."[17]

There is ample evidence that sex was a driving force in the exploration of the Americas.[18] With the discovery of a new continent, a new world was suddenly revealed filled with tropical women whose tribal mores and native-ness left them prey to the more sophisticated and avaricious European males. For the first conquistadors the Americas portended, among other things, freedom from the societal restrictions of Old World culture.

Through time, public lore moved the legend of the Amazon women to whatever location fit the purpose. When they were not in Asia or Europe or Africa or South America, they were said to be elsewhere, including, as we shall see, northwest Mexico. In some instances they were very militant; in others, very alluring and abundantly rich. The women, the legend said, allowed men to visit only once a year. But it was not myths alone that featured the legend of the Amazons reigning in some unknown land. Spanish novels of the day (1491–1504) contributed to the societal whimsy. In *Sergas de Esplandián*, author Garci Rodríguez [or Ordoñez] de Montalvo described the Amazon women as wealthy to the extreme. The women, he wrote, resided on the north mainland of the Indies and possessed weapons "all of gold and there is no other metal on the whole island."[19]

Other Spanish explorers, as well as English, Portuguese, and German aspirants, would become entranced with the legend of El Dorado and scour the challenging South American rainforests for him in vain. Among the searchers were such famous men as England's Sir Walter Raleigh and Germany's Alexander von Humboldt. Eventually, El Dorado's fame spread far and wide, the name becoming a featured town and location identity in many US states and in other countries.[20]

Yet another famous myth known earlier to Europeans told of a supposed "Fountain of Youth." It led Ponce de León to try to find the island of "Bimini," where Puerto Rican natives confided that there was a spring that would restore a person's youth and relieve the pestilence of aging male impotence. The Spaniard's attempt led to the discovery of Florida in 1513. That event was inevitable, but it was prompted by the myth of something that, like a city of gold, is yet to be found.

It is not difficult to see the influence of the myth. Though imaginary, myths helped to provide the initial inspiration for many explorations, and, beyond that, they excited the enlistments of those who joined the New World ventures. Almost always, myths aided and abetted pragmatic incentives that were not personal.

Notably, in 1529 the myths of seven lost cities of gold, as well as of a society of specially endowed women, were regenerated in New Spain. Nuño de Guzmán, the ruthless governor of Nueva España's Pánuco province along the Gulf Coast, heard of great wealth northwest of the present Mexico City in the unpacified province of Nueva Galicia. An interpreter, a young Indian boy named Tejo, recited tales of trading ventures he had made with his father to the unexplored and unknown northern frontier of New Spain. They had traded, he said, at "seven grand pueblos" rich with gold and silver.[21]

Inspired by the hope of great wealth—and, as will be seen, of sexual pleasures—Guzmán led a sizable expedition of 300 to 400 mounted Spaniards and several thousand Mexican Indian allies up the uncharted western coast of New Spain. He ravaged native villages as he conducted a territorial conquest and search for riches. One chieftain, Tangáxuan II, attempted to receive him in peace, providing gifts of gold and silver in addition to supplies and soldiers.[22]

Even this was not enough for the heartless Guzmán, who had set a standard for human cruelty by branding Indian natives on the face with heated irons and selling them as slaves to mine operators in the West Indies. Guzmán tortured the compliant Tangáxuan II until he revealed other caches of gold. This was still insufficient. Guzmán ordered him tied to the tail of a horse and dragged across the plains in an attempt to learn of more gold. When it was finally decided that the ungrateful man had nothing left to give, he was bound to a stake and burned to death.[23]

During a pause in its march, Guzmán's expedition was struck by autumn rainstorms that caused the streams to rise and turn the army encampment into a flood area. Among the casualties was the army's store of foodstuffs, which quickly spoiled. Disease ravaged Guzmán's Indian allies who camped in the low areas. Thousands became ill, and many died; still others deserted and fled, and many were killed in their attempt to escape.[24]

During this time, Guzmán began to hear tales of a place ahead that was inhabited by beautiful women. Surely, he concluded, it must be the land of the Amazon women told of in the early myths. Though Guzmán himself was ill and being carried on a stretcher, his sexual appetites were still at work. When the Indians told of a place called Cihuatlán, a "place of women," he became convinced that the women (young girls, rightfully) among the Indians they were meeting were becoming more and more beautiful. The weak but determined Guzmán pushed on.[25]

But the steep mountains and rough passage, plus starvation among his army, were too much. Finally, he was forced to give up his pursuit of illusory myths. Returning to the conquest of the region that would become Nueva Galicia province, he established San Miguel de Culiacán, today's Culiacán, as its capital. Four years later Guzmán founded the mining town of Compostela as a new capital near the coast below Culiacán; he then founded Guadalajara.[26] In doing so, he continued his practices of slavery and branding the Indians.

Eventually, reports of Guzmán's villainy reached church officials in Mexico City. At the insistence of Bishop Juan de Zumárraga, the Spanish Crown ordered his arrest, and the "most foul and evil man"[27] ever to set foot in New Spain was deposed and imprisoned in Spain, eventually dying there.

A lingering suspicion remained among many citizens of New Spain, however, that even more accumulated treasures lay hidden in the uncharted mountains and forests of northern Mexico. The idea of an Indian city of gold to the north was reignited in 1536 by a significant historical event in northern New Spain. The Cabeza de Vaca group of four Florida expedition castaways arrived that year. Their appearance would cause yet another myth of potential wealth to emerge, this time in Tierra Nueva.

From Culiacán, Guzmán had sent captains with companies of horsemen on sorties to continue the search for the rich cities told of by Tejo. Failing, they turned to capturing natives for slaves and razing their villages. One of the probes, however, did make a spectacular find. A mounted party led by a Guzmán nephew came onto four heavily bearded men dressed in animal skins wandering southward in the mountains of northern New Spain. One was a black man, a slave. The men spoke the Spanish language, and they told an amazing story.[28]

The four wild-looking Spaniards proved to have been remnants of a failed 1528 Spanish expedition to La Florida under Pánfilo de Narváez. When they marched inland from a spot near the present Tampa Bay area, Pánfilo's force became lost from their ships. Suffering severely from hunger and Indian attacks, the Spaniards retreated back to the Gulf Coast. They built five makeshift boats and set sail for New Spain, clinging closely to the shoreline. At sea the flotilla, each craft carrying around 50 men, was already becoming less than seaworthy when it was struck by a hurricane.

Most of the 250 men aboard the boats drowned. Others were swept ashore on a coastal island, where some were killed by Indians and others were held as slaves.[29]

Alvar Núñez Cabeza de Vaca, treasurer of the Florida expedition, escaped to the interior where he survived as a captive, medicine man, and trader among various Indian tribes. After five long years in captivity, he met three other men who had lived through the tragedy at sea and its ensuing ordeal: the Spaniards Andrés Dorantes and Alonzo del Castillo and Dorantes's Moroccan slave, Esteban. During 1533 the four men successfully escaped from their captors near the mouth of Texas's Colorado River and fled westward.

For three more years the men roamed among the Indian bands of southern Texas, New Mexico, and possibly Arizona before turning southward into what is now northern Mexico. There on the Yaqui River they encountered the Guzmán party.

Vaca and his three companions were soon escorted from Culiacán to Mexico City to meet with New Spain viceroy Antonio de Mendoza. They told of their adventures and the many fascinations they had seen in the north: large towns with inhabitants who wore cotton shirts and did metal working.[30]

This trek through unknown lands added to the tales of Tejo and the Antilles myth. It created great excitement in New Spain and elsewhere. Mendoza was impressed with Vaca's story, as were other Spanish notables. From this there sprang a contest among eminent conquistadors. Hernando Cortés; Hernando de Soto; the *adelantado* of Guatemala, Pedro de Alvarado; and even Guzmán began vying with Mendoza for the king's favor in launching an expedition to the alluring vistas of Tierra Nueva.[31]

ABBREVIATION KEY

F/F-*DOCS* = Flint and Flint, eds., trans., annots., *Documents of the Coronado Expedition, 1539–1542*

H/R-*NCE* = Hammond and Rey, eds., *Narratives of the Coronado Expedition, 1540–1542*

W-*CE* = Winship, *The Coronado Expedition, 1540–1542*

NOTES

1. "Coronado to Viceroy," F/F-*DOCS*, 33. See also H/R-*NCE*, 44–45.

2. Leonard, *Books of the Brave*, 11, 37.

3. Flint, *No Settlement, No Conquest*, 19.

4. Brink, "The Function of Myth in the Discovery of the New World," in Everett, ed., *Coronado and the Myth of Quivira*, 15.

5. Ibid., 16.

6. Bolton, *Coronado*, 6.

7. Leonard, *Books of the Brave*, 44.

8. Chapman, *The Golden Dream*, 12.

9. Flint, *No Settlement, No Conquest*, 15.

10. Dunn and Kelley, *The Diary of Christopher Columbus's First Voyage to America, 1492–1493*, 41–44. Prior to setting sail on his way to discover America, Christopher Columbus had carefully read and made marginal notes in his copy of Marco Polo's *The Description of the World*. This book by the famous Venetian traveler told of a mythical palace on an island in the Far East (believed to be Japan) that had gold roofs and floors of gold two fingers thick. It is said that Columbus sought to find the island on his maiden voyage to America. Edwards, "Wonders and Whoppers," 82.

11. Flint, *No Settlement, No Conquest*, 21.

12. Hemming, *The Search for El Dorado*, 97.

13. Ibid., 104–105.

14. Chapman, *The Golden Dream*, 158–159.

15. Carvajal, *Discovery of America*, 114.

16. Columbus, *Journal of First Voyage to America,* frontispiece. The king in the drawing could well represent King El Dorado, reigning over his empire of gold, pointing Columbus to the island of scantily attired Amazon women while the ship's crew members consider which they would like to explore first.

17. Thomas, *Rivers of Gold*, 460, citing Diégo Veláquez in José Luís Martinez, *Documentos, Cortesianos* (Mexico City: Fondo de Cultura Económica, 1991), 45–57.

18. While overt accounts of sexual acts are rare in Spanish documentation, secondary clues of sexual motivation and indulgence are abundant. This subject would merit a study in itself.

19. Cited in Leonard, *Books of the Brave*, 53.

20. States that use El Dorado as a town or location name include Arkansas, California, Colorado, Illinois, Kansas, Maryland, Missouri, Oklahoma, Texas, and Wisconsin. Several Latin America countries, including Mexico, do likewise.

21. "Castañeda's Narrative," F/F-*DOCS*, 386. See also W-*CE*, 188–189; H/R-*NCE*, 195.

22. Bancroft, *History of Mexico* 2: 344–345.

23. Ibid., 346.

24. Ibid., 361.

25. Ibid., 363.

26. Ibid., 366–367.

27. Chipman, *Nuño de Guzmán and the Province of Pánuco in New Spain*, 143.

28. Bandelier, *Journey of Cabeza de Vaca*, 168.

29. Bolton, *Coronado*, 119. It has long been thought that the hurricane swept the Spaniards to Galveston Island, but recent studies point to Louisiana's East Island, south of New Orleans, as the "Isle of Misfortune."

30. Ibid., 11, 12.

31. Flint, *No Settlement, No Conquest*, 42.

2
An Illusion Called Cibola

I dispatched two religious [friars] of the Franciscan Order to reconnoiter along the region of the coast of [the Mar del] Sur. They have returned with news of a very excellent and great land, comprising many settlements.

Viceroy Antonio de Mendoza[1]

Spaniards of the sixteenth century knew Tierra Nueva only as a dark, undefined landmass connected to New Spain on the north. They had learned something of its western coastal line from naval explorations, but they knew nothing of the land's shape, its breadth or depth, its mountains and rivers, or what dire dangers might lurk there. They knew nothing of its inhabitants, landscape, and animal life other than what the Cabeza de Vaca party had said about the region it had wandered through. Some still believed Tierra Nueva might ultimately be land-connected with China, India, or both. Others hoped that a northern water route to the Far East was yet to be found.

Mendoza was determined to win the king's favor as the one to launch an expedition into Tierra Nueva. He was successful in doing so, much to the chagrin of Cortés, who felt strongly that he deserved the prize. Still, the viceroy was cautious about undertaking the venture. With the Spanish

Crown offering no financial support, it would be up to him to bear much of the cost himself. Prudently, he decided that a preliminary reconnaissance of Tierra Nueva was needed. To achieve this, Mendoza turned first to Alvar Núñez Cabeza de Vaca and Andrés Dorantes and asked them to make a return visit to the land they had recently traveled across. Both men refused.

When these efforts failed, the viceroy looked to a Franciscan friar named Marcos de Niza to lead such a party. Marcos was no novice in the Americas. The forty-plus-year-old native of Nice in the Duchy of Savoy had seen missionary service on the island of Santo Domingo, in Guatemala, and in Peru. He had been present in Peru when Francisco Pizarro executed the Inca leader Atahualpa and reaped the fabulous gold and silver booty that had been paid to ransom the leader.[2]

Because Marcos had worked among native peoples, Mendoza felt he could travel among them safely without military protection. In doing so, he would provide an important counter to the swelling criticism of Indian abuse that had been aroused in Europe and elsewhere regarding conquistador behavior. Marcos himself had added to this criticism by contributing to the scathing account of conquistador brutality, *The Devastation of the Indies: A Brief Account*, authored by the Dominican priest Bartolomé de las Casas in 1542 (figure 2.1).[3]

Another Franciscan fray named Onorato was assigned to accompany Marcos on his journey. Also, Mendoza freed Dorantes's slave, Esteban, and enlisted him to guide and aid Marcos. The Moor had established a remarkable rapport with the Indians during the Cabeza de Vaca trip across what is now the southwestern United States. He had shown exceptional ability to learn the natives' speech and achieve special influence over them. He wielded a gourd rattle, decked with red and white feathers and two rows of tinkle bells and other feathers and bells tied about his wrists and ankles, which had greatly impressed the Indians.[4]

It was further arranged that, for assistance and added security, over 100 Indios Amigos would accompany Marcos and Esteban. The party would be escorted north to Culiacán by a military retinue of 200 horsemen and another 100 footmen. Commanding them would be the recently appointed acting governor of Nueva Galicia, Francisco Vázquez de Coronado, who was on his way to assume the duties of his new office as governor.[5]

Coronado, the second son of a ranking military officer, Juan Vázquez de Coronado, had come to New Spain with Mendoza in 1535. Two years

FIGURE 2.1. *Bartolomé de las Casas*

later he married Beatriz de Estrada, the daughter of Alonso de Estrada, former royal treasurer in New Spain. Through the marriage, Coronado received a dowry of considerable value in the form of New Spain *encomiendas*. A favorite of Mendoza's, Coronado was appointed to the governance of Mexico City. When Diego Pérez de la Torre, Guzmán's successor, died after falling from his horse during an Indian battle, Mendoza chose Coronado, still a young man only twenty-eight years old, to replace him as governor of Nueva Galicia.[6]

The combined Coronado and Marcos parties set out from Mexico City in late 1538. Coronado paused at Guadalajara to appoint new officials for the city, then moved on to visit Compostela and other locales in his province. He wrote to the viceroy on March 8, 1539, from Culiacán, telling him that he had heard about a location in an unexplored region of northern Mexico called Topira. His description of the place, which spoke of fabulous excesses of gold and other wealth, fits well into the genre of myths about gold-endowed cities.[7]

Coronado said further that he planned to lead an expedition to the place, though he would "have to travel many leagues to go around very high mountains that rise to the heavens and a river that is so large and swollen there is no place where I can ford it."[8]

He confirmed that Marcos had departed from Culiacán a month earlier accompanied by Onorato, Esteban, and the party of friendly Indians. Instead of leading the expedition to Topira as he had planned, however, Coronado was forced to deal with another matter. An Indian revolt had been led by a war chief named Ayapín. Coronado pursued, hanged, and quartered the man.[9]

While Coronado dealt with these and other affairs of Nueva Galicia province, Fray Marcos led his reconnaissance party northward. The viceroy's instructions had been specific and been put in writing. Marcos was to treat the Indians he met along the way "benevolently," making it clear to them that they would no longer be treated as slaves by the Spaniards. He was to make note of the quality and fertility of the land, especially its rocks and minerals.[10]

In particular, Marcos was to observe the direction of the New Spain coastline along the Mar del Sur (Gulf of California, then mistaken for the South Sea). This was to help a naval party transport supplies Mendoza was considering sending forth in support of a land expedition to Tierra Nueva. Where good ports were offered, Marcos was to erect crosses or carve the emblem into well-located trees, leaving instructional letters at the foot of those trees for Spanish ships. He would also stash crosses and messages at prominent points in his march to give notice of Spain's claim to the land. Because he knew so little about the landmass north of Mexico City, Mendoza thought Marcos would be able to hold to the western coastline. Beyond Culiacán, however, the trail northward on which Esteban took the party bent farther and farther away from the ocean.

The Indios Amigos who accompanied Marcos had been provided mainly for security. The Indians also willingly agreed to transport Marcos's extra clothing, gifts for Indians they would meet, and travel necessities.[11] For food, the party depended upon the generosity of natives they encountered along their march.

A short way into the march at Petatlán pueblo, Fray Onorato fell ill. He remained behind as the party moved on up the coastal plain that linked the sea and the Sierra Madre Occidental range. Along the way, Marcos's entourage was greeted with grand receptions and merrymaking at native villages. The region had suffered drought for several years, and food was scarce. Still, the resident Indians were excited to receive the priest, Esteban, and their Indian allies. They gave what they had to feed the large group of travelers and prepared places of rest.

When he reached a sizable, well-irrigated settlement known as Vacapa, Marcos was informed that after a few days more on his journey he would reach the end of the mountain chain. There he would find a wide, level valley with many more large settlements occupied by people who wore cotton clothes.[12] To Spaniards of the day, cotton clothes indicated an advanced society of much potential. These people became far more interesting when Marcos heard about their wealth of gold and their casual use of it: "Having shown them some pieces of metal which I carried . . . [the natives] told me that there are jars made of that among those people in the valley and that they wear certain round objects made from that [same] gold hanging from their noses and ears. [They also told me that the people of the valley] have a few small spatulas made of [gold], with which they scrape away and remove their sweat."[13]

Though the place the Indians told of was highly intriguing, Marcos concluded that the valley was much too far off his route. He decided that he would investigate it on his return trip.[14]

Because he was uncomfortable with Esteban's habit of accepting the gifts of turquoise jewelry as well as the pleasures of comely women the villagers presented him with,[15] the priest chose to send the Moor on with his two greyhounds and a number of the Indios Amigos to scout the trail ahead.

I arranged with him that if he received word of a settled and rich land (which would be a grand thing), he was not to travel farther but to return in person or send me Indians with this sign which we agreed on. If what [was reported] was of moderate importance, he would send me a white cross [the size] of one *palmo*; if it was grand, he would send one two *palmos* [in size]; and if it was something grander and better than *Nueva España*, he would send me a large cross.[16]

At the same time, Marcos dispatched Indian messengers westward to the sea to bring him natives of the coast and islands so he could learn about them.[17] Marcos was still at Vacapa four days later when the first Indian couriers from Esteban arrived. They carried a cross not merely palm size but so large it was as tall as a man. As if this wasn't enough, the Indians said Esteban had insisted that Marcos hurry forth as quickly as possible. One of the messengers said Esteban had met a native who told him of great things ahead. "He told me," Marcos later reported to Mendoza, "so many magnificent things about it [the land they discovered] that I stopped believing them until later [when] I might see them [myself] or might obtain further assurance about the thing. He told me that it was thirty days' journey from where Esteban was to the first *ciudad* [important community] of the land, which is called Cibola."[18]

Esteban's messenger described Cibola as seven *ciudads* composed of "grand houses made of stone and lime" and decorated with turquoise ornaments. He told, too, of more *ciudads* in other provinces that were even more excellent.[19] Because he had promised to wait for his coastal messengers to return, however, Marcos did not rush on immediately. When the Indians returned as assigned, they brought residents of the offshore islands. These Indians gave Marcos a gift of some of their large war shields. Another delegation of three Indians from territory to the east arrived as well. They described Cibola much the same as had Esteban's messenger.

The visitors continued on with Marcos as he set out to join Esteban. On the way, the friar was met by another messenger. This man carried a cross as large as the first and issued assurances that the land Esteban told of was the best and greatest of all. Again, the priest was urged to hurry forth. Marcos did so, but he always found that Esteban had departed ahead of him. Still, several of the natives Marcos met told him the same stories, describing in detail the seven grand *ciudads*.

Marcos trod on, encountering another settlement, with similar results. Esteban had left another large cross there, and the natives repeated the same stories about Cibola. An ensuing village proved to be an irrigated pueblo whose people wore cotton clothing as well as buffalo hides. Another large cross arrived there, and the messengers who brought it also told of Cibola's grandness.

The headmen of this pueblo were two brothers who wore turquoise ornaments in their ears and noses and turquoise necklaces around their necks. The men were particularly interested in the robe Marcos wore, feeling it with their fingers. Their own garments, they said, were made from the hair of small animals of the region that were about the size of Esteban's greyhounds.[20]

Marcos had now crossed into the present United States, entering an uninhabited region believed to be the upper San Pedro Valley of southern Arizona.[21] Despite its lack of population, he and his people found shelter, food, and water during the four days they were there. The situation was even better in the next heavily populated valley, where the people greeted his party with food and further information on Cibola. Here, to learn his distance from the sea as he went, Marcos sent more Indian couriers to the coast. They returned to tell the friar that the gulf coastline turned sharply to the west.

In his report to the viceroy, Marcos claimed that, to be certain of the distance from his line of march to the coast, he himself had gone in search of it. The erroneous information he provided has led historians to believe he did not actually reach the coast.[22]

Marcos continued to receive glowing reports and descriptions of Cibola from local Indians as his party made its way north up the present Arizona–New Mexico border during May 1539. He erected crosses as he went, leaving notices of the Spanish claim. Yet another messenger from Esteban arrived carrying reassurances about the land ahead.

For twelve days more the Franciscan priest followed a trail spotted by the ashes of campfires left by travelers. He and his followers ate deer, jackrabbits, and partridges. Now close to the end of his journey, Marcos was becoming more and more impatient. "Each day seems like a year to me," he later wrote in his report, "because of my desire to see Cibola."[23]

Then, one day on the trail, Marcos's joy was shattered. His party encountered an Indian boy fleeing down the trail. The boy, who had gone on ahead with Esteban, dripped with sweat, and his face was etched with fear. He had a gruesome tale to relate. Many of his friends, he said, and perhaps Esteban as well, had been attacked and killed by the people of Cibola.

Marcos learned that, upon arriving at Cibola, Esteban, as was his custom, had sent messengers ahead to deliver his belled and feathered gourd to the pueblo's principal man. But the old man threw the gourd to the ground defiantly, declaring that if Esteban and his people tried to enter the pueblo, he would have them all killed.

When Esteban was told of this, he was not alarmed. He said that such incidents had happened often before. Taking the gourd himself, he tried to enter the village. But he and his men, including the boy Marcos had met, were stopped and placed in a building without food or water. All their trade goods were taken from them. The next morning the boy left the building to get a drink from a nearby stream. While there, he saw people from Cibola attack Esteban and his Indians. The boy ran and hid, later fleeing back down the trail. "No one escaped," he said, "except us."[24]

The killing had actually been less general than the boy thought. Most of Esteban's Indios Amigos were captured and later released, but the murder of Esteban had been gory. Information would surface from Indians later met by Mendoza's naval party on the distant Colorado River, where the explorers met and talked with an Indian elder of a local tribe. The old chief had heard about the Cibola affair.

The Indian explained that the Cibola lords were insulted by Esteban's request for women. Also, they were alarmed by his claim that he had behind him "brothers" who had many weapons. The Cibolans killed Esteban, the elder said, and cut his body into many pieces to distribute among the other Cibola lords and prove he was dead. The lords had also killed one of Esteban's greyhounds.

Though he did not then know the full truth, Marcos was greatly disturbed by what the boy had told him. He drew aside to pray over the matter. When he returned, the friar was told that, because it appeared that the Cibolans were prepared to massacre the entire reconnaissance party, his own Indios Amigos were plotting to kill him and flee. To calm them, Marcos emptied his trunk of clothing and trade goods and distributed them among his Indians.[25]

In his report, Marcos states that most of his Indians refused to go to the Cibola village to learn more about the fate of Esteban and the others. Still, he said, two *principales* and interpreters did go with him to a hilltop from which the village could be viewed. There, he told Mendoza, he erected a small cross supported by a pile of stones and declared that he was taking possession of Cibola and other sites in the area for Spain.[26]

"A few times," Marcos admitted, "I was tempted to go there [to the pueblo] myself, for I knew I was only risking my life, and I had rendered that to God."[27]

Whether Marcos actually made it even to the hilltop has long been debated by historians. Some consider his description of Cibola so sparse as to be suspicious and the time of travel too brief for him to have gone that far.[28] Marcos says little else about his return trip. He did mention, however, that he again passed by the wide valley where he had been told the natives had so much gold that they made jars from it. "I did not dare to enter because it seemed to me that it was [first] necessary to come settle this other land of the seven *ciudads* and *reinos* [semiautonomous regions subject to the king] which I am telling about [Cibola]. Then it would be possible to examine [the valley] better without putting my person at risk and, as a result, failing to give a report of what was seen."[29]

When he arrived back at San Miguel de Culiacán, Marcos found that Coronado was not there. The governor had been busy taking possession of Indian villages north of Guadalajara in the name of the Crown. Marcos did contact him at Compostela during late June, however, and made a verbal report of his reconnaissance. He also wrote to Mendoza to notify him of his return and began preparing a report of his journey to Tierra Nueva.

Coronado escorted Marcos to Mexico City where, on September 2, 1539, they were received with great public interest. The friar presented his *Relación* to the viceroy, swearing that "what is included in it did transpire, so that His Majesty may be informed to the truth of what is stated in it."[30]

Marcos's return to Mexico City sparked excited interest among the population. Scholars have presumed as well that Marcos may have spoken even more favorably about Tierra Nueva's wealth in conversations with Mendoza. Apparently, he did so with others. Evidence of this was given when ship passengers from New Spain arrived at Havana, Cuba, in November 1539. They were required to give testimony regarding Mendoza's plans and what Marcos had said about Tierra Nueva.

Several of the witnesses testified that they heard that Marcos had described the land as very wealthy in gold and silver. Andrés Garcia declared that his son-in-law, a barber who customarily shaved Marcos, had told him regarding Cibola, "There were many settlements, *ciudads* and *villas*. The *ciudads* are surrounded by walls and guarded at their gates. [They are] very wealthy, and there were silversmiths. The women were accustomed to wear golden necklaces, and the men, belts made of gold. There were hooded cloaks, sheep, cattle, partridges, a meat market, a blacksmith's forge, and weights and measures."[31]

Imaginary stories such as these, whether originated by Marcos or not, evidently circulated about New Spain and likely worked their way to Mendoza's attention. But the viceroy was still not fully convinced. While Marcos's glowing optimism had been encouraging, his report had not offered tangible proof of the mineral wealth the myths alleged. Still, there was a possibility of such, and the thought that others could reap some of its benefits was worrisome to the viceroy.

Because of this, Mendoza sent word to Melchior Díaz, formerly a captain in Guzmán's conquest of Nueva Galicia and now the *alcalde mayor* (chief judge and administrator) at Culiacán. Díaz was asked to revisit the route Marcos had taken to Cibola and give his take on the friar's report. Unlike Marcos, Díaz would go well armed and prepared to fight.

Díaz departed from Culiacán on November 17, 1539, accompanied by fifteen other mounted Spaniards and a number of Indios Amigos.[32] Riding at Díaz's side was Juan de Zaldívar, who had also fought under Guzmán and later was appointed a *regidor* (municipal official) of Guadalajara by Coronado. The party advanced up the same trail followed by Marcos, also finding the natives hospitable and generous. The village Indians erected straw huts in which to lodge the visitors and supplied corn for the Spaniards' horses.

But as Díaz moved north, the weather grew increasingly cold. By the time the Spanish force had crossed into present Arizona and reached the pueblo of Chichilticale, the weather had turned even colder, the land frosting at night. Neither the Indios Amigos nor the Spaniards were accustomed to such a frigid environment. Some of the Spaniards became seriously ill, and a few of the Indian Amigos died. Díaz was so sick with a persistent fever when he returned to Culiacán that he could barely write his report.[33] The people of Chichilticale were less receptive than others had been. They said that a messenger from Cibola had arrived there to say, "If Christians came, they were to consider them of no importance and were to kill them since they were mortal. This [they said] they knew because they had the bones of the one who had gone there [Esteban]. [They said further] that if [the Chichilticale Indians] did not dare [to kill the Spaniards] they were to send [the messenger] to tell [the people of Cibola] because they would come to do it right."[34]

While, as we shall see, there is no reason to question Díaz's bravery, this dire warning may have reminded him that he and his men were few in this distant land. Regardless, neither the Indios Amigos nor the Spaniards were clothed for the severe cold, and Díaz did not continue farther. While his only information regarding Cibola was secured at Chichilticale, his views of the settlement were far more realistic than those provided by Marcos.

Díaz described the pueblo accurately and told of the inhabitants' social and warring habits, noting that they played flutes, sang, danced, harvested corn and beans, and ate out of bowls. They also consumed human flesh and kept captives as slaves. One such captive, who had come to Chichilticale with the messenger and may have been an information source for Díaz, had been a member of Esteban's party.[35]

Though Díaz and his party would meet an advancing expedition under Coronado on the trail at Chiametla early in the spring of 1540, his report on his trip did not reach the viceroy until the ensuing March 20, when Zaldívar and three other horsemen delivered it to him at Colima.[36] By then, Díaz's observations were virtually moot. Even as he and his men were riding hundred of miles and fighting bitter cold during the fall and winter of 1539–1540, Mendoza had made up his mind to plunge ahead with an elaborate expedition of conquest to Cibola. Coronado was to be its captain general.

Mendoza's decision to proceed had been influenced by a rising clamor among the people of Mexico City to go in search of Cibola's wealth. Pedro de Castañeda said later that word spread around New Spain that the seven *ciudads* Nuño de Guzmán had searched for in vain had finally been discovered.[37]

Everyone in New Spain remembered well the enormous wealth reaped by Cortés and Francisco Pizarro and hearkened passionately to tales of cities of gold that almost surely awaited discovery in Tierra Nueva. Basically, the Coronado Expedition, even more than a grand conquistador escapade, was a business venture—a risky one.

Mendoza and Coronado began recruiting for the Cibola expedition at Mexico City, gathering a small army of Spanish nobles, tradesmen, artisans, and young caballeros who had come from Spain looking for adventure and a calling in life. A virtual "gold rush fever" prevailed. Now idle and bored, they joined the expedition eagerly, impelled by the adventure as well as the potential reward of estates in the newly conquered land where gold and silver lodes were said to abound. Mendoza was generous in handing out gold pieces with which the men could purchase their needs for the journey, including lances, armor, and other warfare items.[38]

Another 800 Mexican Indian allies were enlisted to manage the large herds of sheep and cattle driven along for food. The Indians served the needs of the camp on the march, and their warriors acted as scouts and aided in fighting enemies when the need arose. But Mendoza had sternly ordered that, unlike the former practice of conquistador explorations that forced native slaves to serve as baggage carriers, only Indian volunteers would be taken. They would be allowed to leave the expedition if they wished, and they would be shown the consideration of freemen. Mules would help transport the expedition's burdensome cargoes. Some of the natives brought their wives and children, while Indian families left behind would be paid a subsistence. African slaves, many branded on the cheek, served the needs of the Spanish officers—Coronado among them—and many others.[39]

To avoid disturbing that native population by marching his expedition "army" through their land, Mendoza sent them south in small parties to organize at Compostela. During December 1539, Coronado led a party of sixty horsemen south, among them Captain Juan Jaramillo who later authored a valuable account of the Cibola expedition. Jaramillo described the route—which was probably west from Mexico City to Pátzcuaro and Guadalajara, as the viceroy would follow later—as fully populated and at peace.[40]

Mendoza caught up with Coronado at Guadalajara, and they continued on toward Compostela together. On the way, however, Coronado learned of an Indian uprising at a place called Zacarula in Ávalos province. He turned aside, captured the rebel leader, and had him executed.[41]

Coronado met Mendoza at Compostela, where they and their expedition were hosted by Coronado's lieutenant governor, Don Cristóbal de Oñate, who had made a name for himself during Guzmán's Nueva Galicia campaign. Together, Coronado and Mendoza oversaw the final enlistments and preparations for a daring and historic march into the alluring haunts of Tierra Nueva and Cibola.

ABBREVIATION KEY

F/F-*DOCS* = Flint and Flint, eds., trans., annots., *Documents of the Coronado Expedition, 1539–1542*

H/R-*NCE* = Hammond and Rey, eds., *Narratives of the Coronado Expedition, 1540–1542*

NOTES

1. "Mendoza to Alonso de la Torre, October 1539," F/F-*DOCS*, 91.
2. Bolton, *Coronado*, 17.
3. Flint, *No Settlement, No Conquest*, 31.
4. Bolton, *Coronado*, 19.
5. Flint, *No Settlement, No Conquest*, 39.
6. "Decree of King," F/F-*DOCS*, 51–52. See also H/R-*NCE*, 54–57.

7. "Coronado to Viceroy, March 8, 1539," F/F-*DOCS*, 33–34. See also H/R-*NCE*, 42–43.

8. "Coronado to King, July 15, 1539," F/F-*DOCS*, 33.

9. Ibid., 39.

10. "Instructions to and Account by Marcos," F/F-*DOCS*, 73.

11. Ibid., 74.

12. Ibid., 68.

13. Ibid.

14. Ibid.

15. "Castañeda's Narrative," F/F-*DOCS*, 387.

16. "Instructions to and Account by Marcos," F/F-*DOCS*, 68.

17. Ibid.

18. Ibid., 69.

19. Ibid.

20. Ibid., 71.

21. Ibid., 71–72n128.

22. Ibid., 72.

23. Ibid., 73.

24. Ibid., 75.

25. Ibid., 74–75.

26. Ibid., 75–76.

27. Ibid., 75.

28. Ibid. See discussion, p. 61. It does seem that Marcos would not have claimed that he left behind physical evidence (that is, the cross, pile of stones, and Spain's claim to the land) had he not actually been there. Nothing was said, however, of these objects having been seen when Marcos guided the Coronado Expedition there the following year.

29. Ibid., 76. See also H/R-*NCE*, 80.

30. "Instructions to and Account by Marcos," F/F-*DOCS*, 76.

31. "Testimonies of Witnesses in Habana," F/F-*DOCS*, 100.

32. "Viceroy to King, April 17, 1540," F/F-*DOCS*, 235; Flint, *No Settlement, No Conquest*, 40.

33. "Viceroy to King, April 17, 1540," F/F-*DOCS*, 235, 238.

34. Ibid., 238. See also H/R-*NCE*, 160.

35. "Viceroy to King, April 17, 1540," F/F-*DOCS*, 236–237. See also H/R-*NCE*, 198.

36. "Viceroy to King, April 17, 1540," F/F-*DOCS*, 234. Mendoza, dismayed by Díaz's negative report regarding Cibola, sent Zaldívar back to tell Coronado to stop his expedition and send a captain on to reconnoiter. By the time Zaldívar reached Culiacán, Coronado had already done essentially that.

37. "Castañeda's Narrative," F/F-*DOCS*, 389.

38. Ibid., 45, 50.

39. Ibid., 51.

40. "Jaramillio's Narrative," F/F-*DOCS*, 512; "Castañeda's Narrative," F/F-*DOCS*, 390.

41. Bolton, *Coronado*, 64–65.

3
Off to the Land of Treasure

Across strange seas deep valleys lie, which hide strange temples,
wondrous sights, great mountains towering to the skies.

Capt. Gaspar de Villagrá[1]

On the brisk Monday morning of February 28, 1540[2] (Julian calendar; March 2, Gregorian calendar), the mining town of Compostela, perched along Mexico's west coast, stirred with excitement in witness of its moment of history. The small silver- and gold-mining village that Nuño de Guzmán had founded in 1535 as the capital of Nueva Galicia rested comfortably on a palm-treed plateau swathed in early morning by the shadows of the Sierra Madres to the east.

Resident Spaniards and Indian natives, many wrapped in blankets against the morning chill, gathered to watch as the governor of Nueva Galicia and captain general of the Cibola expedition, Francisco Vázquez de Coronado, marshaled together his disparate force of Spanish citizens of many callings: black and Indian servants, a number of whom were slaves; and friendly Mexican Indians (Indios Amigos) who had been recruited as a potential fighting force for the expedition.

This was the conglomerate of disaffected personnel Coronado was to lead into the mysterious but promising lands to the north. This was no ordinary event for New Spain. Many of those involved had contributed their all. The challenge of their venture was great, expectations were high, and excitement abounded as the expedition formed into marching order.

Coronado had come dressed befitting his role as a new-generation conquistador replete with glistening body armor. His long Spanish sword swung at his leg, a red cape swathed his shoulders, a feathered plume topped his golden helmet, and spike-toothed spurs sparkled at his boot heels. His charger, a beautiful, high-spirited black stallion that pranced and snorted against its commanding restraint, caught the admiring eye of all.

The horse, valued at 100 gold pesos, had been presented to Coronado by his lieutenant governor, Don Cristóbal de Oñate, who would officiate over Nueva Galicia during Coronado's absence.[3] The stallion would serve Coronado well on the expedition until it died during the return to New Spain in 1542.

With his black beard neatly trimmed beneath his glistening war helmet, the twenty-nine-year-old captain general presented a firm, determined posture when seated on the stallion. Still, he, too, was inwardly filled with the excitement of the moment. The monumental scope of his assignment stood to be the true measure of a Spanish conquistador. The task before Coronado was to lead this *entrada* of largely untried people northward through a wilderness land. He had been told that for a time they would be served by the well-worn paths that connected Indian villages. He would soon learn, however, that waiting ahead were coastal forests to conquer, dangerous mountainside trails to cross with his animals, and arid deserts to survive to reach the mysterious world the Spaniards called Tierra Nueva. Once there, he was to conquer and pacify seven Indian settlements about which little was known, install his authority, and establish Spain's claim to the land.

Situated at the lead with Coronado were Lope de Samaniego, the *maestre de campo* (second in command), and Pedro de Tovar, a nephew of Viceroy Mendoza, as *alférez mayor* (chief lieutenant), both also serving as captains of horsemen companies. Other captains were Rodrigo Maldonado, the twenty-five-year-old *encomendero* of Guadalajara; Diego de Guevara, son-in-law of the first conqueror of Nueva España, who served as *alcalde mayor* of Nueva Galicia; Tristan de Arellano, in his mid-twenties, who had once served as captain general of an unsuccessful expedition to La Florida; García López de Cárdenas, a kinsman of Viceroy Mendoza and a former *alguacil mayor* (chief law enforcement officer) of the Audiencia and Chancilleria de Mexico; and Diego López, formerly a councilman of Seville, Spain. Hernando de Alvarado, twenty-three years old, served as the expedition's captain of artillery; and Captain Pablos de Melgosa, a native of Burgos, Spain, also twenty-three, commanded the footmen.[4]

With the Royal Treasury providing no financial support, the expedition became purely a private endeavor. Outfitting such an expedition with animals, equipment, and supplies was expensive. Coronado scholar Shirley Cushing Flint calculated Mendoza's contribution at 85,000 silver pesos, all from moneys borrowed against his landholdings. Coronado, meanwhile, invested another 71,000 pesos that he secured using the inherited estate of his wife, Beatriz de Estrada, as collateral. Another heavy investor was Pedro de Alvarado, governor of Guatemala.[5]

The rest of the expedition financing came from property owners and merchants of means who joined the venture, donating money, materials, and livestock to the cause. Melchior Pérez, son of the former Mexican governor Pérez de la Torre, invested close to 5,000 silver pesos.[6] For everyone, including the captains and other members who contributed slaves, stock, supplies, armament—at times, everything they had—these contributions were calculated to be an investment against the great rewards they would reap in the north. The Coronado Expedition, even more than a grand conquistador escapade, was a high-risk business venture. For many, it was a chancy gamble, but the call of becoming a conquistador was paramount.

Mules would be used to transport the expedition's burdensome cargoes.[7] Coronado and his guard, having attended civic functions at Guadalajara, joined Mendoza at Compostela where they were hosted by Cristóbal de Oñate. Together, Mendoza and Coronado oversaw the final enlistments and preparation of the massive expedition. When that was done, Mendoza ordered that a formal review of the expedition would be held.

> There were present the governor Cristóbal de Oñate, the *factor*
> Gonzalo de Salazar, Pedro Amildes Cherinos the *veedor*, Barrios
> *comendador* of the order of St. John, learned in holy theology, and many
> other gentlemen, residents and conquerors of that city and province.
> The aforesaid review was carried out with fine order, harmony, and a

display of trappings of great value. With the same order, uniformity, and rejoicing, the standard, the royal insigne of the army was shown.[8]

The muster roll of the expedition details Coronado as taking twenty-two or twenty-three spare horses. One member of the expedition later recalled Coronado as having seven good horses and twelve or fifteen others for use by his retinue, plus fifteen mules. Another expeditionary remembered later that in addition to the cattle, sheep, and pigs, Coronado's supply train included hardtack, wheat, and a supply of oil and vinegar. Also available were medicines for anyone who fell sick or was injured. Trailing behind in the procession, seven slaves—four men and three women—oversaw Coronado's animals as well as his many fine clothes and other goods.[9]

The cattle, sheep, and pigs were to provide fresh meat for the expedition during its long march and after. But the pigs did not drive well, and rocky portions of the trail were so damaging to the sheep's feet that they had to be turned back.

Coronado held his mount in position as his captains ushered their cavalry neophytes, over 225 of them, into marching formation behind the company standards. Mostly, they were young hidalgos recruited in Mexico City, their eyes flashing with hopes of great adventure ahead. Thus far, for them the world of New Spain had been largely aimless and unrewarding as they idled slothfully about in Mexico City. They had seen nothing of the riches and adventure that had brought them across the sea from Spain. Their presence in Mexico City had been less than productive, and many of the city's older citizens were glad to see them leave. The young men had become a nuisance with their gambling, drinking, marital problems, and occasional dueling with outraged husbands.[10]

Spanish historian Mota Padilla described them as social parasites "bobbing up and down like corks on the water, without having anything to do, constantly pestering Mendoza for estates and rich maidens to wed."[11] Indeed, they seemed a sorry lot to fit the glorified mold of past conquistadors.

But now the young caballeros were embarking on a great, promising venture of which they had long dreamed. Their spirits were buoyed further by the sturdy mounts beneath them, as well as by the lances, swords, shields, armor, and colorful dress the generous viceroy had provided. Camp talk of the great discovery of golden treasures they expected to make at the seven cities of Cibola had caused them to feel more like true, gallant conquistadors and less like inexperienced urbanites who had

FIGURE 3.1. *Mexican cart with wheels*

seriously overloaded themselves with personal goods for the long, challenging march ahead.

Coronado's army of eight companies was described as "two hundred and seventy mounted men with lances, swords, and other hand weapons, some with coats of mail and sallets with visors, both of iron and of raw cowhide, and the horses with bardings of native blankets; and seventy infantrymen, both musketeers and harquebusiers, and others with swords and bucklers."[12]

One of the more notable items the Spanish had brought to the New World was the transportation wheel and pulleys. The Spaniards had used two-wheeled carts to move artillery during Cortés's invasion of Mexico (figure 3.1).[13] The wheel, however, had not become widely adopted in New Spain in Coronado's day, even for the famous donkey or mule carts with their two large wheels of solid wood. They would not have lasted long on the trail to Tierra Nueva.

Next came the pack animals loaded with provisions, equipment, extra arms and armor, munitions, and six pieces of light artillery. Massed behind them were the Indian allies, pacified to Spanish rule but still bound by their traditional war ethic and ready, if not eager, for combat with other tribes. They have been estimated to have numbered between 900 and

1,300, but some scholars believe there were as many as 2,000 or more. A sizable number were warriors. Armed with their usual weapons of war—bows and arrows, spears, clubs, javelins, slings, and leather shields—they would provide the Spanish troops with a dominating force in conflicts ahead.

As historian Richard Flint astutely observed, the presence of these Indios Amigos—the largest segment of the expedition—has been slighted in accounts of the Coronado Expedition. Spanish documents say very little about them, even, or perhaps especially, regarding conflicts that erupted during the expedition. Likewise, the role of the Indios Amigos has been virtually ignored by many historians of the past, who have recounted conquistador adventures almost purely through the prism of Spanish heroism.[14]

Mixed in among the entourage were black and native servants to herd the large remuda of spare horses and mules, as well as the food animals that would provide fresh meat along the way. Because of the slower pace of the stock, they arrived late at each campsite. Personal slaves would arrange camps along the march, preparing meals, tending the soldiers' horses, and doing other chores. "The army, then," Padilla observed, "was divided in this manner, with more than a thousand horses, not counting the pack-animals, and others loaded with six field-guns [*pedreros*], powder, and shot, and more than a thousand Indian allies and Indian servants, and horse-handlers, cowmen, and shepherds."[15]

Coronado's departure from Compostela had been carefully programmed. After the captains were assigned to their companies, everyone had taken Sunday mass at the San Jago church. The building, erected only a year earlier of volcanic red stone native to the region, has stood through the centuries to the modern day. It was there that Mendoza held his review and delivered an eloquent speech reminding the soldiers of the loyalty they owed to their captain general. He spoke of the expedition's potential to effect the religious conversion of the people of Cibola, as well as the "profit to those who conquered that land." He also stressed "the service it would be to His Majesty and the obligation they were placing [the king] under to always aid and support them."[16]

After this, the entire army—captains and soldiers alike—swore their oaths on a Bible, vowing that they would follow and obey their captain general in everything he commanded them to do in the days ahead. When the long caravan had finally been organized for the march, Coronado was joined at the front by Lope de Samaniego and Pedro de Tovar, the expedition's chief standard bearer. The moment of departure came, and Don Francisco gave the signal to march. With colors flying above his cavalrymen's bobbing heads, their lances aslant skyward, he led his civilian army off northward toward the mystic land of Cibola to the hearty cheers of "Granada" from the Spanish spectators.

As the Coronado Expedition marched boldly and proudly out of Compostela up the trail northward, however, no one in the expedition, from Coronado down to the lowest Indio Amigo—all of whom were accustomed to central New Spain's balmy climate—then realized that they had made a serious oversight. They had not foreseen how deadly cold it would be in Tierra Nueva during the forthcoming winter. Overlooked were the warm clothing and blankets they would so desperately need. Even without these items, however, transporting the cumbersome goods up the difficult trail ahead would be a challenge.

The route of the expedition's march from Compostela followed along the primordial slopes of the Sierra Madre, whose white peaks trim the horizon along the Pacific Coast of Mexico (figure 3.2). On this initial stretch of still raw country, the uninitiated volunteers from Mexico City were introduced to the burdens and hard facts of life on the trail. They left behind a telling track of discarded excess items they had soon learned were more of an impediment than a benefit to them on the march.

Two days out from Compostela, Coronado issued a proclamation. There was to be no licentiousness, blasphemy, living in concubinage, or other vices such as excessive gambling on the expedition. It was announced publicly that no one would be permitted to take any Indian slaves, male or female, in Tierra Nueva, under pain of certain penalties. This, it was later testified, caused the army to be very well governed on its march to Cibola.[17]

Because Mendoza had removed the Indians from rendering many of the manual services they normally performed, the coddled sons of Spanish families were forced to serve themselves. Even those who had personal slaves were required to tend their own horses, pack their own baggage, bake their own bread, make their own camp arrangements, and perform many of the other chores of simple survival on the trail.[18] They would soon learn as well that they had entered a harsh, primitive land where many dangers lurked. Gradually, the rough life of the trail would harden them as men and make them better soldiers.

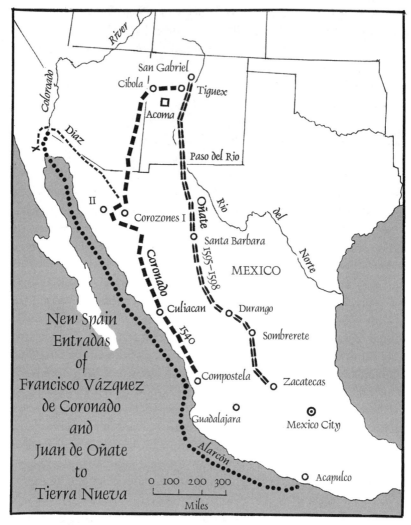

FIGURE 3.2. *Coronado and Oñate routes to Tierra Nueva (map by author)*

The animal herds, the sheep in particular, held the march to a slow pace through the yet unbroken countryside. The cavalcade was detained for several days at the Rio Grande de Santiago, where the sheep had to be carried one by one across the cascading mountain stream.[19]

The standard historical portrayal of Coronado has been as a congenial, temperate man. While this may well have been true, there is clear evidence that he was also a determined commander, a severe disciplinarian,

and a merciless deliverer of punishment to anyone who defied his authority. His treatment of captive offenders was often as brutal as that exercised
by his conquistador predecessors. While it was claimed that all his men
loved him greatly, members of the Cibola expedition later testified that
the captain general exercised such threatening restraint on the march that
no one dared act against or without his approval: "If any individual from
the army disobeyed, committing any outrage or taking corn or property
from [the Indians] Francisco Vázquez imprisoned and punished that person. [The witness] said that he saw that for very slight infractions individuals were kept in shackles for two or three days' travel."[20]

Coronado's three-year visit to Tierra Nueva covered the same time
period, 1540–1542, as New Spain's Mixon War. Some have claimed that
this bloody insurrection against Spanish rule was initiated by the march of
Coronado's Cibola expedition through the Mexican provinces. Coronado
disputed this, but an incident that occurred on his way to San Miguel de
Culiacán may have been an opening shot in the long, bloody war that
revealed the Mexican Indians' deep resentment of the Spanish system of
demanding tributes. It was also the first hostile encounter for many of
Coronado's men.

During a camping stop at Chiametla, camp master Samaniego led
a detachment of soldiers into the countryside to collect tributes of food.
They found the Indians unaccommodating, at times even belligerent. At
one village a soldier who had strayed was taken prisoner. When Samaniego
rushed into the brush to rescue the screaming man, he was killed by an
arrow that entered his brain through an eye while his helmet visor was
raised. Some suspected that Samaniego's killing may have been related to
his previous service in the area with the ruthless Guzmán.

Several other soldiers were wounded in the fracas. Coronado
responded furiously with punitive raids that netted a number of Indian
captives. Again, he applied the standard rule of conquistador conquest—
merciless punishment and fear. By his order, several Indians, both men
and women, who were thought to be guilty of fostering insurrection were
hanged and—again as a dire warning to others—left dangling from tree
limbs. As an even more horrific warning against rebellion, other captives
were quartered—that is, victims were decapitated and their arms and legs
dismembered—and left for others to see.[21]

At Chiametla, Díaz and his men, returning from their reconnaissance
to Tierra Nueva, met and joined with the Coronado Expedition. The

trail-weary captain reported his findings in private. But even though an attempt was made to keep the findings secret, expedition members likely heard accounts from Díaz's men around the campfire. The news was not good. Díaz had found only two or three poor villages whose inhabitants had insisted there was nothing ahead but rough, mountainous country.[22]

This was not at all what Marcos had claimed it to be. Among other things, Marcos had said the way north would be "plain and good," with only one small hill to ascend. Members of the vanguard were disturbed, and grumblings were heard among the men. But the ever exuberant Marcos stepped forward to dispel doubts, with assurances that they were truly on their way to a place "where their hands would soon be filled," presumably with gold. Somewhat heartened, the Cibola expedition pushed on. Still, Captain Diego López said later that after the meeting with Díaz, he "held no hope that they would come across anything [worthwhile] in that new land."[23]

The expedition continued north, reaching Culiacán just prior to Easter in March 1540. Upon its arrival there, the expedition participated in a unique, farcical event. Coronado was met by a delegation of the city's Spanish citizens, who requested that he withhold his entrance until they could prepare a pretend defense. Agreeably, Coronado paused while the town's Spanish officials put seven brass cannons in place. A sham battle ensued, with Coronado taking the outpost city captive. A good time was had by all except the artilleryman, who had not finished priming his cannon when the order was given to fire. He lost his hand.[24]

At Culiacán, Spanish members of the expedition discarded more of their most disposable baggage. They reluctantly gave citizens their spare equipage: furniture, dress clothing, and other items that were detriments on the trail. Some of the goods were left to be put aboard two supply-laden vessels Mendoza was sending up the coast under Hernando de Alarcón's leadership for the expedition.[25] These items were never recovered, and even the light clothing would be desperately missed during two trying winters in Tierra Nueva.

An incident of note occurred while the expedition was at Culiacán. A young man named Trujillo made the surprising claim that he had had a prophetic vision while bathing in the river. The devil, he said, had appeared before him and declared that he was to kill the general, after which Trujillo would marry Coronado's wife, Doña Beatriz, and she would reward him with many treasures.[26]

Not unexpectedly, Trujillo was dismissed from the expedition. His story became the subject of sermons and New Spain gossip. Culiacán, nonetheless, proved a happy respite for the weary expeditionaries. In recent years the outpost town had prospered from bountiful harvests and, in addition to providing comfortable quarters and entertainment, willingly re-supplied its guests. Additional corn and other provisions were obtained from ships at anchor in Culiacán's harbor.[27] As a result, Coronado remained there for nearly a month, not departing until April 22.[28]

Because of the reports he received from Díaz on the trail ahead and the serious lack of food supplies, Coronado made an important decision. Leaving the main portion of his expedition at Culiacán, he opted for a smaller group to go in advance. He selected seventy-five or eighty mounted soldiers and twenty-five or thirty foot soldiers, with each man carrying his own eighty days' worth of provisions. Captain Tristan de Arellano was given command of the portion of the expedition that was left behind. The advance party included a particularly conspicuous member, Francisca de Hozes, who was accompanied by her husband, Alonso Sánchez, and their son.[29] The outspoken Francisca, the only woman in the advance party, would eventually prove to be one of Coronado's most outspoken critics.

Coronado took his African servants and most of the Indian allies, who provided a security force that some historians believe numbered more than 1,000 men. Two friars, Fray Marcos and Fray Antonio Vitoria, eager to reach potential converts in the new land, also joined the advance party. Vitoria, however, broke his leg and was forced to remain behind with the main body of the army.[30]

According to participant testimony, Coronado rigidly obeyed Mendoza's order to treat natives they met along the way generously. When a village was approached, men were sent ahead with a cross as a sign that the Spaniards meant no harm. Coronado made his camps well outside the settlements, issuing stern orders that none of his men were to take food or other goods from the natives unless he so directed. Guards were placed around the camps at night to prevent any of the soldiers from slipping away for a mercenary or romantic visit.[31] Participants also agreed that on the march the natives of all the towns visited between Culiacán and Cibola made the Spaniards "very welcome." The natives gave of the foodstuffs they had and "rendered obedience to His Majesty and to the general in his royal name."[32]

The march, however, proved even more difficult than expected and was often perilous as the advance made its way up the Mexican coast to the Sinaloa River. Both the men and their horses were severely worn by the rough country and lack of food. At places, the mountains were so difficult that "even if the trail is well repaired, it cannot be traversed without great danger of the horses rolling [down] there."[33]

The toll on the vanguard was significant. Not only had the expedition lost a number of horses, but, as Coronado reported, "some of my Indian allies died, as well as a Spaniard named Espinosa and two Moors, who died from eating a certain plant because they were lacking food supplies."[34]

The expedition was now into what had become known to Spanish explorers as the Valley of Hearts, so named after natives there supplied the Cabeza de Vaca foursome with "six hundred hearts of deers" their village kept for eating.[35] Coronado tried to keep his march close to the sea (the Gulf of California) but was constantly pushed farther inland by Marcos and the terrain. He again sent some horsemen double-speed ahead to search out a pass through the mountain chain to the Yaqui River beyond the present city of Alamos, Mexico. On the basis of information secured by the scouting horsemen, the advance followed the Yaqui north until it was possible to cut across to the Sonora River and the village of Corazones near, it is thought, present Ures, Sonora.[36]

From Jaramillo's descriptions, the expedition is believed to have turned north near the site of present Cananea and continued along the Rio San Pedro. Following this stream northward, they crossed what is now the US-Mexico border below present Palominas, Arizona.[37]

On June 17 (Julian calendar; June 27 Gregorian), the expedition camped on the San Pedro before swinging northeastward along the Chiricahua Mountain range, going into camp at an Indian village called Chichilticale. The site is backdropped to the east by the Chiricahua National Forest, with its rugged volcanic rock spires. But for the Spaniards, the most interesting feature of Chichilticale was an ancient ruin known as the Red House.

This roofless adobe structure, an archaeological site known today as the Kuykendall Ruins, featured thick standing walls that led Pedro de Castañeda to think it had once been a fort destroyed by the people who now resided there. Archaeologists now believe the brick-red color of the walls resulted from the building's destruction by fire.[38]

The Chichilticale natives had no food they could provide for the expedition, but fortunately there were springs in the region, and the settlement itself contained a shallow well with sloping sides that permitted easy access to its water.[39]

The villagers at Chichilticale told Coronado that he was a fifteen-day journey from the sea. Marcos had said it was only five leagues away, and everyone's distrust of the friar was renewed. Natives, who habitually went to the coast to fish, said they had seen a ship pass by recently; but the Spaniards did not know if it was a Spanish ship or a much-dreaded Portuguese vessel.[40]

Marcos's error in placing the gulf much closer than it was would later anger Coronado, who wrote Mendoza: "Thus, when I reached Chichilticale, I found myself fifteen days' travel from the sea. The father provincial had been saying that the distance was only five leagues and that he had seen it. We all experienced great distress and confusion on seeing that we found everything to be contrary to what he had told Your Lordship."[41]

After resting for two days, Coronado and his vanguard headed north from Chichilticale, entering a wilderness of dense forests, punishing deserts, and nearly impassable mountains—the *despoblado* (uninhabited region) that straddles the border between southeastern Arizona and southwestern New Mexico.

ABBREVIATION KEY

F/F-*DOCS* = Flint and Flint, eds., trans., annots., *Documents of the Coronado Expedition, 1539–1542*

H/R-*NCE* = Hammond and Rey, eds., *Narratives of the Coronado Expedition, 1540–1542*

W-*CE* = Winship, *The Coronado Expedition, 1540–1542*

NOTES

1. *A History of New Mexico*, 39.

2. This date differs from the Tuesday, February 24, 1540, offered in Flint, *No Settlement, No Conquest*, 75. Bolton says he started off "the next day," which would have been Monday, February 23; *Coronado*, 78. Winship also gives that date; W-*CE*, 64. In the absence of any proven date of departure provided in the Spanish documents, consideration must be given to the "Hearing on

Depopulation Charges" (F/F-*DOCS*, 171–184), according to which five witnesses gave testimony on February 26 and one, Cristóbal de Oñate, on February 27. Not once did any of them speak of the expedition's departure in the past tense. Instead, thirty-five times they used the future tenses of "are going," "is going," and "are leaving." The fact that the expedition did not leave later than February 29 (1540 was a leap year) was established by a letter from the viceroy to the king on April 17, 1540, in which Mendoza refers to a report he sent to the king on the "last day of February" 1540. Then he stated that Coronado and his people had already departed from Compostela (Viceroy to King, April 17, 1540, F/F-*DOCS*, 235). Therefore, if the depopulation testimony is accepted as applicable evidence, the departure would have occurred on either February 28 or 29. By reasoning that Coronado would have wished to have the depopulation charges effectively countered before he departed and that Mendoza would have waited until the day after the departure to write the king, a February 28 departure seems the more likely candidate.

3. Simmons, *The Last Conquistador*, 22–23.

4. Flint, *Great Cruelties*, 277. Biographical information was found in ibid., appendix 2, and F/F-*DOCS*, appendix 1.

5. Richard and Shirley Cushing Flint, "The Financing and Provisioning of the Coronado Expedition," in Flint and Flint, eds., *The Coronado Expedition*, 45–47.

6. Ibid.; Flint, *Great Cruelties*, 207.

7. Flint, *No Settlement, No Conquest*, 56–57.

8. Hammond and Rey, eds. and trans., *Obregon's History*, 14.

9. Flint, *Great Cruelties*, 364; F/F-*DOCS*, 118.

10. Day, *Coronado's Quest*, 70.

11. Padilla and de la Matías, *Historia de la Conquista*, 111.

12. Day, "Mota Padilla," 91.

13. Thomas, *Rivers of Gold*, 490.

14. Flint, "What's Missing from This Picture," 59–66.

15. Day, "Mota Padilla," 91–92.

16. "Castañeda's Narrative," F/F-*DOCS*, 390. See also W-*CE*, 194, 199; H/R-*NCE*, 203.

17. Flint, *Great Cruelties*, 361, 363, 391.

18. Ibid., 392; Bolton, *Coronado*, 81.

19. Day, "Mota Padilla," 92.

20. Flint, *Great Cruelties*, 110.

21. Ibid., 330, 463.

22. "Coronado to Mendoza, August 3, 1540," F/F-*DOCS*, 252–253. See also W-*CE*, 319; H/R-*NCE*, 163.

23. Flint, *Great Cruelties*, 396.

24. "Castañeda's Narrative," F/F-*DOCS*, 392. See also W-*CE*, 201; H/R-*NCE*, 205.

25. "Historical Introduction," W-*CE*, 71–72.

26. "Castañeda's Narrative," F/F-*DOCS*, 392. See also W-*CE*, 201; H/R-*NCE*, 205.

27. "Castañeda's Narrative," F/F-*DOCS*, 392.

28. "Coronado to Viceroy, August 3, 1450," F/F-*DOCS*, 254. See also W-*CE*, 318; H/R-*NCE*, 162.

29. Bolton, *Coronado*, 96.

30. "Castañeda's Narrative," F/F-*DOCS*, 392. See also W-*CE*, 201; *H/R-NCE*, 206.

31. Bolton, *Coronado*, 96–97.

32. "Rodrigo Ximón Testimony," in Flint, *Great Cruelties*, 128.

33. "Coronado to Viceroy, August 3, 1450," F/F-*DOCS*, 255. Winship interpreted this as: "There are mountains where, however well the path might be fixed, they could not be crossed without there being great dangers of the horses falling over them." "Coronado to Mendoza," W-*CE*, 319. See also H/R-*NCE*, 164.

34. "Coronado to Mendoza, August 3, 1540," F/F-*DOCS*, 256.

35. Bandelier, *Journey of Cabeza de Vaca*, 160; "Jaramillo's Narrative," F/F-*DOCS*, 512. See also W-*CE*, 373; H/R-*NCE*, 296. Winship interpreted this statement as: "Ten or twelve of the horses had died of overwork by the time that we reached this Valley of Hearts, because they were unable to stand the strain of carrying heavy burdens and eating little. Some of our negroes and some of the Indians also died here." W-*CE*, 320. See also H/R-*NCE*, 166.

36. Based on field research and studies by Nugent Brasher, as stated in "The Chichilticale Camp of Francisco Vázquez de Coronado," 436.

37. Ibid., 436–437. See "Map of Coronado Trail," ibid., 440.

38. Ibid., 441–449.

39. Ibid., 446–447.

40. "Coronado to Viceroy, August 3, 1450," F/F-*DOCS*, 255. See also W-*CE*, 320; H/R-*NCE*, 165.

41. "Coronado to Viceroy, August 3, 1540," F/F-*DOCS*, 255. See also W-*CE*, 320–321; H/R-*NCE*, 165.

4

"We Ask and Require"

They [the Hopi Indians] had received word that Cibola had been overrun by the most ferocious people who rode animals that ate people.

Castañeda[1]

Coronado's precise route beyond Chichilticale has never been resolved with certainty. It is clearly determined, however, that he marched north to the Zuni settlements on the Zuni River in present New Mexico just across its border with Arizona. A direct route thereto would have taken the expedition along the east side of the border through Apache Pass, past the Peloncillo Mountain range and the Apache-Sitgreaves National Forest, past the site of present Eagar and St. Johns, Arizona, and across the Little Colorado River to the known location of Cibola on the Zuni River.

A participant in the march, writing from Cibola at about the same time as Coronado, described the perils of the journey: "[Vázquez de Coronado] reached this *provincia* on Wednesday, the seventh of this past July [1540], with the whole troop he took from the valley of Culiacán (highest praise to Our Lord), except one Spaniard who died of hunger four days' journey from here and some Blacks and Indians who also died of hunger and thirst."[2]

Coronado describes an equally harrowing journey, as in his account describing the deaths of some of his Indian allies, a Spaniard named Espinosa, and two Moors. That same account also records the loss of horses: "We lost more horses in this last unsettled region than we had farther back."[3]

Along with their hunger, disillusionment had been mounting steadily among Coronado's party as they struggled through the harsh, sunbaked countryside that spoke scant of wealth or other reward. Still, for all those who had dreamed of a city with streets of gold, the sighting of this first pueblo city was even more disheartening: "When they saw the first *pueblo*, which was Cibola, such were the curses that some of them hurled at fray Marcos that may God not allow them to reach [his] ears."[4]

Just beyond the crossing of the Zuni River at the present New Mexico border, the Cibola expedition caught its first glimpse of the fabled city, the Indian name of which was Hawikuh. Pedro de Castañeda described it as "a small pueblo crowded together and spilling down a cliff." He wrote: "It is a *pueblo* with three and four upper stories and with up to two hundred fighting men. The houses are small and not very roomy . . . A single patio serves a neighborhood."[5]

Juan Jaramillo observed that "the houses have flat roofs, and the walls are made of stone and mud."[6] The *Relación del Suceso* noted that "in many places the *pueblos* present defensive walls formed by the buildings."[7]

Captain García López de Cárdenas, now *maestre de campo*, was ordered to scout ahead with fifteen horsemen. While doing so, he encountered four natives walking near a lake. Presenting them with a cross, he told them through sign that his party came peacefully in the name of the king to defend and aid them. The Indians responded in friendly fashion, assuring the Spaniards that when they arrived at the village they would be provided with food.

This was a critical matter, for at this point in the march both the men and their animals were famished. Coronado took two of the Cibolan Indians hostage and sent the other two, along with a Sonora Indian who spoke their language, back to their village. They carried instructions for the inhabitants to tell the leaders that the Spaniards were coming "on behalf of His Majesty to bring them to his obedience and so that they might know God."[8] The people were to remain quietly inside their homes when the Spaniards arrived, and they would be done no harm.

Coronado next dispatched Cárdenas to scout out the trail ahead to look for a place where the Indians might launch an ambush. Such a spot was found and occupied. That night the Indians came to the place, afterward known as "Bad Pass" near the present Arizona–New Mexico border, to attack the Spaniards. The Indians soon retreated to their village. When notified of the attack, Coronado hurried forth to join Cárdenas with the remainder of his command, then pushed on the next morning toward the pueblo village. Coronado later wrote: "I was worried that if we had to delay one more day, we would all be dead of hunger. [This was] especially [true of] the Indians because among us all we had no more than two mine [*sic*] of corn."[9]

As he and his horsemen advanced on the pueblo, smoke signals appeared against the sky, and a native warrior began sounding a warning on a "conch trumpet." An estimated 300 Indians, armed with bows and arrows and round war shields, appeared to confront the Spaniards, indicating their defiance vocally and tossing handfuls of dirt into the air.

Cárdenas, Frays Daniel and Luis, Hernando Bermejo, and some horsemen were sent forward with rosary beads and small cloaks for presents. Also sent were the two remaining captives who were to be released to their people.[10] Melchior Pérez later testified that the defiant resident Indians were told they would be given knowledge about Jesus Christ and how they would be saved while Cárdenas was to deliver the *Requerimiento* to the Indians.

The *Requerimiento* was the official Spanish demand of submission regularly presented to New World natives by conquering expeditions following its adoption in 1513. In part, the edict read: "We ask and require . . . that you acknowledge the Church as the ruler and superior of the whole world, and the high priest called Pope, and in his name the king and queen . . . our lords, in his place, as superiors and lords and kings of these islands and this mainland."[11] If the natives failed to obey, the *Requerimiento* declared, "the deaths and losses which shall accrue from this are your fault, and not that of their highnesses, or ours."[12]

Bewildering though the message may have been to the Cibolans, its essential idea was probably understood: "We are here to take over your land and your lives. We will punish you if you resist." If not clear at that moment, it would soon become so when the Spaniards began demanding the Cibolans' homes, food, clothing, and women.

The Cibola natives remained belligerent, however, and began raining a shower of arrows toward the emissaries. One arrow pierced the robe of Friar Luis but failed to do him bodily harm. Other arrows struck some of the horses.[13] Coronado later testified: "Although they [the natives] were summoned three times to offer peace and made to understand, through the interpreter who had been sent to speak with them and went to them, they were never willing to come in peace nor to render obedience to His Majesty. Nor did they stop shooting arrows."[14]

In his report to Mendoza, Coronado insisted that he held back from offensive action for as long as he could, doing all he could to persuade the natives to surrender. But, with the approval of the friars, he finally ordered his cavalry to charge the Indians, none of whom had ever seen a horse. The force of the animals bearing down on them, with the Spaniards wielding their swords and lances, quickly drove the defenders back to their village. The Spanish onslaught was severe. One Spanish soldier said later that "the general attacked them with the whole force, and they lanced up to forty men."[15]

This was the first known encounter between Indians and horses within what is now the United States of America. To them, the horses gave the Spaniards a fearsome advantage. It would take well over another century for the Spanish horse to multiply in the American Southwest and drastically alter the fighting technique, the value system, and, indeed, the very life of tribal natives.

Still unable to negotiate a surrender, Coronado divided his forces for an attack on the pueblo. Dismounting his men, he ordered his musketeers and crossbowmen to fire their weapons. But the Spaniards were unable to drive the Indians from their rooftops, from where they were still loosing a volley of arrows. When the Spaniards came close enough to the base of the pueblos, the Zunis hurled a barrage of large stones down upon them.

Coronado had now taken the lead, and his gleaming armor drew special attention from the Indian archers, who saw him as a target of choice. An arrow struck him in an unprotected leg, and he suffered small facial wounds and bruises on his arms and legs. He was pelted by rocks until finally a large missile struck his plumed helmet, driving him from his mount. He lay sprawled on the ground unconscious, his nose bleeding and a leg badly bruised, until Cárdenas came to his rescue. The captain threw his body over that of his captain general until others arrived to drag Coronado away to safety.[16]

Coronado remained unconscious. He had suffered three wounds in the face and bruises all over his body. The arrow wound caused his leg to remain swollen for some time before it healed.[17] When he finally awoke in a tent, the battle was over.

Two soldiers and several horses were injured and three mounts were killed before the Spaniards finally won the day. Because he was incapacitated and not further involved, Coronado does not tell more about the battle. He does say that some of the Indians were killed and others might have been slain if pursuit had been made.

Cárdenas said no more than twelve Indians died; another said it was "many." Still another participant summarized the battle from the point of Coronado's misfortune: "Because of the great injury they were doing to us from the flat roofs, we were compelled to draw back. From a distance the artillery and arquebuses [*sic*] began to do them harm. That afternoon they surrendered."[18]

After this, the Zunis fled the village en masse, taking refuge atop a mesa north of present Zuni, New Mexico.[19] When they entered the vacated pueblo, the famished Spaniards gorged themselves on the food supply left behind—maize, beans, the turkeys the natives kept mostly for their feathers, all well seasoned with precious white salt. Coronado's men rested and recuperated.

Eventually, a delegation of Zuni chiefs returned to the village to talk. Coronado lectured them on how they had done wrong by opposing him, again demanding that they pledge their allegiance to the Spanish king and take up the Christian religion. The chiefs humbly admitted their great error in resisting and vowed future obedience to their new lords. The Zunis brought modest gifts of turquoise, a few small cloaks, and edible game such as rabbits. Still, when Coronado asked that their people return to the village, it was some time before the Spaniards saw any Indians under age fifteen or over sixty, and none of them were women.[20]

While the famished expedition was much relieved to find food in the pueblo, they were sorely disappointed at turning up nothing made of any metal, none of the riches for which they had come. Coronado wrote Mendoza, "From what I am able to conclude, there does not appear to me to be any prospect of obtaining gold and silver, but I trust in God that if it exists here we will obtain it. And it will not remain unlocated for lack of seeking it . . . In this place some gold and silver have been found. Those who understand mining have thought it not bad. To this point I have been unable to extract from these people where they dug it up."[21]

It was a false hope indeed. The only metal found, it was later learned, had been carried to Cibola by a member of the vanguard. But Coronado added a hopeful note in his report to the viceroy: "I think they have turquoise in quantity."[22] He also informed Mendoza that he had given the pueblo he had captured the name Granada because of its similarity to the Spanish town.[23]

The Spaniards found considerable indication of Esteban's death scattered about the pueblo. The Zunis had killed the Moor there, the natives said, because he assaulted their women, whom they loved even more than themselves. Reluctantly bending to pressure, the Indians turned over an Indian boy named Bartolomé who had been with Esteban. Coronado put him to use as an interpreter.[24]

Having never received the provisions aboard the two support ships Mendoza had sent up the coast under Captain Hernando de Alarcón, Coronado's advance party had barely made it to Cibola. But the Cibola pueblos offered limited food supplies, and Alarcón's goods were desperately needed. Driving cattle from New Spain to Cibola, Coronado later wrote Mendoza, would take an entire year on the road. Alarcón had meanwhile sailed his way up the Gulf of California along Mexico's western coastline, failing to find any sign of the Cibola expedition but making contact with Indian tribes—some friendly and some hostile—along the way.

In late August, Alarcón reached the apex of the gulf and in doing so became the original discoverer of the mighty Colorado River. He advanced up the river in small craft as far as the present border of California, seeking a juncture with Coronado. In doing so, he contacted more Indian tribes along the stream, including the interesting, tall Yuman tribe of Southern California. Though still far from Coronado at Cibola, Alarcón did meet an old Indian who knew of the place and told about an African man who had been killed there. The black man, the Indian said, had worn "certain things on his feet and arms that made sound."[25] Alarcón's effort up the Colorado was prodigious; but, failing to find Coronado, he returned to his ships and headed back south.

Though dejected that no great stores of precious metals had been found at Cibola, Coronado had set about the conquest of other pueblos in the region. At the same time, he and his men explored the surrounding countryside, ever on the lookout for new discoveries worthy of reporting to Mendoza. The first of these side explorations beyond the pueblos of Cibola land was one to the west under Captain Pedro de Tovar. Tovar was accompanied by seventeen soldiers and Fray Juan Padilla and guided by Zuni scouts. Coronado dispatched the party on July 15 to investigate a place he had heard called Tusayán, the homeland of the Hopi Indians that is now embodied in the Hopi Indian Reservation of northeast Arizona.[26]

The bearded men in glistening armor, riding on the backs of strange animals and carrying long, shiny lances, presented an astounding and frightening sight to the Hopis. They quickly massed in combat formation before their town and rejected all peace efforts by Tovar. During the parley, the Spaniards crossed a line the Hopis had drawn on the ground with sacred cornmeal. A Hopi warrior responded by striking one of Tovar's horses on the head with a club, and the fight was on.

In the Spanish lead was none other than Father Padilla. The Spaniards charged, killing some of the Indians and driving the remainder back into their town. Following this, Tovar dismounted his men to fight afoot. The Hopis came forth, bringing presents and expressing their desire to be friends. After touring the other Hopi pueblos, Tovar returned to Cibola, carrying stories of a large river on which a tribe of giant people resided downstream. Presumably these were the Yumans, whom Alarcón was encountering even then on the lower Colorado River.

To deliver a lengthy progress report to Mendoza back over the 3,000-mile route to Mexico City, Coronado called upon the dependable Juan Gallego. Gallego's small party was accompanied by Melchior Díaz as far as Corazones. The main expedition had moved there from Culiacán and, as instructed, awaited further orders. Also departing from Cibola with Gallego was the badly discredited Fray Marcos, whose fanciful stories had proved so fallacious that he deemed it unsafe to remain among Coronado's men.[27]

Díaz had been sent back to the main command at Corazones for two reasons: one was to take charge of a detachment from the expedition's army and begin a settlement in the Sonora Valley; the other was to lead a party in search of Alarcón and his supply ships.[28] Initially, Díaz established himself as *alcalde* of a second San Gerónimo settlement in the Sonora Valley and then saw the remaining Cibola expedition off to join Coronado.

But locating Alarcón was an urgent matter. Appointing Captain Diego de Alcaráz to command the post during his absence, Díaz set off in late September with twenty-five mounted soldiers, Indian allies, servants, a herd of sheep, and his greyhound. He did not go directly west to the coast but rather headed northwest to the present Arizona border, following it to the Colorado River. There Díaz discovered a tree into which a message had been carved: "Alarcón reached this point. At the foot of this tree there are letters."[29] The messages were retrieved, and they told of Alarcón's efforts to contact Coronado's army and that he had finally given up and returned to New Spain.

While constructing rafts to cross the Colorado River, Díaz became suspicious of Indians who lurked about. He ordered one captured and, by torturing the man, learned that the natives planned to attack while the party was midstream. The captive was killed, weighted down, and thrown into the river during the night. Further aroused by the disappearance of their missing man, the Indians attacked the next morning. Díaz's cavalry charged and drove them away with lances and harquebuses.[30]

The Spaniards came out of the fracas unscathed, but a freak, tragic event soon followed on the return march. Seeing a dog chasing one of the sheep that provided food for his expedition, Díaz spurred his mount in pursuit. In a moment of anger, he hurled his lance at the dog. The lance missed his target and embedded itself in the ground at an angle. Díaz's horse, at full gallop, charged down upon the weapon. The quivering shaft missed the horse but struck Díaz in the groin, piercing his bladder.

His men placed Díaz on a litter and tried to get him back to a priest for last rites. The severely injured Spaniard lived for nearly three weeks, but on January 18, 1541, somewhere on the trail back to San Geronimo, he died and was buried on a hilltop in a gravesite now lost to the ages.[31]

On August 25, not long after Tovar had returned to Hawikuh, Coronado dispatched Cárdenas with twenty-five men to search beyond the Hopi settlements for the large river and giant people of which Tovar had been told. Cárdenas found the Hopis generous to the extreme, with gifts of food, lodging, and guides to take them to the great river. It took twenty days from there for Cárdenas and his party to come onto a stupendous discovery—the Grand Canyon and, far away at the bottom, the Colorado River.[32]

The Spaniards' attempts to descend to the bottom of the great chasm proved futile. After three days of unrewarded effort and needing water badly, Cárdenas turned back for Cibola. The only prize he carried with him was some salt crystals the group had gathered. Others would find it difficult to fathom the fantastic descriptions of the magnificent gorge he had discovered. Still, Cárdenas and his party won a place in history as the first men of the outside world to set eyes on one of America's great wonders of nature.

In the meantime, Captain Tristan de Arellano had set off from New Spain's Sonora Valley to rejoin Coronado with the main portion of the Cibola expedition. He departed during mid-September 1540, leaving eighty men behind under Alcaráz. Following Coronado's trail, the caravan reached Cibola during mid-November, having endured severe hunger, a driving snowstorm, freezing temperatures, and other hardships that caused much suffering—especially among the poorly clad Indian allies.

Coronado had been waiting anxiously for Arellano to arrive. While he waited, he learned of a group of twelve pueblos to the east that greatly interested him. By what he had been told, the place offered the potential of good lodging, friendly natives, fine pastures, and good water. The Indian settlement was known as Tiguex, and Coronado made plans to winter there. The river on which it was located, he would later learn, was the upper waters of a stream Spaniards first knew as the Rio de Nuestra Señora and later as the Rio del Norte, eventually the Rio Grande.

ABBREVIATION KEY

F/F-*DOCS* = Flint and Flint, eds., trans., annots., *Documents of the Coronado Expedition, 1539–1542*

H/R-*NCE* = Hammond and Rey, eds., *Narratives of the Coronado Expedition, 1540–1542*

W-*CE* = Winship, *The Coronado Expedition, 1540–1542*

NOTES

1. "Castañeda's Narrative," F/F-*DOCS*, 396. See also W-*CE*, 208; H/R-*NCE*, 212. Coronado said he traveled 40 days from Culiacán to Cibola. The "Relacíon del Suceso," F/F-*DOCS*, 497, said the march took 73 days. April 22 to July 7 is 77 days.

2. "Translation of the *Traslado De Las Nuevas*," F/F-*DOCS*, 291. See also W-*CE*, 336; H/R-*NCE*, 179.

3. "Coronado to Mendoza, August 3, 1540," F/F-*DOCS*, 256. See also W-*CE*, 323; H/R-*NCE*, 166. The Jaramillo narrative states that Espinosa and two others died from consuming poisonous plants, which they ate because of their

great hunger. "Jaramillo Narrative," F/F-*DOCS*, 513. See also W-*CE*, 374; H/R-*NCE*, 298. Bolton concluded that the poisonous plants were likely wild parsnips that grow near McNary, Arizona. *Coronado*, 110–111.

4. "Castañeda's Narrative," F/F-*DOCS*, 393. See also W-*CE*, 203; H/R-*NCE*, 208.

5. "Castañeda's Narrative," F/F-*DOCS*, 393.

6. "Jaramillo's Narrative," F/F-*DOCS*, 513. See also W-*CE*, 374; H/R-*NCE*, 298.

7. "Relación del Suceso," F/F-*DOCS*, 498. See also W-*CE*, 351; H/R-*NCE*, 286.

8. "Troyano's Testimony," in Flint, *Great Cruelties*, 167.

9. "Coronado to Mendoza, August 3, 1540," F/F-*DOCS*, 256–257. Flint and Flint (*DOCS*, 654n51) state that one "mina" [*sic*] amounted to "slightly more than 3 bushels." See also W-*CE*, 324; H/R-*NCE*, 187. Hammond and Rey (*NCE*, 167) translate the measure as "two bushels of maize." Winship (*CE*, 324) calls it "two bushels of corn."

10. "Coronado to Mendoza, August 3, 1540," F/F-*DOCS*, 257. See also W-*CE*, 323; H/R-*NCE*, 167.

11. Flint, *Great Cruelties*, 518.

12. Weber, *The Spanish Frontier*, 22, citing several translations.

13. "Castañeda's Narrative," F/F-*DOCS*, 396. See also W-*CE*, 208; H/R-*NCE*, 168.

14. Flint, *Great Cruelties*, 280.

15. "Pedro de Ledesma's Testimony," in ibid., 236.

16. Ibid.; "Coronado to Mendoza, August 3, 1540," F/F-*DOCS*, 257. See also W-*CE*, 325.

17. Flint, *Great Cruelties*, 366, 397.

18. "Relacion del Suceso," F/F-*DOCS*, 497. See also W-*CE*, 351; H/R-*NCE*, 285.

19. Bolton, *Coronado*, 181.

20. "Coronado to Mendoza, August 3, 1540," F/F-*DOCS*, 259. See also W-*CE*, 335; H/R-*NCE*, 177.

21. "Coronado to Mendoza, August 3, 1540," F/F-*DOCS*, 262. See also W-*CE*, 335; H/R-*NCE*, 177–178.

22. "Coronado to Mendoza, August 3, 1540," F/F-*DOCS*, 259. See also W-*CE*, 326; H/R-*NCE*, 171.

23. "Coronado to Mendoza, August 3, 1540," F/F-*DOCS*, 258.

24. "Troyano's Testimony," in Flint, *Great Cruelties*, 168.

25. "Narrative of Alarcón's Voyage," F/F-*DOCS*, 199. See also H/R-*NCE*, 143.

26. "Castañeda's Narrative," F/F-*DOCS*, 396. See also W-*CE*, 208; H/R-*NCE*, 213–214.

27. "Castañeda's Narrative," F/F-*DOCS*, 394. See also W-*CE*, 204; H/R-*NCE*, 210.

28. "Castañeda's Narrative," F/F-*DOCS*, 394. See also W-*CE*, 204; H/R-*NCE*, 210.

29. "Castañeda's Narrative," F/F-*DOCS*, 394. See also W-*CE*, 206; H/R-*NCE*, 211.

30. "Castañeda's Narrative," F/F-*DOCS*, 395. See also W-*CE*, 206; H/R-*NCE*, 212.

31. Day, "Mota Padilla," 95–96.

32. "Castañeda's Narrative," F/F-*DOCS*, 397–398. See also W-*CE*, 209–210; H/R-*NCE*, 210.

5

Curse of the Golden Bracelet

He [the Turk] was given credence [and is even] now, because of the ease with which he spoke and because they showed him tin jewelry and he smelled it and said that it was not gold. He was very familiar with gold and silver, and he took no notice of the other metals.

Castañeda[1]

During the fall of 1540, a delegation of Indians arrived at Hawikuh to confer with Coronado. They were from a place to the east called Cicuye (Cicúique), today the site of Pecos, New Mexico. At their lead were two men, one of whom was a young warrior—tall and handsome with a fine physique. Because of his long mustache, the Spaniards dubbed him "Bigotes," the Spanish word for whiskers. The other, a much older man, was known to the Spaniards as "Cacique" (chief), as he was head man of his pueblo. The visitors said they wished to meet the black-bearded men who wore shiny attire and rode about on animals.

The Indians brought some of their finest objects as offerings of friendship: dressed skins, decorated war shields made from thick buffalo hide, and feathered ceremonial headgear. Coronado responded by presenting them with items the likes of which the guests had never seen: a string of pearl beads, glass dishes, and little bells that greatly amused the guests with their tinkling.[2] Still, the Indians would eventually regret that they had made this visit.

Coronado, anxious for a discovery of material value that would reward those who had invested so heavily in the expedition and serve as a worthy find to report to the viceroy, was especially interested in knowing more about the great herds of prairie cattle (buffalo) about which he had heard so much. A member of the visiting party displayed the crude drawing of one such animal tattooed on his body.

Coronado assigned Captain Hernando de Alvarado to take twenty men on a sojourn eastward to witness the herds, ordering him to report back within eighty days. Bigotes, Cacique, and their men were taken along as guides. Also with them was the determined Fray Padilla.

Five days out from Hawikuh in what is now western New Mexico, Alvarado and his party came onto one of the most distinctive landmarks they had yet encountered—the massive, towering rock plateau still known today as Acoma, atop of which a band of Indians maintained a fortress-like pueblo village. Pedro de Castañeda described it well:

> The *pueblo* was extremely strong because it was [immediately] above
> the entrance to the rock, which everywhere was sheer stone of such
> great height that it would take a well-handled arquebus to shoot a ball
> onto the top. There was only one way up, a stairway cut out by hand. It
> began at the top of a short, steep incline which that part formed. Near
> the ground this stairway was wide for about two hundred steps, until
> it reached the rock [itself]. Then there is another [stairway from that
> point], narrow and next to the rock, of about one hundred steps. At
> the top of this they have to climb up the rock [for a distance of] about
> three times the height of a man by means of cavities into which they
> insert their toes. And [the same] is done with their hands. At the top is
> a large, dry-laid stone wall. From there, without exposing themselves,
> they can knock down so many [people] that no armed force would be
> strong [enough] to win entrance from them.[3]

The pueblo houses also contained large rooms called *estufas*. These rooms had stone floors, were located underground, and were entered into by a ladder from a hole in the roof. The rooms featured pine pillars, bench-like seats around the bare walls, and a hearth. Castañeda saw the *estufa* principally as the domain of young males. The rooms were usually square or circular with floors made of large, smooth stone slabs and featuring a fireplace.[4]

FIGURE 5.1. *Bird's-eye view of Acoma and its mesa, looking northeast*

Seemingly, Acoma was an impregnable stronghold (figure 5.1). One day in the future, the Spaniards would fight a desperate battle to ascend the plateau and, indeed, would capture the village. But for now Alvarado's small force chose not to make war with the native warriors who came down to face them. Peace was eventually made, and the residents brought the Spaniards tanned skins, cloth, and turquoise as well as bread, nuts, corn, cornmeal, and turkeys to eat.

From Acoma, Alvarado continued on to the east, reaching a river called the Nuestra Señora on September 7, the eve of the Catholic Feast of Our Lady.[5] The stream is today's Rio Grande, which they reached below present-day Albuquerque. From there, Bigotes led the Spaniards north to a group of twelve pueblo towns known as Tiguex, spread along both sides of the Rio Grande a few miles above present Bernalillo, New Mexico (figure 5.2).

The party then traveled east to the Indians' home village of Cicuye. The four-story pueblo sat in a valley between mountain chains surrounded by pine forests. Nearby ran a stream with an abundance of trout and populated by otters and black bears. Square in form and surrounded by a low stone wall, the pueblo held a dominant defensive position on the fringe of the buffalo plains. Its four-story dwellings were interconnected around a

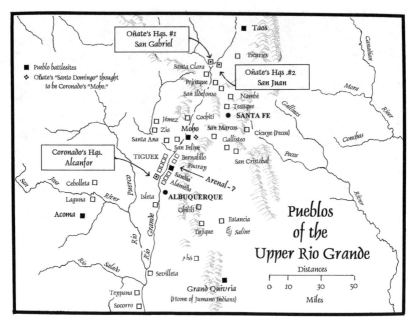

FIGURE 5.2. *Pueblos of the Upper Rio Grande (map by author)*

central patio, with overhanging balconies reachable with movable ladders, which stood ready against the pueblo's mud walls. Residents moved about on the balconies or across the continuous rooftops. The town had been built around a natural spring whose waters could be diverted to individual homes, giving it a vital defensive advantage.[6]

The inhabitants of Cicuye gave Cacique, Bigotes, their men, and their Spanish companions a rousing welcome. In a gala celebration of their return, drums were beaten and flute-like pipes played. The Spaniards enjoyed such a pleasant respite at Cicuye that they remained there for several days.[7]

During their stay, they were provided with two Indian slaves, both natives of the prairies, whom they took along as guides to seek the buffalo. One of the slaves was called Sopete (Ysopete). Castañeda referred to him as a "tatooed Indian."[8] The other slave, the Spaniards decided, resembled the Muslims who had once lived in Spain, so they called him "El Turco" (the Turk). He was a native, Castañeda noted, of the land that extends toward Florida.[9] The men spoke to them through the sign language in which the Indians were so fluent.[10]

The unknown author of the *Relación del Suceso*, who was with the Alvarado party, wrote: "He [Alvarado] continued onto these plains. At the beginning of them he found a small river which flows to the southeast. After four days' journey he found the [bison], which are the most extraordinary kind of animal that has been seen or read [about]. He followed this river a hundred leagues (±260 miles), each day finding more [bison]."[11]

The two slave guides would have a profound effect on the Coronado Expedition and on history. What the Turk told Alvarado and his party of Spanish soldiers as they moved eastward along the Canadian River to hunt buffalo was startling. The Turk said his original home, called "Arahey" (also "Harahey" or "Haraee"), was on the prairies to the northeast in a country called Quivira.[12] It was a city filled with an abundance of gold, silver, and fabrics. Proof of this, he said, could be found in a gold bracelet and other jewelry his Puebloan master, Bigotes, had taken from him. But, the Turk insisted, Alvarado was not to mention the matter to Bigotes or Cacique, for they would likely kill him for telling the secret.[13]

Gold and silver! Nothing could have grabbed Alvarado's attention more intensely. All the excitement that had earlier quickened his pulse now returned. His interest in the "cattle" he and his men were finding in immense herds on the prairies east of Hawikuh was quickly washed away by plans to witness and obtain the gold bracelet and jewelry. Castañeda wrote, "Such and so many were the things that he [the Turk] said about riches of gold and silver, that there were in his land that [Alvarado's company] did not diligently pursue the search for [bison] beyond seeing a few."[14] The Turk's imagination did not stop there. He filled the Spaniard's ears with tales that surpassed the conquistador's own imagination:[15] "He said [as well] that they [the Quivira warriors] took the chief out to war in a litter, and that when he wished, he unmuzzled some greyhounds that tore the enemies to pieces; that they had a very large house, where everyone attended to serve him; and that in the doors were hung cotton blankets."[16]

Alvarado swung his command about and hurried back to tell his general the exciting news. Coronado had already begun to move his army from Hawikuh to Tiguex, sending Cárdenas ahead to prepare the way for the expedition's army. The captain general prepared to follow, leaving instructions that once Arellano's group had arrived at Hawikuh, he was to rest his people and horses for twenty days and then bring them on to Tiguex.

Coronado and the remainder of his advance command then followed. As he passed Acoma, the natives were again generous with their corn and turkeys. Some of the soldiers, wishing to see the top of the rock mesa, struggled up the ascent path with great difficulty. After doing so, they were amazed that Acoma women could carry loads of water up the wall in ollas on their heads and never touch the containers with their hands.[17]

When Coronado and his party arrived at Tiguex, they found that Cárdenas had complied with his orders and cleared a pueblo, Alcanfor (also known as Coofor), of its Indian inhabitation to provide quarters for the Spanish army. Spanish accounts imply that the native residents happily complied with Cárdenas's polite request. But, considering the conquistadors' habits and the discontent Coronado found in the Tiguex area, it may well have happened differently.[18]

Losing their homes was not the only hurt the Indians suffered. The Spaniards, so it seems, did just about everything they could do to disrupt the cooperation and food supplementation the pueblo leaders had provided previously. One signal misstep was related to the treatment of Bigotes and Cacique. Upon arriving at Alcanfor, Coronado summoned Alvarado and the Turk to his quarters to hear firsthand the story of the golden bracelet. The wonders of the Turk's tale had become even more magnificent. Castañeda wrote:

> The celebrations he [Coronado] made were not few as a result of such good news because [El Turco] said that in his land there was a river in a plain which was two leagues wide. There were fish as large as horses there. And [there were] a great many exceedingly large canoes with more than two rowers on each side, which also carried sails. The lords traveled on the poop, seated beneath awnings. On the prow [there was] a large eagle of gold. He said further that the lord of that land slept during siesta under a great tree on which a great number of small golden bells hung. In the breeze they gave him pleasure. Further, he said that generally everyone's common serving dishes were worked silver. And the pitchers, plates, and small bowls were [made] of gold. [El Turco] called gold "*acochis*."[19]

Coronado and his men were elated at the renewed hope of finding a city of gold. Still, one must wonder how much of the story was the Turk's, how much of it was construed through interpretation of the sign language the Indian used, and how much of it was an embellished response to leading questions. We are left to wonder how the (supposedly) prairie-raised

Turk even knew about canoes, poops, prows, awnings, sails, and dishes of wrought plate.[20]

No one listened when the slave Sopete protested that nothing the Turk said was true. Clearly, the Turk had read the Spaniards' weakness for gold and played to it. For anyone as fully possessed and filled with hope as they, his story was very convincing.

Coronado ordered Alvarado to hurry back to Cicuye and procure the gold bracelet. There, Bigotes and Cacique reacted with great surprise to the Turk's story, both swearing—no matter how hard the Spaniard quizzed them—that there was no gold bracelet or jewelry and insisting that the slave was lying. Alvarado was far from convinced as to who was telling the truth, but the potential evidence of treasures was too alluring to ignore. He had to have that bracelet! The two Pueblo men were politely invited back to his tent. When they arrived, he seized them and placed them in chains with an iron collar around their necks.[21]

The ironing of Bigotes and Cacique alarmed the people of Cicuye, who saw it as a gross betrayal of the friendship and assistance they had provided the Spaniards. Warriors rushed forth with bows and arrows, prepared to rescue their leaders. At the moment, however, their pueblo was threatened by an enemy tribe. Alvarado calmed the anger directed at him by offering his help in fighting Cicuye's enemy. The intertribal disturbance subsided, however, and the Spaniards marched back to Tiguex with Bigotes and Cacique led behind the soldiers' horses in iron collars and chains.[22]

At Tiguex, Coronado called forth Fray Padilla, who had become acquainted with Bigotes on the buffalo search, and asked him to interview the Pueblo warrior. The priest did so, only to report that the man continued to deny adamantly that there was any such bracelet. The Spaniards decided that he was surely lying. To find out, new, more drastic measures were needed. The problem was passed back to Alvarado. Apparently on Coronado's order and almost certainly with his knowledge, Alvarado took Bigotes and Cacique to a field beyond the pueblo of Alcanfor, where dogs were set on the chain-restrained Bigotes in an attempt to force a confession. The Indian was bitten on an arm and a leg.[23]

Still, he continued to insist that the Turk's story was a blatant lie. Cacique was likewise threatened by Alvarado, who constructed a gallows and threatened to hang him unless he told the truth about the bracelet. The old man, who likely could not admit to something that did not exist, was terrified.[24]

The myth of the golden bracelet remained unresolved throughout the winter while the three men—Bigotes, Cacique, and the Turk—were kept in irons. Both the chaining and the "dogging" of the two Pueblo leaders created a great distrust and dislike for the Spaniards among the people of Cicuye. Even so, Coronado and his men continued to add fuel to the smoldering fire of discontent among the pueblo settlements.

ABBREVIATION KEY

F/F-*DOCS* = Flint and Flint, eds., trans., annots., *Documents of the Coronado Expedition, 1539–1542*

H/R-*NCE* = Hammond and Rey, eds., *Narratives of the Coronado Expedition, 1540–1542*

W-*CE* = Winship, *The Coronado Expedition, 1540–1542*

NOTES

1. "Castañeda's Narrative," F/F-*DOCS*, 400. See also W-*CE*, 217; H/R-*NCE*, 221.

2. "Castañeda's Narrative," F/F-*DOCS*, 398. See also W-*CE*, 210; H/R-*NCE*, 217.

3. "Castañeda's Narrative," F/F-*DOCS*, 398. See also W-*CE*, 215; H/R-*NCE*, 218.

4. "Castañeda's Narrative," F/F-*DOCS*, 418. See also W-*CE*, 284, 289; H/R-*NCE*, 254.

5. "Alvarado's Narrative," F/F-*DOCS*, 305–306. See also W-*CE*, 384–385.

6. "Castañeda's Narrative," F/F-*DOCS*, 420–421. See also W-*CE*, 346; H/R-*NCE*, 257.

7. "Castañeda's Narrative," F/F-*DOCS*, 399. See also W-*CE*, 275; H/R-*NCE*, 219.

8. This may indicate that Sopete's face was painted with stripes in the manner of the Indians Coronado would later meet on the plains; "Castañeda's Narrative," F/F-*DOCS*, 409. Winship translated Sopete's description of *"indio pintado natural de quivira"* as "painted Indian of Quivira" ("Translation of Castañeda," W-*CE*, 235). The translation in Flint and Flint (*Documents*, 464) reads "do no havian visto otra cosa sino/vacas y çielo yba en el campo o- / tro indio pintado natural de qui- vira que se deçia sopete este in- / dio siempre duo que el turco men- / tia y por esto no haçian caso de el y a- / unque en esta saçon tambien lo / deçia como los quercos havian / informado con el y el ysopete no / era creydo [rubrica]." Winship's translation (*Coronado Expedition*, 143) reads "y çielo yba en el campo otro indio pintado natural de quiuira que se deçia sopete este indio

siempre dixo que el turco mentia y por esto no haçian caso del y aunque en esta saçon tambien lo deçia como los querchos auian informado con el y el y sopete no era creydo." Whether Sopete's face was tattooed or painted could give clues to his original home.

9. "Castañeda's Narrative," F/F-*DOCS*, 399–400. See also W-*CE*, 215; H/R-*NCE*, 219.

10. Castañeda states that the Turk was given credence "because of the ease with which he spoke"; "Castañeda's Narrative," F/F-*DOCS*, 400. Bolton claims that "he [the Turk] supported his hand signs occasionally with the Mexican [tongue] of which he knew a little"; *Coronado*, 189. Bolton gives no source, however.

11. *Relación del Suceso*, F/F-*DOCS*, 499. See also W-*CE*, 356; H/R-*NCE*, 289. If the river referred to is the Canadian and if Alvarado followed for 100 leagues (ca. 260 miles), his buffalo-hunting party would have gone well beyond the present New Mexico–Texas border.

12. "Jaramillo's Narrative," F/F-*DOCS*, 514–515. See also W-*CE*, 376; H/R-*NCE*, 301.

13. "Troyano's Testimony," in Flint, *Great Cruelties*, 169.

14. "Castañeda's Narrative," F/F-*DOCS*, 400. See also W-*CE*, 215; H/R-*NCE*, 221. Castañeda is contradicted by other testimony regarding the extent of the hunt. On the basis of this statement, Bolton concludes that the party turned back at a point on the Canadian River just west of the present New Mexico–Texas border. But the author of *Relación del Suceso*, who indicates that he was a member of Alvarado's party, states that they followed the river for 100 leagues, as does Alvarado, and Melchior Pérez says they followed it for 80 leagues (Flint, *Great Cruelties*, 212). If the river they were following was the Canadian and they followed it east for 100 leagues (±260 miles), then they were well beyond the point just west of the New Mexico–Texas border where Bolton reasoned they turned back. One hundred leagues east from the New Mexico bend of the Canadian could have taken them near the latitude of Amarillo, Texas. Bolton describes the point where the hunters turned back as being "where the trail to Quivira swung northeast" (*Coronado*, 189). But the choice of that point is hypothetical based on Coronado's projected return route from Quivira.

15. Bolton, *Coronado*, 198.

16. Day, "Mota Padilla," 99.

17. "Castañeda's Narrative," F/F-*DOCS*, 401–402. See also W-*CE*, 218; H/R-*NCE*, 223.

18. Coronado testified that Cárdenas started to build a house for the Spaniards but the Indians of the pueblos told him not to do so, that they would vacate their homes for them and move to other pueblos nearby (Flint, *Great Cruelties*, 286). The overall behavior of the Coronado Expedition casts considerable doubt on this statement.

CURSE OF THE GOLDEN BRACELET

19. "Castañeda's Narrative," F/F-*DOCS*, 400. See also W-*CE*, 217; H/R-*NCE*, 221.

20. In their *Documents* notes (676n228), Richard and Shirley Flint call attention to canoes filled with Indian warriors witnessed by the De Soto Expedition on the Mississippi River, suggesting that the Turk might have experienced that region. Still, an Indian warrior would hardly have known about sails or golden bells or poop decks. Bolton (*Coronado*, 189) suggested that the Turk even knew some of the Mexican language (i.e., Spanish). Just how and where he would have come by that knowledge prior to meeting Alvarado's party is curious.

21. "Troyano's Testimony," in Flint, *Great Cruelties*, 169.

22. Ibid., 283–284.

23. Rodrigo de Frías testified that he later saw that "Bigotes was not well and had an arm and a leg crippled"; "Rodrigo de Frías' Testimony," in Flint *Great Cruelties*, 194.

24. Ibid., 196. Juan Troyano said that after being bitten by the dog, Bigotes "admitted to having at Cicuique (Cicuye) a gold bracelet, a dog, an earthenware flask, and other jewelry"; "Troyano's Testimony," in Flint, *Great Cruelties*, 170. There is no supportive evidence of this, however.

6

Terrorizing Tiguex

Because the general had ordered that the [Indians] not be taken alive, so as to be a punishment and to make the rest of the Indians afraid, [López de Cárdenas] ordered that two hundred posts be planted in the ground right away in order to burn the [Indians] alive.

Castañeda[1]

When winter came, Coronado sent for a Tiguex chief he had met and declared that he needed clothing for his poorly clad, shivering troops. He demanded that he be furnished with about 300 mantas, or robes. The chief said he could not possibly provide them, suggesting that the matter be put before the various town governors. Instead, Coronado sent parties of soldiers to round up—by force—the needed cloaks and blankets from among the twelve Tiguex villages. At times, when people hesitated to give up the garments they were wearing, the soldiers stripped them from the person's back and made off with them.[2]

Still another issue arose when an Indian accused a soldier of violating his wife at a pueblo called Arenal. When the soldier spied a pretty Indian woman at the pueblo, with audacity he called her husband down to hold his horse while he climbed to the upper story. There he assaulted the woman, then came back down, took his horse, and departed. When

Coronado learned of the matter, he made all of his soldiers appear before the husband so the offender could be identified. The man could not pick out the soldier. When he did identify the horse he had held, the owner argued that if the Indian could not recognize the culprit, he could be wrong about the horse. Because of this flimsy defense, no one was charged and the husband's complaint was left unaddressed. The incident caused great concern among the Indians for the safety of their wives and daughters.

This was by no means the only such transgression. Juan de Contreras, Coronado's head groom, who ate in Coronado's tent and slept at the entrance at night, testified, "It was widely known and publicly acknowledged that a [certain] Villegas, a brother of the Villegas who is *regidor* of the city of Mexico, went to a pueblo in the Tiguex province with other soldiers from don García de López Cárdenas's company and took a quantity of clothing, poultry, and mats without the natives' permission. He also seized an Indian woman with whom it was said he had sexual relations."[3]

On the day following that event, the natives revolted. A band of Indians attacked the men guarding the army's horses and mules, killing one of the guards and driving off the stock. This last may have been an effort to rid the Spanish soldiers of their enormous advantage in waging war. The Spaniards' horses and mules posed a threat to the Puebloans in another way. The Spanish practice of grazing their animals on the stubble of pueblo cornfields destroyed a vital source of winter fuel for the Indians. This was a perilous loss to the shivering natives, who were at the same time sacrificing their limited clothing to the Spaniards.[4]

Many of the horses and mules were never recovered. Cárdenas discovered some of them, however, when he was sent to Arenal to talk with the Indians. With a command of sixty mounted men, some foot soldiers, and a number of Mexican Indian allies, he arrived during late December 1540 to find that barriers had been erected to close off the village. He heard a great hubbub inside the enclosure and discovered that the Indians were chasing some of the stolen horses about the improvised arena and shooting them with arrows.[5]

Efforts were made to read the *Requerimiento* to the pueblo, but the Indians shrieked and sang war songs so loudly that it could not be delivered.[6] When they totally rejected Cárdenas's call to surrender, he surrounded the village and launched his attack. Some of his troops fought their way to the top of the pueblo, while others used battering rams to crush holes in the pueblo walls. The soldiers then lit smudge fires to drive the Indians out of their places of refuge. Rodrigo Ximón, a seasoned soldier, declared that "as many as eighty or a hundred Indians were captured alive from among those who had fled [from the pueblo] and others who had been dragged out by their hair and had been hiding in the rooms that had been taken. He saw that [the Spaniards] lanced, stabbed, and set dogs on [those Indians], so that very few survived."[7]

Other Indians atop the pueblo put forth a determined resistance with bows and arrows, but the Spanish crossbows, swords, lances, and harquebuses were overwhelming. The soldiers were ordered not to take prisoners but instead to kill anyone who resisted so that others would greatly fear the Spaniards. But when the soldiers reached the pueblo rooftop, a large number of the inhabitants made a cross with their hands, signifying their wish to surrender peacefully, and laid down their weapons. Cárdenas, who had been wounded in the foot, answered by making his own sign of a cross as his promise for a truce whereby the Indians would not be killed.[8]

Melchior Pérez, the son of a previous governor of Nueva Galicia who served as *alguacil mayor* of the expedition, testified that he saw Cárdenas make the sign. Suspicious that the *maestre de campo* would not keep his word and concerned that a religious vow was being betrayed, Pérez objected and warned Cárdenas, "Do not show them the cross unless you expect to fulfill your promise."[9]

Cárdenas shrugged him off, replying that it did not matter because he had made the sign incorrectly. As Pérez suspected, the officer blatantly betrayed his word when the Indians emerged without weapons and were taken to a tent. The officer later insisted that he was merely complying with Coronado's orders when he ordered his men to drive stakes in the ground for the purpose of burning the captives alive. Contreras described the carnage that followed:

> When the Indians who remained in the tent saw this, they began to defend themselves with poles that were there and stakes they pulled up, because they expected [the Spaniards] to do to them what they were doing to their companions. There, inside the tent, [the Spaniards] lanced and put to the sword everyone who was there and defending themselves, in such a way that none of them survived. [The witness] saw that when this had been done, they set fire to the others, who were still tied to the posts, and burned them all alive.[10]

Soldier Juan Troyano testified that after the surrender he saw Coronado come from his nearby camp and talk with Cárdenas. Troyano felt certain that the captain-general then issued instructions concerning the prisoners' fate. Coronado declined to execute the Indians until the Turk and Sopete could be sent there to witness the event so they would tell about the Spanish doings and spread terror among the other Indians.[11]

Castañeda said that afterward the mounted soldiers chased anyone who tried to escape, slashing them down with swords until not a man remained alive.[12] Not even those who had taken refuge in the *estufas* were spared. Men, women, and children not driven from the pueblo by smoke died in the ensuing fire.

Castañeda's account does not speculate as to how many Indians burned to death; nor does he dwell on the butchery of the Spanish cavalry hacking the fleeing natives with their swords. Gruesome details of the event, however, would eventually resurface as charges in the Spanish court against Coronado and Cárdenas. Thirty or more victims were burned at the stake, while many more were killed in the battle and the torching of Arenal.[13] Mota Padilla wrote, "Our people endeavored to avenge the outrage [that of stealing the Spanish horses], and after some battering, the poor wretches surrendered. When they had been tied up, our people cruelly killed more than one hundred and thirty braves, treating them as beasts because they did not understand them, since they had no interpreter. This action was looked upon in Spain as deplorable, and with good cause, because it was an act of great cruelty."[14]

Several witnesses testified that ten of the twelve Tiguex pueblos were destroyed by fire. In part, this was done to prevent the Indians from returning and refortifying them.[15] But before the pueblos were set afire, the Spaniards, who were shivering in the winter cold of the mountains, ripped timbers from the Indian homes to use for their own fires.[16]

The misfortunes of Bigotes and the other captives continued when Coronado ordered them taken through a snowstorm to Arenal so they could witness the wrath of Spanish punishment firsthand and spread word of it among their people.[17] But Coronado was far from finished. With his forces supplemented by the arrival of Arellano and the remainder of the Cibola expedition at Alcanfor, he moved to crush the revolt that had spread among the Tiguex pueblos.

Again he sent Cárdenas forth with forty cavalrymen and a number of foot soldiers to demand submission from the other pueblos along the Rio Grande. At one town, several carcasses of the stolen Spanish horses lay dead in the plaza. As an object lesson, the pueblo was set afire. Cárdenas found that most of the other villages had been vacated following the Arenal mayhem, with the inhabitants retreating to Moho, the largest of the pueblos.

Located near today's San Felipe on the Jémez River just above its junction with the Rio Grande, Moho was also known to the Spaniards as Pueblo del Cerco. During the winter of 1540–1541, the Indians had gathered there and fortified it as a defensive position. The pueblo's walls sat atop towering basalt cliffs, giving its defenders a dominant position that looked down on any attacking force.[18]

When Cárdenas arrived at Moho, he had with him his forty cavalrymen, some Spanish foot soldiers, and, as Coronado later acknowledged, a force of Indios Amigos. From his mount at the fore of his cavalry, Cárdenas yelled his demand that the Pueblos surrender. The leader of the Pueblos, Juan Alemán, responded with a request to talk, provided the Spaniards withdrew their horsemen and moved their other people away.[19] The Spaniards complied, and Juan Alemán came down with two of his men. Even as the two leaders embraced, Pueblo warriors attacked Cárdenas with clubs. Coronado later gave his account of the affair:

> It was common knowledge and widely known that the Juan Eman [*sic*] referred to in the question told [Cárdenas] that he should dismount and leave his weapons, helmet, and beaver because [the Indians] wanted to meet and talk with him, which would have happened [already] except that they were afraid of the others. After he had dismounted [the Indians] seized him and did violence to him, and they would have killed him, if it had not been for those who came to his aid.[20]

This move ignited action from warriors who suddenly appeared at the walls above. Emitting a din of insults and war calls, they showered their arrows down on the Spanish forces, wounding many as they rushed to retrieve their embattled captain. Coronado said later that a number of Spaniards and Indian allies were killed.[21]

One of the Spaniards killed during the siege was Captain Francisco de Ovando, who made the mistake of trying to crawl through a small opening in the pueblo wall. Even as his head emerged beyond the wall, he was seen by the Indians and dragged out. He was evidently killed immediately. Castañeda wrote that Ovando's body was later found by the Spaniards, lying unmolested among the dead in the pueblo.[22]

Leaving a small force at Moho, Cárdenas took the rest of his command to another fortified pueblo nearby, where his demand for surrender was met by another chorus of shouted insults and a rain of arrows. Unable to achieve his purpose he returned to Moho, leaving Captains Diego de Guevara and Juan de Zaldívar to hold the second pueblo under siege.

Upon his return, the people of Moho came out in force against the Spaniards. Making a pretense of fleeing so as to draw them out onto the flat countryside, the Spaniards wheeled their horses about suddenly and attacked. Several warriors were downed before the remainder fled back to their pueblo roofs.[23]

Cárdenas returned to the Tiguex headquarters where Coronado ordered him to go back to Moho and place the pueblo under siege.[24] At Moho, the captain set up the tents of his camp, his *real*, and prepared for an impressment of the defiant pueblo. He took with him several scaling ladders. According to Castañeda's account, the ladders were not a good idea: "Because . . . the enemies had had many days to prepare themselves, they threw so many stones onto our people that they knocked many [of them] to the ground, and they wounded about a hundred men with arrows. Afterward several died from [their wounds], because of poor treatment by an unskilled surgeon who was traveling with the expedition."[25]

Though the sequences of events are unclear between Castañeda's account and that of Mota Padilla, the latter tells of other efforts Coronado attempted to overcome the pueblos: "One was to build some engines with timbers, which they called swings, like the old rams with which they battered fortresses in times before gunpowder was known; but they did no good. Then, lacking artillery, they attempted to make some wooden tubes tightly bound with cords on the order of rockets; but these did not serve either."[26]

The soldiers failed in their attempts to ram the walls of the pueblo, finding them heavily reinforced with tree trunks lashed together with tough willow saplings.[27] The Spaniards now saw a powerful advantage, however. Though Moho held a strong defensive position and was well stocked with stones and stored foodstuffs, it suffered a disastrous defect. Situated 440 yards from the Jémez River, it was set off from the stream by a flat, barren bank once created by an ancient lava flow.[28] Those inside the pueblo walls had no natural source of water.

During the fifty days of wintry siege, the Moho defenders depleted their stored supply of water and attempted to survive on rainwater and melted snow. But neither was sufficient. Desperately, they undertook the digging of a well—a very deep one—to reach water. But the sides of the well caved in, killing thirty of the workmen.[29]

Eventually, the people of Moho were forced to surrender. They initiated peace talks, this time offering to give up their women and children because of the scarcity of water. An agreement was reached, and a squad of Spanish horsemen under Don Lope de Urrea began receiving Indian children. Fewer than 100 young boys and girls were brought forth and no women, who chose to stay with their men. A fracas erupted when the Spaniards refused to back away until a shower of arrows forced them to do so.[30]

The siege continued unabated under the watch of forty horsemen, who stood ready in case the embattled Indians attempted to escape. Then one night they did so. Just before daybreak a party of women surrounded by warriors emerged from the pueblo and headed for the river. The alarm sounded in the cavalry camp of Captain Rodrigo Maldonado, and the attack was on.

Though one horse and its rider were knocked down and killed, the Spaniards broke through the defenders and began to slaughter them with their swords. The Indians were driven into the freezing, rapidly flowing river, where the killing continued. Only a few of those attempting to escape survived the onslaught. "The next day the people from the *real* crossed over the river and in the countryside found many wounded [Indians] whom the severe cold had felled. They brought them back in order to heal [them] *and to be served by them*. Thus that siege came to an end, and the *pueblo* was taken. Some [Indians], however, who had remained in the *pueblo*, made a stand in one section [but] were captured in a few days."[31]

During Coronado's trial, which was conducted when he returned to Mexico, Pérez testified that he knew and saw "at the pueblo besieged by Francisco Vázquez [de Coronado that] he ordered about thirty Indians to be killed, set upon by dogs, and have their hands cut off."[32] Coronado's culpability was examined during his trial. Virtually every witness firmly agreed that no one would dare disobey him or do such a thing without his permission and order.[33]

The siege of Moho was brought to an end in late March when the last remaining Indians who had holed up inside the pueblo were flushed out and captured. The second refuge village, which Diego de Guevara and Juan de Zaldívar had been left to conquer, was taken in early March 1541.

The two captains had observed that warriors of the pueblo would come forth each morning to make a show of their willingness to do combat. At times, people of the pueblo would come behind them. Spies were stationed to keep an eye on the place, waiting for an opportunity to strike. Then one morning it came: "[The Spaniards] came out of ambush and went to the *pueblo*. They saw the people fleeing and followed them, working slaughter among them. When news of this was delivered, the troop left the *real* and went through the *pueblo*, looting it and taking prisoner all the people who were in it. There were about one hundred women and children."[34]

Coronado was still not finished. When he learned that Indians had returned to some of the pueblos and were building defensive fortifications, he ordered his forces to destroy the structures once any food and clothing that could be found had been taken from the houses.

Though Coronado later claimed he gave no order to do so, several of the pueblos were burned to the ground as a result of this action.[35] Once again in the interest of instilling fear in the hearts of the native population, he sent Bigotes, Cacique, the Turk, and Sopete to Moho where they could witness the harsh punishment and devastation that was sure to come as a result of defiance of Spanish rule.[36]

So, in the brutal way of the conquistadors, Coronado had struck against the Indian insurrection through the winter and won victory. Yet even as he was so engaged, thoughts of the Turk's story and the potential of a golden city awaiting his discovery on the eastern plains agitated his ambitions.

On April 20, 1541, Coronado wrote a letter to the king that has been lost and a report to Antonio de Mendoza apprising them of Díaz's death and events at Tiguex. He sent the documents south with couriers led by Pedro de Tovar, who was to restore order at San Gerónimo and bring back some of the soldiers stationed there.

This done, he turned to the review he planned to hold for his expedition to Quivira.[37] Because he expected to be on his way to Quivira when Tovar returned, Coronado sent word for Tovar to catch up with him on the plains, saying he would erect crosses as he went and leave messages of instruction. As Bolton noted, the treeless prairies ahead offered little wood for making crosses. Coronado may have found a way to leave word along the trail, but it did not matter. He would be back in Tiguex before Tovar returned.

ABBREVIATION KEY

F/F-*DOCS* = Flint and Flint, eds., trans., annots., *Documents of the Coronado Expedition, 1539–1542*

H/R-*NCE* = Hammond and Rey, eds., *Narratives of the Coronado Expedition, 1540–1542*

W-*CE* = Winship, *The Coronado Expedition, 1540–1542*

NOTES

1. "Castañeda's Narrative," F/F-*DOCS*, 403. See also W-*CE*, 220–221; H/R-*NCE*, 226.

2. "Castañeda's Narrative," F/F-*DOCS*, 402. See also W-*CE*, 219; H/R-*NCE*, 224.

3. "Contreras's Testimony," in Flint, *Great Cruelties*, 112. Mota Padilla gives the captain's name as García Lopez; Day, "Mota Padilla," 100.

4. "Troyano's Testimony," in Flint, *Great Cruelties*, 171.

5. "Castañeda's Narrative," F/F-*DOCS*, 403. See also W-*CE*, 219–220; H/R-*NCE*, 226.

6. "Diego López's Testmony," in Flint, *Great Cruelties*, 394.

7. "Rodrigo Ximón's Testimony," in Flint, *Great Cruelties*, 132.

8. "Troyano's Testimony," in Flint, *Great Cruelties*, 174; "Melchior Pérez's Testimony," in Flint, *Great Cruelties*, 216.

9. "Melchior Pérez's Testimony," in Flint, *Great Cruelties*, 216.

10. "Contreras's Testimony," in Flint, *Great Cruelties*, 113–114.

11. "Troyano's Testimony," in Flint, *Great Cruelties*, 174.

12. "Castañeda's Narrative," F/F-*DOCS*, 403. See also W-*CE*, 221; H/R-*NCE*, 226–227.

13. Various numbers were given by witnesses. See Flint, *Great Cruelties*, 131, 240, 258.

14. Day, "Mota Padilla," 100.

15. "Domingo Martin, Juan de Contreras, and Rodrigo Ximón Testimonies," in Flint, *Great Cruelties*, 96–97, 113, 131.

16. "Melchior Pérez's Testimony," in Flint, *Great Cruelties*, 215.

17. "Troyano's Testimony," in Flint, *Great Cruelties*, 175,

18. "Coronado's Testimony," in Flint, *Great Cruelties*, 362–363; Flint, *No Settlement, No Conquest*, 150–151; "Castañeda's Narrative," F/F-*DOCS*, 404. See also W-*CE*, 221; H/R-*NCE*, 227.

19. "Castañeda's Narrative," F/F-*DOCS*, 404. See also W-*CE*, 222; H/R-*NCE*, 227. Mota Padilla identifies the Indian leader as D. Juan Lomán, whom the Spanish nicknamed after a Mexican citizen with that name. Day, "Mota Padilla," 160n41.

20. "Coronado's Testimony," in Flint, *Great Cruelties*, 363. For Castañeda's account of this affair, see F/F-*DOCS*, 404. Mota Padilla tells the story still

another way: "Under this agreement, D. Garcia [Cárdenas] dismounted his horse and turned over his sword to his soldiers, whom he ordered to retire. Then, approaching the walls, he was confronted and embraced by Juan Lomán, and immediately six Indians who had been coached in their parts seized him bodily and would have dragged him into the pueblo if the door had not been small, for there he made a stand, and was able to resist until some troopers arrived, who defended him"; Day, "Mota Padilla," 100.

21. "Coronado's Testimony," in Flint, *Great Cruelties*, 363.

22. "Castañeda's Narrative," F/F-*DOCS*, 419. See also W-*CE*, 270; H/R-*NCE*, 256.

23. "Castañeda's Narrative," F/F-*DOCS*, 404.

24. Contradicting Castañeda, Mota Padilla implies that, seeing that things were not going well, Coronado went to Moho and took charge. If so, it may have been at this point.

25. "Castañeda's Narrative," F/F-*DOCS*, 404.

26. Day, "Mota Padilla," 101–102.

27. Bolton, *Coronado*, 223.

28. Flint, *No Settlement, No Conquest*, 152.

29. "Castañeda's Narrative," F/F-*DOCS*, 404.

30. Ibid., 405.

31. Ibid (emphasis added).

32. "Melchior Pérez's Testimony," in Flint, *Great Cruelties*, 218.

33. "Juan Gómez de Paradinas and Domingo Martin Testimonies," in Flint, *Great Cruelties*, 81, 95.

34. "Castañeda's Narrative," F/F-*DOCS*, 405. See also W-*CE*, 224–225; H/R-*NCE*, 230–231.

35. Bolton, *Coronado*, 229.

36. Ibid., 228.

37. Ibid., 236–237.

1

Swallowed by a Sea of Grass

I arrived at some plains so without landmarks that it was as if we were in the middle of the sea. There [the guides] became confused, because on all of [the plains] there is not a single stone or hill or tree or bush or anything that looks like that.

Coronado[1]

While Coronado was engaged in pacifying Tiguex, he could hardly wait until the Indians were quelled and warm weather came so he could continue his quest onward to the wondrous place the Turk called Quivira. Surely, Coronado reasoned, in everything the Turk told, there was enough truth to overcome the disappointments he and his men—and the viceroy who had invested so much money and faith in him—had thus far suffered.

The Turk, great prevaricator and storyteller that he was, had become suspect to some as a witch doctor of sorts who was in league with Satan. A superstitious Spanish guard claimed he had witnessed the Turk talking into a jug to the devil. The soldiers were further convinced of the Turk's supernatural capacity when, despite his isolated confinement, he claimed to know how many Christians had been killed at Moho. The figure he gave was correct.[2]

Coronado's captains advised him that it would be wise to send some-one ahead to Quivira to check out the Turk's claims. After all, had not they been badly deceived by the fanciful stories of Friar Marcos?[3]

But Coronado would not listen. In a letter to the king on April 20, 1541, Coronado had expressed skepticism regarding the Quivira reports: "Since it was a report from Indians and mostly by signs, I did not give them credence until I could see it with my own eyes (their report seeming very exaggerated to me)."[4]

In another letter to Mendoza written at around the same time, however, Coronado was evidently less restrained. Mendoza, based on Coronado's letter, wrote: "Regarding what concerns gold and silver and 'fair-complected' and handsome women and food, up to the present [the Coronado expeditionaries] have found [them] in abundance . . . with news that farther on there are many jars of gold and pearls, as well as grand *ciudads* and houses and a land very productive of food."[5]

But by fall Coronado had made up his mind to send a full expedition in search of Quivira. If there truly were golden treasures there, he wanted to be the one who found them. And what if King Tatarrax did not wish to give up his gold and silver? Coronado's entire fighting force might be needed to wrest the treasure from him.

Throughout the long, cold winter, Coronado had puzzled over who was lying and who was telling the truth about the gold bracelet. The totally innocent (most likely) Bigotes had been held in chains and iron collar, as had the Turk and Sopete. Cacique, because of his age, was spared such harsh treatment. Imprisonment of the captives had caused a serious reversal in relations with the people of Cicuye, where Bigotes and Cacique were still revered as leading men. The highhanded arrest of the two men and the dog baiting, not only of them but also of a delegation sent to plead their case with Coronado, had cast the Spaniards in a much different light.

The natives had good cause to feel their generosity had been inad-equately rewarded. Now, though, as Coronado laid plans for a journey to the prairies, he realized that Cicuye, sitting on the road to the east with a large warrior force, posed a potential hazard.

Coronado had actually begun making plans for an expedition to the buffalo prairies even before Moho was captured. During the siege, he set out to make amends with the people of Cicuye. Keeping Bigotes safely in irons at Alcanfor, he and an escort of soldiers took Cacique back to Cicuye and released him.[6] The townspeople were very relieved but pleaded for the return of Bigotes as well. Coronado promised that when the Tiguex war was finished, he would set Bigotes free. In addition, he offered them one of the Tiguex villages—all of which had been vacated by their inhabitants—as a reward for their support. The Cicuye leaders listened quietly, but inside they held a deep distrust and dislike of the Spaniards.

Returning to Alcanfor, Coronado first sent men to establish friendly relations with other pueblo communities, hoping to have harmony in the region while he was gone.[7] Coronado also dispatched Pedro de Tovar to the San Gerónimo, Mexico, outpost to bring back some soldiers to supplement his New Mexico army.[8] Tovar was then to return and join Coronado on the road to Quivira by following a trail of crosses that would be left for him. Tovar would not return in time to do so, but in any event Coronado's trail across the prairies of the Texas Panhandle would be a blind one at best. Finding wood from which to build crosses would prove hopeless on the treeless plains.

Two couriers who rode with Tovar were to go on from San Gerónimo to Mexico City and deliver Coronado's April 20, 1541, report to Mendoza. After seeing Tovar off, the expedition's military conducted a review before setting off from Alcanfor southeastward on April 23 for what would prove to be a wandering, nearly fatal search for Quivira (see figure 7.1). Counting the Mexican Indian allies, 1,500 people were under Coronado's command, among them Friar Juan Padilla and lay brother Luis de Escalona, as well as the Turk, Sopete, and Bigotes. Remarkably, three women—wives of Spanish soldiers—and their children were members of the expedition. These hardy women were Señoras Sánchez (Francisca de Hozes), Paradinas (Maria Maldonado), and Caballero.[9]

Black and Indian slaves herded the estimated 1,000 horses, 500 cattle, and 1,000 sheep behind the expedition personnel. Pack animals carried the cargoes of necessary supplies and equipment. The Turk asked slyly why they were placing such heavy loads on the horses and mules, since it might make them too tired to carry back all the gold and silver the Spaniards would find at Quivira.[10]

Because of its impediments of stock and pack animals, the Quivira caravan moved slowly, with scouts riding ahead to investigate the route and find choice campsites. Always there were the tasks of making and breaking camp and taking meals. Making camp involved gathering firewood (with no wood, it was necessary to use buffalo chips on the prairie), building cooking fires, and preparing food. This last task often required

FIGURE 1.1. *Timeline and projection of Coronado's march to Quivira, 1541, Julian and Gregorian calendars*

	Jul.	Greg.	
1	4-23	5-3	start at Tiguex[1]
2	4-24	5-4	
3	4-25	5-5	
4	4-26	5-6	reach Cicuyé[2]
5	4-27	5-7	
6	4-28	5-8	
7	4-29	5-9	reach Pecos R.[3]
8	4-30	5-10	bridge built[4]
9	5-1	5-11	
10	5-2	5-12	
11	5-3	5-13	
12	5-4	5-14	reach Plains
13	5-5	5-15	
14	5-6	5-16	
15	5-7	5-17	
16	5-8	5-18	
17	5-9	5-19	
18	5-10	5-20	exp. becomes lost
19	5-11	5-21	on Llano Estacado;
20	5-12	5-22	find buffalo, meet
21	5-13	5-23	Querecho Indians[6]
22	5-14	5-24	
23	5-15	5-25	
24	5-16	5-26	
25	5-17	5-27	
26	5-18	5-28	
27	5-19	5-29	
28	5-20	5-30	

	Jul.	Greg.	
48	6-9	6-19	
49	6-10	6-20	
50	6-11	6-21	
51	6-12	6-22	
52	6-13	6-23	
53	6-14	6-24	
54	6-15	6-25	
55	6-16	6-26	
56	6-17	6-27	
57	6-18	6-28	
58	6-19	6-29	
59	6-20	6-30	
60	6-21	7-1	
61	6-22	7-2	
62	6-23	7-3	
63	6-24	7-4	
64	6-25	7-5	
65	6-26	7-6	
66	6-27	7-7	
67	6-28	7-8	
68	6-29	7-9	Coronado reaches
69	6-30	7-10	Quivira River, moves
70	7-1	7-11	on to Quivira village[10]
71	7-2	7-12	
72	7-3	7-13	
73	7-4	7-14	
74	7-5	7-15	
75	7-6	7-16	

	Jul.	Greg.	
96	7-27	8-6	
97	7-28	8-7	
98	7-29	8-8	
99	7-30	8-9	
100	7-31	8-10	
101	8-1	8-11	
102	8-2	8-12	Turk is killed;
103	8-3	8-13	return begun[12]
104	8-4	8-14	
105	8-5	8-15	Coronado obtains
106	8-6	8-16	supplies/guides at
107	8-7	8-17	first Indian town;
108	8-8	8-18	leaves cross/message
109	8-9	8-19	
110	8-10	8-20	
111	8-11	8-21	
112	8-12	8-22	
113	8-13	8-23	
114	8-14	8-24	
115	8-15	8-25	
116	8-16	8-26	
117	8-17	8-27	
118	8-18	8-28	advance marches
119	8-19	8-29	on good roads amid
120	8-20	8-30	buffalo to Querecho
121	8-21	8-31	village then Cicuye[13]
122	8-22	9-1	
123	8-23	9-2	

No.	Date	Date	Event
30	5-22	6-1	
31	5-23	6-2	
32	5-24	6-3	
33	5-25	6-4	
34	5-26	6-5	reach Canyon #1,[7]
35	5-27	6-6	hit by hail storm;
36	5-28	6-7	march for Canyon #2
37	5-29	6-8	
38	5-30	6-9	
39	5-31	6-10	reach Canyon #2[8]
40	6-1	6-11	
41	6-2	6-12	
42	6-3	6-13	exp. rests, divides;
43	6-4	6-14	main party turns
44	6-5	6-15	back/Coronado leads
45	6-6	6-16	advance party north[9]
46	6-7	6-17	
47	6-8	6-18	
95	7-26	8-5	

No.	Date	Date	Event
77	7-8	7-18	reach first Quivira
78	7-9	7-19	town, Coronado goes
79	7-10	7-20	on north past other
80	7-11	7-21	villages to river
81	7-12	7-22	at end of Quivira[11]
82	7-13	7-23	
83	7-14	7-24	
84	7-15	7-25	
85	7-16	7-26	
86	7-17	7-27	
87	7-18	7-28	
88	7-19	7-29	
89	7-20	7-30	
90	7-21	7-31	
91	7-22	8-1	
92	7-23	8-2	
93	7-24	8-3	
94	7-25	8-4	

No.	Date	Date	Event
125	8-25	9-4	
126	8-26	9-5	
127	8-27	9-6	
128	8-28	9-7	
128	8-29	9-8	
129	8-30	9-9	
130	8-31	9-10	
131	9-1	9-11	
132	9-2	9-12	
133	9-3	9-13	
134	9-4	9-14	
135	9-5	9-15	
136	9-6	9-16	
137	9-7	9-17	
138	9-8	9-18	
139	9-9	9-19	
140	9-10	9-20	Coronado returns to Tiguex[14]

1. Coronado to king, Winship, Coronado Expedition, 364.
2. Flint, "Reconciling the Calendars," 156, "Narrative of Jaramillo," Winship, Coronado Expedition, 375; Day, "Gómora," 352; Day, "Mota Padilla," 103.
3. Flint, "Reconciling the Calendars:" 156.
4. "Narrative of Castaneda," Winship, Coronado Expedition, 232.
5. Flint, "Reconciling the Calendars," 156.
6. "Narrative of Castaneda," Winship, Coronado Expedition, 232.
7. Day, "Mota Padilla," 105.
8. Flint, "Reconciling the Calendars," 159.
9. "Narrative of Jaramillo," Winship, Coronado Expedition, 379.
10. Ibid.
11. Ibid., 380.
12. Ibid., 381.
13. Ibid.
14. "Narrative of Castaneda," Winship, Coronado Expedition, 248

slaughtering and butchering sheep or cows or, later, buffalo. Horses had to be saddled and unsaddled, pack animals unloaded and reloaded, necessities unlimbered, and animals taken to watering holes and tethered to graze. Tents for those who had them had to be erected and taken down, beds tended, and armor and arms stowed at the ready overnight.

Physical needs were addressed away from the camp area. It can be supposed that when a stream or pond presented itself, the hot and weary expedition members took the pleasurable opportunity to bathe. Almost assuredly, the Indian allies and African servants camped and ate apart from the Spaniards.

A day's march was seldom more than six or seven leagues (fifteen or eighteen miles) and less than that through challenging country. It required four days to travel the sixty-some miles from Alcanfor around the Sandia Mountains to Cicuye. Through the entire journey, a man was assigned the task of counting the steps taken during each day's march to have an as-precise-as-possible measurement of the distance traveled to record.[11]

At times with important expeditions, an official chronicler (sometimes others, although often a friar) kept a daily log of the events that occurred, what was seen, and any encounters with other people during the day's march. Coronado's report of the journey, as well as accounts by Pedro de Castañeda, Captain Juan Jaramillo, and the author of the *Relación del Suceso*, were written afterward from memory. Others, such as Mota Padilla, based their accounts on participant recollection (that of Captain Pedro de Tovar, it is believed).[12]

Padilla states that from Tiguex the expedition encountered four pueblo villages, the last of which was Cicuye, where "all barricaded themselves and would scarcely speak with them."[13] But when Coronado gave Bigotes his freedom there, either in gratitude or simply to encourage the Spaniards to move on, the pueblo fathers rewarded them with food supplies—corn, calabashes, beans, and turkeys.[14]

Bigotes further presented Coronado with another captive boy named Xabe, who, like the Turk and Sopete, was a native of Quivira. When the boy was interviewed about Quivira and the wonders of which the Turk had spoken, he said in effect (at least the Spaniards heard him to say) that yes, there was gold and silver at Quivira, but not quite as much as the Turk claimed.[15]

Just why the boy went along, even in part, with the Turk's grandiose lie is not known. Perhaps in doing so, he, too, saw a chance to escape his slavery and return to Quivira. Or he may have been connected to a devious scheme the Cicuye leaders had concocted with the Turk. The Turk later confessed that during Coronado's visit, he had met secretly with Bigotes's people. They encouraged him to mislead the expedition out onto the vast, landmark-void buffalo prairies to the east. There, it was hoped, the Spaniards would become lost, whereupon their horses and with luck they themselves would perish. Abetted by the Spaniards' passion to find new treasures, the scheme came very close to working.

Castañeda tells us that from Cicuye, Coronado's Quiriva expedition moved south around the mountain range, taking four days to reach the Pecos River. There, probably at Anton Chico (as historian Herbert E. Bolton noted) or below, the soldiers took another four days to bridge the stream so the livestock and everything else could cross.[16] Historian Richard Flint suggests that artilleryman Juan Troyano, who had bridge-building experience and to whom Coronado often went for advice on military matters, was likely involved in construction of the bridge.[17]

Moving eastward from the Pecos River, expedition members began to see large numbers of buffalo. Coronado commented on the immense buffalo herds that would continue to astound visitors to the plains for the next three centuries: "To count them is impossible. [I say this] because never for a single day did I lose sight of them as I traveled through the plains, until I returned to where I [first] found them."[18]

The Spaniards discovered still another subject of great interest in the Querecho (Apache) Indians, whom they began meeting as they marched through eastern New Mexico. Much unlike other tribes the Spaniards had met thus far, the Querechos followed and lived from the buffalo, resided in portable tents made of tanned buffalo hides, and conveyed their goods on two long poles dragged behind dogs, of which they had a great many.

The French would give the pole-dragging technique the name "travois." Castañeda found the Querechos to be a friendly but fearless, intelligent people who were so adept at sign language that no interpreter was needed. The tribespeople were expert at tanning buffalo hides and deerskins, which they took along with dried buffalo meat to the pueblos of the Rio Grande to trade for corn and cloth.[19]

Following the meeting with the Querechos, two incidents occurred: Cárdenas was injured when his horse fell, and a soldier who went off hunting became lost on the boundless plains. Evidently, the man was not seen again.[20] Castañeda commented, "It is something worth noting that because land is so flat, if at midday they have wandered foolishly following their prey from one place to another, they must stay calmly near their prey until the sun lowers, in order to see by what course they must return to where they departed from. Even so, these had to be knowledgeable men."[21] Coronado directed Captain Diego López to take a few men and proceed ahead "toward the sunrise for two days" to locate a supposed village, then to return immediately and report his findings.[22] The army continued on behind López, its advance guard hunting and killing buffalo as it went. On one occasion a buffalo herd stampeded into a ravine, with some of the animals falling into it and others atop them. Three of the hunters also plunged into the gorge. Castañeda wrote:

> There were so many grazing animals [bison] that, with some difficulty, those who traveled in the advance guard overtook a large number of bulls ahead of them. Because [the bulls] fled and were pushing one another, [when] they came upon a ravine, so many of the animals fell in that they filled it level and the rest crossed over the top [of them]. The horsemen who went in pursuit of them, without knowing what [the bulls] had done, fell on top of them. Three saddled and bridled horses, among those that fell, went in among the [bison] and could not be retrieved.[23]

Castañeda fails to say whether the riders survived, but historians have since wondered where is the ravine that possibly still holds the animal bones and horse accouterments lost by the Spaniards.

When the allocated time had passed and López had not returned, search parties were sent out. Some of the expedition's Indians who were searching for fruit—likely sand plums, wild grapes, or persimmons—eventually found López, who had been held up by the loss of his horses. The captain reported that he had traveled twenty leagues (over fifty miles) up the river but found "nothing except [bison] and the sky."[24]

Coronado, as well as other Spaniards, was puzzled and confused. When the Turk insisted once again that eastward was the right way, Coronado continued on in that general direction. But apparently he soon cut away from the river valley and followed a Querecho trail southward onto the endless prairies of the Texas Panhandle. Again Sopete protested, but to no avail.[25] Coronado later admitted that for five days he went wherever the Querechos led him, eventually becoming hopelessly lost on what is believed to be the prairie grassland of West Texas. Later, that grassland would become frontier famous as the Llano Estacado, or Staked Plains.

FIGURE 7.2. *Image of an American buffalo*

Food supplies began running low. The corn they had brought was gone, and for days expedition members had nothing to eat but bison meat (figure 7.2). "I drank [water] so bad it contained more mud than water," Coronado told the king. "[We] traveled for many days without water, cooking our food with [bison] dung."[26]

It became necessary to hunt buffalo every day, at times killing as many as sixty or seventy animals. This was very dissipating for the horses, which no longer had corn to eat. Occasionally during hunts the Spanish mounts were gored by buffalos and killed. Further, there was always a very real danger that hunters would become lost from the main caravan.[27] As Castañeda reported:

> Many of the people who went out to hunt during this time got lost. They did not return to the camp for two or three days, foolishly traveling from one place to another without knowing how to return to the place from which they had departed. [This happened] even with that barranca [canyon] being such that either upstream or down they had to hit upon [it]. Because every night a report was made of those who were missing, they fired the artillery, sounded trumpets, and beat drums. And they built huge, bright bonfires. Some [of the lost men]

were so far away and so imprudent that none of this benefited them, although it was worthwhile for others.[28]

Coronado's visit to the area, generally believed to be the Texas Panhandle, occurred two centuries before the Comanche or Kiowa Indians arrived to join the Plains Apaches below the Canadian River. But one must wonder if there could be an ensuing connection between Coronado's lost conquistadors, who may have died on the plains, and the Plains Indians in the existence of coats of mail found among them. During February 1786, New Mexico governor Don Juan Bautista de Anza met in Santa Fe to talk peace with a band of Comanche Indians led by Chief Ecueracapa, known in Texas as Cota de Malia (Coat of Mail).[29]

Another Comanche leader, Pohebits Quasho (Iron Jacket), was killed by Texas Rangers during the Battle of Little Robe Creek just northeast of the Antelope Hills of present Oklahoma in April 1858. His captured coat of mail was cut into pieces for souvenirs, with one part taken back to Texas governor Hardin Runnels.[30] Leading a Union force from New Mexico into the Texas Panhandle in 1864, Colonel Kit Carson fought a force of Comanches and Kiowas on the Canadian River near Adobe Walls. Among the Indians killed in the fight was a young warrior wearing a Spanish coat of mail.[31] A Plains Apache chief from the Texas Panhandle named Iron Shirt was a signatory to the Treaty of the Little Arkansas in October 1865.[32]

With some desperation, Coronado ordered Captain Rodrigo Maldonado and a company of cavalry to go forward and search the land for something to guide the expedition. Maldonado was in luck. After marching for four days and laying a trail of stones and buffalo dung to mark his path, he suddenly came upon a large ravine (*barranca*) and along a small stream in its bottom a sizable Indian village. The Spaniards learned that this was a camp of the Teyas Indians, enemies of the Quiviras.[33]

An old, blind, bearded Indian man conveyed an interesting story to Maldonado through sign language. He said that many days before in the south he had met four other men similar to Coronado's men. Tangible evidence of this encounter was the presence of a young girl among the Teyas who, though her chin was painted in the tribal fashion, "was as white as a Castilian lady."[34] Moreover, the Teyas expressed pleasure at being visited again by Spaniards, presenting them with a huge pile of cured hides along with a large tent.

When Coronado arrived with the main expedition, he immediately posted guards over the mound of hides. The expedition discovered, however, that the captain general was allowing certain parties to have access to the hides. This led to a general stampede to take the hides by expedition members and Teyas natives alike, and the pile quickly disappeared.[35]

While still camped with the Teyas at the bottom of the *barranca* during the month of May, the expedition was struck by a sudden 3:00 p.m. "whirling storm." Its driving winds carried a heavy barrage of hailstones "as large as small bowls and larger and as dense as rain, that in one place they covered the ground [to a depth of] two or three *palmos* and more."[36] Many tents were ruined, helmets were battered, irreplaceable camp crockery was broken, and panicked horses were sent flying up the sides of the *barranca*—some climbing high up the canyon walls.

African servants, wearing helmets, managed to hold two or three of the horses, protecting them as best they could with shields or nets. The banks of the canyon prevented the animals from scattering on the open prairies, and, though some were injured, only one was missing. Unfortunately, the Teyas—a roving, buffalo-hunting tribe—could provide no replacement pottery or even gourds to hold the expedition's corn, which lay scattered on the ground.

"If the storm had caught them on the plains above," Castañeda surmised, "as it did within the *barranca*, the expedition would have been placed at great risk, without horses, because many would not have been recovered."[37]

Bolton firmly believed this *barranca* was the Texas Panhandle's Tule Canyon below present Amarillo. Recent archaeological excavations further south in Blanco Canyon near Floydada, Texas, however, have produced Spanish artifacts such as chain mail, copper crossbow arrow points, nails, and other items common to the Coronado period that make it a prime candidate as the site of the hailstorm.[38]

From the Teyas, Coronado learned that he was marching toward a place that had none of the rewards the Turk had promised: no great towns, no abundant supply of maize, and, doubtless, no treasure troves. If the expedition were to be saved, it required not only a new direction but a new guide as well.

It is both interesting and revealing that at the very moment the Coronado Expedition was wandering lost on the prairies of West Texas in its quest to find Quivira, miles away to the south the expedition under Gonzalo Pizarro had become hopelessly engulfed by the tropical rainforests of western Brazil in a search for El Dorado.[39]

Both Coronado and Pizarro had fallen victim to their own ambitions, as well as to the ancient but resilient myths that wafted formidably through the air in the sixteenth century.

ABBREVIATION KEY

F/F-*DOCS* = Flint and Flint, eds., trans., annots., *Documents of the Coronado Expedition, 1539–1542*

H/R-*NCE* = Hammond and Rey, eds., *Narratives of the Coronado Expedition, 1540–1542*

W-*CE* = Winship, *The Coronado Expedition, 1540–1542*

NOTES

1. "Coronado to King," F/F-*DOCS*, 319. See also W-*CE*, 367; H/R-*NCE*, 186.

2. "Castañeda's Narrative," F/F-*DOCS*, 407. See also W-*CE*, 231; H/R-*NCE*, 234.

3. *Relacion del Suceso*, F/F-*DOCS*, 500. See also W-*CE*, 359; H/R-*NCE*, 290–291.

4. "Coronado to King, October 20, 1541," F/F-*DOCS*, 319. See also W-*CE*, 364; H/R-*NCE*, 185. The April 20, 1541, letter to the king has not been found, but Coronado refers to it in his October 20, 1541, letter.

5. "Mendoza to Fernández de Oviedo, October 6, 1541," F/F-*DOCS*, 312. Flint points out that though Coronado's letter has been lost, Mendoza refers to it twice in his own letters.

6. "Castañeda's Narrative," F/F-*DOCS*, 407. See also W-*CE*, 226; H/R-*NCE*, 233.

7. "Castañeda's Narrative," F/F-*DOCS*, 407. See also W-*CE*, 231; H/R-*NCE*, 233.

8. "Castañeda's Narrative," F/F-*DOCS*, 406. See also W-*CE*, 226; H/R-*NCE*, 232.

9. Flint, *No Settlement, No Conquest*, 57; Bolton, *Coronado*, 258.

10. "Castañeda's Narrative," F/F-*DOCS*, 414. See also W-*CE*, 248; H/R-*NCE*, 246.

11. "Castañeda's Narrative," F/F-*DOCS*, 410. See also W-*CE*, 238; H/R-*NCE*, 240.

12. Day, "Mota Padilla," 88.

13. Ibid., 103.

14. "Castañeda's Narrative," F/F-*DOCS*, 407–408. See also W-*CE*, 232; H/R-*NCE*, 234.

15. "Castañeda's Narrative," F/F-*DOCS*, 408. See also W-*CE*, 232; H/R-*NCE*, 235.

16. "Castañeda's Narrative," F/F-*DOCS*, 408. See also W-*CE*, 232.

17. Flint, *Great Cruelties*, 162.

18. "Coronado to King, October 20, 1541," F/F-*DOCS*, 319. See also W-*CE*, 364; H/R-*NCE*, 186.

19. "Castañeda's Narrative," F/F-*DOCS*, 423. See also W-*CE*, 279; Bolton, *Coronado*, 247.

20. "Castañeda's Narrative," F/F-*DOCS*, 408. See also W-*CE*, 235; H/R-*NCE*, 236.

21. "Castañeda's Narrative," F/F-*DOCS*, 411. See also W-*CE*, 238, 241; H/R-*NCE*, 241.

22. "Castañeda's Narrative," F/F-*DOCS*, 408. See also W-*CE*, 235; H/R-*NCE*, 236.

23. "Castañeda's Narrative," F/F-*DOCS*, 408. See also W-*CE*, 235; H/R-*NCE*, 236.

24. "Castañeda's Narrative," F/F-*DOCS*, 408. See also W-*CE*, 235.

25. See appendix A for a discussion of Coronado's route.

26. "Coronado to King, October 20, 1451," F/F-*DOCS*, 320. See also W-*CE*, 387–388; H/R-*NCE*, 187.

27. *Relacion del Suceso*, F/F-*DOCS*, 500–501. See also W-*CE*, 349; H/R-*NCE*, 291.

28. "Castañeda's Narrative," F/F-*DOCS*, 411. See also W-*CE*, 238; H/R-*NCE*, 241.

29. Richardson, *Comanche Barrier*, 62–63.

30. Hoig, *Tribal Wars of the Southern Plains*, 174–175.

31. Sanchez, "Historiography," 298.

32. Kappler, *Indian Treaties*, 892–895.

33. "Castañeda's Narrative," F/F-*DOCS*, 409. See also W-*CE*, 235; H/R-*NCE*, 237.

34. "Castañeda's Narrative," F/F-*DOCS*, 409. See also W-*CE*, 236; H/R-*NCE*, 238.

35. "Castañeda's Narrative," F/F-*DOCS*, 409. See also W-*CE*, 236; H/R-*NCE*, 237.

36. "Castañeda's Narrative," F/F-*DOCS*, 409. See also W-*CE*, 236; H/R-*NCE*, 238.

37. "Castañeda's Narrative," F/F-*DOCS*, 409. See also W-*CE*, 236; H/R-*NCE*, 238.

38. Blakeslee and Blaine, "The Jimmy Owens Site," 208–213; Blakeslee, Flint, and Hughes, "Una Barranca Grande," 370–385.

39. Hemming, *Search for El Dorado*, 111–123.

8
A Place Called Quivira

Here he [Coronado] wrote a letter to the governor of Harahey and Quivira, having understood that he was a Christian from the shipwrecked fleets bound for La Florida.

Jaramillo[1]

The Teyas's information regarding the expedition's course received dramatic support from Sopete. The much-ignored "other" slave from the plains now caused a great commotion. Throwing himself on the ground, he made signs indicating that before he would continue to follow the Turk any further, he would let the Spaniards cut off his head. Finally, Coronado was ready to listen. He had the Turk and Xabe brought forth and demanded the truth. Though none of the expedition narratives reveal such, effective intimidation was likely applied. The Turk broke down and put his life at risk by revealing that, indeed, he had been misleading the expedition. Even more threatening to his survival, he admitted that what he had said about riches in Quivira was false. The Spaniards suspected that the people at Cicuye had put him up to it in an effort to get them lost on the prairie. Because of a lack of food, they and their horses would become weak and vulnerable.[2]

Expectedly, the captains voiced their desire to kill the Turk and be done with him. But Coronado hesitated. Until the expedition had extricated itself from the *barrancas* (canyons or ravines) and found the true way to Quivira, the Turk might still be useful. Thinking correctly that he had been led too far south, Coronado sent scouts northward and began considering what to do next.

Calling together his officers and others, Coronado discussed their plight.[3] Everyone agreed on a plan whereby the main portion of the expedition would return to Tiguex under Arellano while Coronado—with thirty chosen horsemen, six foot soldiers, servants, some Teyas guides, and spare mounts—would press on to Quivira. Forging into unknown territory with such a small force was risky at best, but to turn back now and leave the mystery of a potentially gold-filled Quivira unresolved was unthinkable.

When the scouts returned, they guided the expedition north to another deep *barranca*, bottomed by a small stream. Another large Teyas village was camped there. By Bolton's theory, this was the main branch of Palo Duro Canyon, but others have suggested it could have been the North Concho because of its prevalence over other canyons for nut-bearing trees, which the expedition is said to have encountered.[4]

For two weeks the army rested and reorganized, both for the return to Tiguex and for Coronado's venture ahead. Hunters killed buffalo by the hundreds, the meat jerked for sustenance on the trail. Coronado also chose the men who would go with him to Quivira. With the Turk now in chains, Sopete was chosen to lead the way. He agreed to do so but asked that the Turk, who might be troublesome, be left behind. Coronado refused to abandon the Turk, but he did agree that when they reached Quivira, Sopete would be freed to remain there. The deposed Turk was thereafter towed at the back of the advance party.

Shortly before June 1, 1541, Coronado and his select group found a path out of the canyon and set forth on the final leg of their fateful journey. *Maestre de campo* López de Cárdenas was not among them, however. His arm had been thrown out of joint when his horse fell, and he was suffering great pain.[5] His position as Coronado's second in command was taken by Captain Diego López, formerly an alderman at Seville. Cárdenas was forced to return to Tiguex with the main party.

The route Coronado and his advance party followed from the second canyon to Quivira has long defied a provable answer. The *Relación del*

Suceso account states that from the second canyon the party proceeded many days "following the compass,"[6] presumably to the north. Convinced that canyon number 2 was Palo Duro Canyon, Bolton concluded that the march took place from that point northward across the Oklahoma Panhandle to the lower bend of the Arkansas River and northeastward up the river's north bank to Quivira.

Other scholars have puzzled about compass deviations and precisely what traveling "by the needle" (as Winship states) implies. It seems unreasonable, for instance, that "a straight line due north" is meant. Early foot and horseback travelers on the open plains were often guided in part by topographical features. One such feature was the tree line of streams and rivulets that promised sorely needed water for the Coronado party and their horses. Captain Juan Jaramillo, a member of the select thirty, implies that the party's march followed a line that offered an ongoing supply of water: "We pursued our journey, from here turning always toward the north for 30 days or nearly 30 days of travel . . . However, [they were] not long days of travel, [and] we never lacked water during any of them. [We were] always among the [bison], some days more numerous than others, depending on the streams we encountered. In this way we ended up striking a river there on the day of San Pedro and San Pablo [June 29], which we named accordingly [Quivira]."[7]

If the advance group departed on its march from Palo Duro, Tule, or Blanco Canyons, it would have encountered a number of streams on its march northward. The first major stream would have been the Canadian River. North of that west-east watercourse, Palo Duro Creek runs northeast into the Beaver extension of the North Canadian River and seemingly offers such a water-rewarding route. Beyond the Beaver, the Cimarron would have been encountered. Still, Coronado's route will likely remain unproven and suppositional until more concrete archaeological evidence emerges. (See appendix A for a discussion of Coronado's route.)

It is generally thought that the stream the advance party reached on Saint Peter and Saint Paul's Day was the Arkansas River and that it was crossed near the present town of Ford, Kansas, at the southern bend of the river (figure 8.1).[8] From there, it is reasoned, Coronado's party marched northeastward along the river's north bank for three days—perhaps forty to fifty miles—before they came onto a group of Indian buffalo hunters near present Great Bend, Kansas: "Here where we found the Indians and

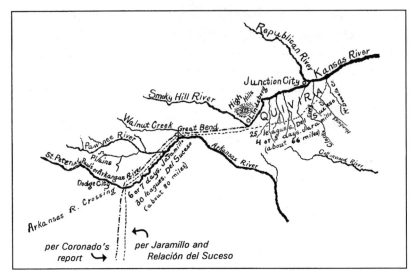

FIGURE 8.1. *Coronado's march in Kansas, 1541 (map by George A. Root)*

they saw us, they began to utter yells and appeared to fly, and some even had their wives there with them. The Indian Isopete began to call them in his language, and so they came to us without any signs of fear."[9]

Spanish historian Francisco López de Gómara, who had never been to the New World yet whose account of Coronado's expedition reflects a firsthand source, said the Spaniards were told that Quivira had a king who was bearded, gray-haired, and rich and "who prayed from a book of hours, worshiping a golden cross and an image of a woman, queen of heaven."[10]

Meeting the Indians was a moment of much satisfaction. Coronado, who still held high hopes for a great discovery, was so elated with the meeting that he penned a letter to the governor of Harahey and Quivira, of whom he had heard much from the Turk, Sopete, and Xabe. From what he had been told of the manner of government and the general character of the Quiviran people, Coronado wrote, it was his understanding that the governor was a Christian from the lost army of Florida. This last was apparently in reference to the failed 1528 Florida expedition under Pánfilo de Narváez, of which Cabeza de Vaca was a member.[11]

Some of the soldiers, remembering Marcos's misrepresentations, thought such a king could be another fantasy made up by the friars. But Coronado did not agree.

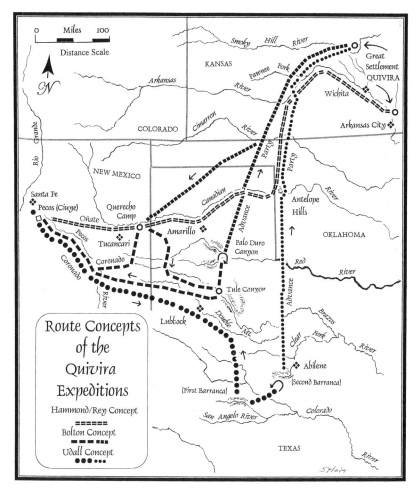

FIGURE 8.2. *Route concepts of Quivira Expeditions (map by author)*

Sopete, who accompanied the hunters to their village, was sent to deliver the letter. Coronado and the others followed, taking three or four days before they encountered an Indian settlement. The location of this village (the first of the Quivira group visited by the Spaniards) required some consideration.

A pertinent source for this segment of Coronado's march was advance party member Juan Jaramillo. His Spanish narrative has been translated differently by different scholars, their versions leading to a divergence of Coronado's march (figures 8.2, 8.3). Winship interprets

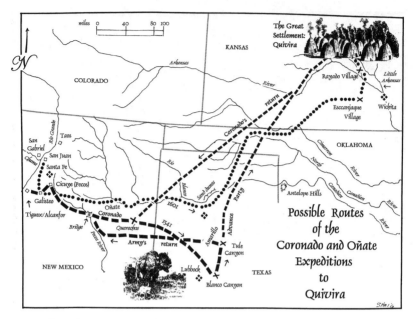

FIGURE 8.3. *Possible routes of the Coronado and Oñate Expeditions to Quivira (map by author)*

him to say: "After marching three days (from the river crossing) we found some Indians who were going hunting, killing the cows to take the meat to their village, which was *about three or four days still farther away from us.*"[12] Flint and Flint, however, take his statement to read: "After traveling three days [from the river crossing] we found some Indians who were out hunting, killing [bison] to supply meat to their pueblo, *which was three or four days of our travel further downstream.*"[13] Hammond and Rey also translate this as "about three or four days from us farther down [implying downstream]."[14]

Assuming the advance marched three days (±45 miles) down the Arkansas River from near the site of Ford, Kansas, to the vicinity of Larned (where the hunters were encountered), the question arises as to which direction they went from there. By Winship's translation, they could have turned away from the Arkansas northerly or northeasterly, as has often been assumed, to reach the first Quivira village.

But the Flint and Flint and Hammond and Rey translations, which have Coronado's advance moving on "downstream" for three or four more days (±45–60 miles), refute this. Moving downstream would have taken Coronado's advance party past the site of present Great Bend, Kansas, and well toward Hutchinson.

Jaramillo provides a further clue by stating that, after meeting the hunters, "we also proceeded at our rate of marching until we reached the settlements, which we found along good river bottoms, although without much water, and good streams which flow into another, larger than the one I have mentioned [presumably the Quivira River, i.e., the Arkansas]."[15] This implies that the advance group cut away from the Arkansas and crossed some smaller streams that flowed into the Arkansas River basin. These could have been Walnut Creek, Cow Creek, and the Little Arkansas or lesser streams.

The Flint and Flint translation reads: "We found [the houses] on pleasant streams, although not with much water, with good riverside gardens. [These streams] flow into the other, larger one I have mentioned."[16]

By both translations, the Quivira settlements were found on a series of small streams. By the Flint and Flint reading, these streams fed into the larger one (the Quivira, i.e., Arkansas). But by Winship's translation, they fed into some large stream other than the Quivira. This last seems implausible, since all the streams immediately north of the Arkansas drain southeasterly into that river basin.[17]

The advance party discovered that Quivira was not one large single village but instead a series of several settlements—Jaramillo says six or seven—of straw huts considered to be separate towns. Neither Coronado nor anyone else mentions an ensuing meeting with the chief at Quivira to whom the letter had been sent.

Because of archaeological evidence—bits of mail—found at the sites, it is believed today that Coronado had reached what is now known as the Cow Creek and Little River junctures with the Arkansas River in the vicinity of Hutchinson, Kansas. The captain general tells little of his meetings with native leaders, though he did report to the king of Spain that the Quivirans "rendered obedience to Your Majesty and were placed under your royal dominion."[18]

"The houses are round, without fence[s]," Castañeda wrote of the Quivira domiciles. "They have upper stories like buildings on stilts; [up there] underneath the roof [is] where they sleep and have their belongings; the roofs are made of thatch."[19]

"These [people] of Quivira," Coronado reported, "have an advantage over the others because of the houses they have and because they plant corn."[20]

"In some villages," another Spanish observer wrote, "there are as many as 200 houses; they have corn and beans and melons; they do not have cotton nor fowls [as did the Pueblo Indians], nor do they make bread, which is cooked, except under the ashes."[21]

Coronado reported to the king that the Quivira natives ate the flesh of buffalo raw and wore no clothing other than the animal skins they tanned. The men were tall, some measuring ten palms in height, he said, and the women were well proportioned, "with faces more like Moorish women than Indians."[22]

After traveling among the villages for four or five days, the Spaniards came to the end of Quivira. When the natives were asked if there was anything of significance beyond that point, they said that another place called Harahey was farther on. Coronado asked that the lord of that place be brought to him, and in a few days a large, well-proportioned Indian called Tatarrax arrived, accompanied by 200 warriors. During this mid-summer month of July, the visitors wore only narrow breechclouts that covered their private parts. Feathered bonnets decked their heads. All of the warriors carried bows and arrows.[23]

Significantly, the visiting Indians possessed nothing that hinted of mineral wealth. A piece of copper—the only metal found—hung about Tatarrax's neck. When Coronado inquired about it, signs were made that indicated that more could be found farther on. None was ever discovered, however. Coronado took the copper piece with him when he departed from Quivira and later sent it to Mendoza.[24]

Citing his lack of interpreters to handle the diversity of languages from one native village to another, Coronado wrote to the king to say: "Because [of this] I have been forced to send captains and men in many directions in order to find out whether there might be some place in this land where Your Majesty would be served."[25] He added: "In this *provincia* of Quivira I spent twenty five days, both to see and ride about the land and to obtain a report as to whether there was anything farther on which might be of service to Your Majesty."[26]

Though he was well aware that his small Spanish force was alone in a potentially hostile land, almost assuredly Coronado would have sent his men about the Quivira area proper to ascertain whether there was any treasure to be discovered. He was severely criticized later, however, for not pushing on farther north to Harahey to see if there truly was, as the Turk had claimed, gold waiting to be found there. The appearance of his visitors made it seem fairly certain that there was none.

Modern archaeological finds have supported research scholars in determining that the Quivira villages were spread along the Arkansas River from its Cow Creek juncture to the Little Arkansas, as well as up those streams to the north. It is believed that Coronado and his men explored as far north as the Quiviran town of Tabiás, which was then on the Smoky Hill River near Lindsborg, Kansas.

This theory is based on a prominence, now known as Coronado Heights, that rises from the Lindsborg countryside and provides a panoramic overview of the Smoky Hill valley. In 1915 a college professor found a piece of Spanish chain mail at a nearby Indian village site, giving support to Castañeda's statement that the expedition had reached a point where "as far as Quivira the land is level, but at that place there begin to be some mountain ranges."[27]

Having found no treasures and well aware that they were a very small force surrounded by various Indian tribes with large numbers of warriors, the expedition ended its exploration and turned back.

There had been ominous signs of danger. The Turk was still in shackles when the Spaniards reached the first Indian village at Cow Creek. There, the dethroned guide had pointed at Alvarado's mount and called out in his native tongue for his fellow tribesmen to "kill him." At Tabiás, the Indians refused to supply the Spaniards with much-needed maize for their horses. The Turk, it was learned, had persuaded the villages not to provide the grain, without which the horses might die and leave the Spaniards to become easy prey on the prairie.[28]

Coronado's captains had long been suspicious that the Turk was not to be trusted. Coronado, seeing him as a potential link to fortune and fame, had shielded the imaginative Indian from harm and trusted him far too much. But now it was clear that the man had been lying, that there was no golden treasure at Quivira. Coronado relented, ordering Captain Diego López to interview the Turk again and learn why he had led them astray. López did so and, by whatever means, secured a confession from the prisoner. The Turk, Coronado told the king, had been persuaded to lead them onto the plains where they and their horses might die and had done so "by the advice and order of the natives of these *provincias*."[29]

Presumably, Coronado had good reason to suspect the much-wronged Bigotes and the people of Cicuye.

The Turk's confession finalized his death warrant. But the Spaniards knew they must be discreet. If it became known that they had murdered the Turk, his fellow tribesmen might strike back. Thus under darkness of night in Alvarado's tent, where the Turk was kept, a rope was put around his neck and he was garroted to death. His body was buried among the soldiers' tents and the mound over it carefully concealed. Still, the Spaniards knew the execution might become known to the Quivirans.

In preparing to depart, Coronado left behind a historic memento of his presence. At the last village on his retreat back through Quivira—at Tabiás on Cow Creek, it is thought—he ordered that a cross be erected and at the foot of it an inscription be chiseled to the effect that Francisco Vázquez de Coronado, general of the Spanish army, had been there. The records do not tell us the precise wording of the inscription or whether it was chiseled into wood or rock.[30] Whichever it was, the cross and legend have thus far been lost to the ages.

It had begun to rain in the region, and fall was setting in.[31] Sopete was released as promised, and six Quiviran Indians were recruited to guide the expedition back across the prairie to New Mexico. Jaramillo summarized the return trip:

> Thus it was that we returned by the same route until [the place] where I said earlier we had struck the river San Pedro and San Pablo. From this point we diverged from the one by which we had come, bearing to the right. They [the Indians] led us along streams and among the [bison]. [It was] a good path, although there is none through one area or another except the path of the [bison].
>
> As I have said, we ended up leaving, and finally we recognized the land where at the beginning I said we had found the *rancheria* where El Turco led us away from the route we needed to take.[32]

Sopete vanishes from the historical record at this point. It can only be surmised that he may have lived on to regale tribal listeners around campfires at night with stories of his experiences as a slave with the Puebloans and a guide for the Spanish intruders. If so, even he may have enjoyed telling how the Turk filled their heads with dreams of riches and very nearly led them to their deaths on the prairie.

Coronado arrived back at Tiguex during mid-September and reported on his expedition in a letter to the king on October 20, 1541. Of Quivira he observed: "The soil [of Quivira] itself is the most suited for growing all the [crops] of Spain that has been seen because in addition to its being deep and black and having very excellent water from streams, springs, and rivers, I found plums like those in Spain, walnuts, excellent sweet grapes, and mulberries."[33]

He went on to say that the best place he had found in Tierra Nueva was the Tiguex area, but even there it would be impossible to establish a settlement because of its remoteness and lack of firewood and clothing during the cold winters. Still, despite his failure to find gold, Coronado considered returning to Quivira to explore further. Evidently, he was encouraged in this by Fray Padilla, who had found there a "treasure trove" of heathen souls waiting to be Christianized. Others still insisted that if Coronado had only searched a little bit farther, he would have found the El Dorado he sought. But fate was against the captain general. His future would continue to be shaped by bad fortune: a tragic accident, incapacitated health, trying events, and bitter disruptions within his expedition.

ABBREVIATION KEY

F/F-*DOCS* = Flint and Flint, eds., trans., annots., *Documents of the Coronado Expedition, 1539–1542*

H/R-*NCE* = Hammond and Rey, eds., *Narratives of the Coronado Expedition, 1540–1542*

W-*CE* = Winship, *The Coronado Expedition, 1540–1542*

NOTES

1. "Jaramillo's Narrative," F/F-*DOCS*, 516 (emphasis added). See also W-*CE*, 380; H/R-*NCE*, 303.

2. "Jaramillo's Narrative," F/F-*DOCS*, 515. See also W-*CE*, 376; H/R-*NCE*, 301; "Castañeda's Narrative," F/F-*DOCS*, 411. See also W-*CE*, 241; H/R-*NCE*, 241.

3. "Castañeda's Narrative," F/F-*DOCS*, 410. See also W-*CE*, 238; H/R-*NCE*, 240.

4. Sanchez, "Historiography," 289.

5. *Relación del Suceso*, F/F-*DOCS*, 500. See also W-*CE*, 359; H/R-*NCE*.

6. *Relación del Suceso*, F/F-*DOCS*, 501. See also W-*CE*, 359; H/R-*NCE*, 291.

7. "Jaramillo's Narrative," F/F-*DOCS*, 515. See also W-*CE*, 379; H/R-*NCE*, 302–303.

8. One argument for this assumption was that "the explorers must have crossed the bend below Dodge City in order to follow the river eighty miles in a northeast direction, which distance would have taken them to the site of Great Bend, where the river changes direction"; Richey, "Early Spanish Exploration and Indian Implements," 156. See also Bolton, *Coronado*, 285.

9. "Translation of Jaramillo," W-*CE*, 379. See also F/F-*DOCS*, 516; H/R-*NCE*, 303.

10. Day, "Gómara on the Coronado Expedition," 351.

11. "Translation of Jaramillo," W-*CE*, 380. See also F/F-*DOCS*, 516; H/R-*NCE*, 303.

12. "Translation of Jaramillo," W-*CE*, 379 (emphasis added).

13. "Castañeda's Narrative," F/F-*DOCS*, 516 (emphasis added).

14. H/R-*NCE*, 303. This conflict in translations is based on Jaramillo's phrase as given in "Jaramillo's Narrative," F/F-*DOCS*, 522: "A su pueblo que Estava como tres U quarto hornadas [jornadas?] de/las nuestras mas abaxo [abajo?] aqui donde hallamos los yindios." Neither Winship nor Hammond and Rey gives a reading of the original Spanish.

15. "Translation of Jaramillo," W-*CE*, 380.

16. "Jaramillo's Narrative," F/F-*DOCS*, 516.

17. Ibid., 523. The Spanish text to the key phrase as given by Flint and Flint reads: "buenas rriberas [stet] que Van a Entrar estotro mayor que tengo dicho."

18. "Coronado to King, October 20, 1541," F/F-*DOCS*, 320. See also W-*CE*, 368; H/R-*NCE*, 188.

19. "Castañeda's Narrative," F/F-*DOCS*, 423. See also W-*CE*, 280, 283; H/R-*NCE*, 263.

20. "Coronado to King, October 20, 1541," F/F-*DOCS*, 320. See also W-*CE*, 368; H/R-*NCE*, 188.

21. *Relación del Suceso*, W-*CE*, 359. See also F/F-*DOCS*, 501; H/R-*NCE*, 292.

22. "Coronado to King, October 20, 1541," F/F-*DOCS*, 320. See also W-*CE*, 368; H/R-*NCE*, 188.

23. "Jaramillo's Narrative," F/F-*DOCS*, 516. See also W-*CE*, 380; H/R-*NCE*, 188.

24. "Coronado to King, October 20, 1541," F/F-*DOCS*, 320–321. See also W-*CE*, 369; H/R-*NCE*, 188.

25. "Coronado to King, October 20, 1541," F/F-*DOCS*, 321. In their notes to this quotation (664n49), Flint and Flint argue that Coronado was specifically searching for "populous and wealthy places over which conquistadors could exercise jurisdiction for the crown and be recompensed through tribute." In translating, Winship (W-*CE*, 369) uses the phrase "to find out if there was *anything in this country*" of worth to the king rather than "*in this place*." Flint and Flint see this as a "subtle though fundamental misunderstanding" about the "targets of subjugation

and conquest." Hammond and Rey (H/R-*NCE,* 169) use the phrase "anything farther on by which your majesty might be served." Still another interpretation could be that Coronado actually meant "anything of value," including *encomienda* opportunities or simply the "golden treasures" he had come to Quivira to find.

26. "Coronado to King, October 20, 1541," F/F-*DOCS,* 321. See also W-*CE,* 369; H/R-*NCE,* 321.

27. "Castañeda's Narrative," F/F-*DOCS,* 423.

28. Ibid., 516. See also W-*CE,* 380; H/R-*NCE,* 304.

29. "Coronado to King, October 20, 1541," F/F-*DOCS,* 321. See also W-*CE,* 369; H/R-*NCE,* 189.

30. "Jaramillo's Narrative," F/F-*DOCS,* 516. See also W-*CE,* 381; H/R-*NCE,* 305.

31. Jaramillo (W-*CE,* 380) said that if he remembered correctly, when the Spaniards departed from Quivira it was "past the middle of August"; "Jaramillo's Narrative," F/F-*DOCS,* 516. Castañeda stated that "it was early in August" when Coronado began his return and "it had already begun raining"; W-*CE,* 248. An extrapolation of data from Coronado's report (see Coronado's timeline projection, figure 7.1) and other accounts indicates that the departure occurred on or about August 3, Julien Calendar, or August 13, Gregorian Calendar (see figure 7.1).

32. "Jaramillo's Narrative," F/F-*DOCS,* 517. See also W-*CE,* 381–382; H/R-*NCE,* 305–306.

33. "Coronado to King, October 20, 1541," F/F-*DOCS,* 321. See also W-*CE,* 368; H/R-*NCE,* 189.

9

Winter of Disasters

This mental image of his [own] death gave him [Coronado] the desire to go back to where he had a wife and children, to die. His own physician and surgeon, who was treating him (and was also a gossip), learned about the grumblings that were going on.

Castañeda[1]

After Coronado departed, Arellano and the main army rested for fifteen days in the second ravine. While there, they killed 500 bison and dried the meat to take with them on the trip back. Famished for fresh greenery, the Spaniards feasted on the wild but not yet ripe grapes, currants, mint-flavored wild marjoram, and the fruit of a rose-like plant that grew there.

During this rest period a tattooed Indian woman who was held as a slave by Juan de Zaldívar hid in a ravine and ran away. Her escape is particularly notable in that, by fleeing eastward, she was eventually taken up in eastern Texas by remnants of the exploring Spanish party of the conquistador Hernando de Soto, thereby establishing a link between the two expeditions.[2]

The main army made its way back more directly westward to the Pecos River, striking it south of the bridge the men had built earlier. Finding Cicuye now hostile and defiantly inhospitable, Arellano and his people continued on to Tiguex. There they set about wresting food and clothing for the coming winter from the pueblos up and down the Rio Grande. One command was sent to scour the pueblos north to the Taos area and another southward as far as Hot Springs (now called Truth or Consequences), New Mexico.[3]

In anticipation of meeting Coronado on his return from Quivira, Arellano led a party of forty horsemen back to Cicuye, whose inhabitants had been hoping to see nothing more of the Spaniards. They were again met by hostile warriors, and a battle ensued. Several Indians, including two leading men, were killed—some on the field outside and others by shots fired into the pueblo.[4]

When Coronado and his party arrived, Arellano escorted them on to Alcanfor. There the captain general was hailed with great joy. The elation quickly faded, however, when it was learned that no treasure of any kind had been found at Quivira. From that point on, things grew steadily worse for Coronado.

When the expedition returned to Tiguex, there had been talk of going back to Quivira with the entire army to make a full discovery of all the Indian settlements there.[5] But the colony and the army at Tiguex were in disarray. Soldiers and colonists alike suffered from the lice that abounded in the confiscated pueblos. Though the Spaniards had adapted somewhat to the Indian mode of wearing animal skins, they suffered from a lack of clothing.

Moreover, the once very popular Coronado had fallen into disfavor with many of his men. They complained that the officers who gathered cloth and apparel from the natives were allowed to take the best for themselves and their friends, and they left only scraps for them. Coronado's favorites were exempted from guard duty and other chores. These practices were even more critical regarding the allocation of foodstuffs.[6]

Then, in addition to everything else, Coronado suffered a serious personal injury at Alcanfor, one that would mark the beginning of the end of his expeditionary days. On Saint John's Day, December 27, 1541 (a Tuesday), he went out with an officer for a horseback ride in the countryside. The two men were having a friendly race, and Coronado was in the lead on his spirited sorrel when his saddle girth broke. The captain general was thrown to one side in the path of the other man's galloping mount. As the officer's horse passed over him, a hoof struck Coronado in the head. It was a near-death injury. Coronado remained confined to his bed in his

Alcanfor pueblo through the rest of the winter, undergoing a very slow and uncertain recovery.[7]

This was a period of extreme travail for Coronado. Held to his bed in the heatless and likely flea-infested pueblo room during one of the coldest winters on record, he was unable to rise and move about to attend to the affairs of his command. There was no medicine to relieve his throbbing head and little other of the comforts ordinarily provided to the sick or injured. His mental state during this period can only be speculated upon, but it is apparent that he yearned with all his soul to be back at his Mexico hacienda in the arms of his wife and family.

Moreover, for him, the inspiring expectation of discovering golden treasure was woefully gone. In a letter written to the king on his return to Tiguex, he said he had become convinced there was no gold to be found at Quivira or its environs, only small settlements with houses made of hides or grass straw. He had been led astray by his guides, he claimed, failing to distinguish between the advice he had received from Sopete and that of el Turco. He also failed, when speaking of the Turk, to mention the night-time garroting of the guide.[8]

Gone were all of the grand dreams for which he had sacrificed himself and his expedition during the past two years. He knew he had been badly duped twice, both at Cibola and at Quivira, and undoubtedly his disappointment cast a bitter spell over his disconcerted thoughts. He was left to lie helpless day after day, only to stare at the adobe ceiling and consider his failure before the world.

Following the accident, Castañeda and others reported that Coronado underwent a change of personality. Before, he had been outgoing and certain of himself; now, he was melancholy and suspicious. Moreover, his deterioration of spirit was exacerbated by the conflict that developed between those who wanted to return to Mexico and a faction who still heard the siren song of unfound treasure or who simply wished to remain in Tierra Nueva.

Castañeda describes a ploy the bedridden Coronado used to secure support for a return to Mexico. While he wished to do so, he did not want it to appear that returning was his idea. Even as he pretended he was opposed to the idea of returning, he sent loyal friends to persuade his soldiers to favor doing so and to encourage them to submit a signed petition to him in support of abandoning the Tierra Nueva colony. This was done; but when his deception became known, an enclave of resentment formed against the captain general. Some of the officers and others who wished to stay attempted to steal the petition from his room. Coronado, however, had placed a strong guard to protect the petition.[9]

George Winship summarized the situation in the camp:

> Two parties formed in the Spanish camp at Tiguex during the winter of 1541–42 . . . Many persisted in the belief that a more thorough exploration [of Quivira] would discover some of the things about which they thought the Turk had told them. On the other hand, there were many besides the leader who were tired of this life of hardship, which had not even afforded the attractions of adventure and serious conflict. Few of them, doubtless, had wives and estates waiting to welcome them home, like their fortunate general, but most of the gentlemen, surely were looking forward to the time when they could win wealth and glory, with which to return to old Spain, and add new luster to their family name.[10]

The original *entrada* had been planned on the basis of the expedition being resupplied by sea, but the inability of Hernando de Alarcón's ship to make contact drastically changed the situation. The failure of both Cibola and Quivira to produce a dramatic discovery, combined with Coronado's deteriorating health, further exacerbated the pain of remaining in Tierra Nueva. Coronado is said to have felt a gnawing fear that death might soon visit him, making him yearn even more to be back in Mexico with his wife, Doña Beatriz, and their children.[11]

More bad news came when word arrived that conditions had suffered greatly at the San Gerónimo, Mexico, outpost under Diego de Alcaráz, whom Melchior Díaz had left in charge there. Alcaráz's heavy demands for tributes and the appropriation of Indian women as slaves and sexual partners—himself the worst perpetrator—created great offense among the Indians.

It was later testified that "he [Alcaráz] cut off many Indians' hands, noses, and tongues and took women and girls by force and against their will, in order to have sex with them."[12]

The Sonora Indians rebelled, fighting the Spaniards with poisoned arrows that caused the flesh to rot away with a foul odor. Within twelve hours, victims died in great agony, bloated and raving.[13] When he arrived at San Gerónimo, Pedro de Tovar learned that the Indians had killed a soldier there with a poisoned arrow and then resisted a small detachment sent to investigate. On Tovar's orders, Alcaráz sent a larger force to make arrests; seventeen more soldiers were killed. Tovar moved the post to another location thought to be stronger defensively. He then headed back to Tiguex, taking many of the post's better soldiers, who were filled with high anticipation of sharing in Quivira's wealth.[14]

Arriving back at Tiguex, Tovar's party found that Coronado had returned without discovering any treasure. Their disappointment and anger only added to that already fomenting at Tiguex. The failure of Coronado's expedition to find gold at Quivira had greatly demoralized members of his colony. Their dreams of a great treasure there, however, were reignited by Xabe, the Quiviran slave who had returned to Tiguex with the main army. He insisted that there were indeed abounding riches to be found had Coronado only explored on a little bit further.[15]

Tovar had brought a package of letters from Mexico. Among them was one informing Cárdenas, who still wore a sling on the arm he had broken, that his brother in Spain had died, leaving him a worthy inheritance. With Viceroy Antonio de Mendoza's permission, Cárdenas headed for Mexico City with a small party. Upon reaching the new post Tovar had established, they found it deserted, its streets strewn with bodies. The bodies included Alcaráz's arrow-ridden corpse, as well as those of two soldiers, a number of allied Indians, horses, and livestock. Half of the soldiers at the post had mutinied, whereupon the Indians had attacked and overwhelmed the garrison. Some of the soldiers stationed there had escaped south to Culiacán, and others now joined Cárdenas, who returned to Tiguex.[16]

Because of Coronado's deteriorating health, *maestre de campo* Diego López, who was now essentially in charge at Tiguex, withheld news of the San Gerónimo disaster from the captain general until he improved. When they did tell him the news, Coronado suffered a relapse.[17]

As spring approached, Coronado conceded to a council decision and issued orders for a return to Mexico in early April 1542 for the entire expedition: the army, colonists, clergy, servants, and Indian allies. A dissident group of expedition members, numbering sixty or more, expressed their wish to remain in Tierra Nueva. These people had lost faith in Coronado's leadership and felt their futures were better served by remaining in the north rather than returning to Mexico, where many were now in debt because of their heavy expedition investments.[18]

An angry Coronado vowed to place in irons anyone who refused to leave. Francisca de Hozes, who had ridden from Mexico City to Cibola and Tiguex with her husband and son and out onto the Texas prairie as far as the *barrancas*, later testified that the captain general threatened to hang her and her husband if they talked further about remaining.[19]

But a group of friars succeeded in staying. Father Juan Padilla informed Coronado that he and some of the other friars wished to remain. Padilla declared that he personally hoped to return to Quivira, where he believed his teachings would bear fruit in drawing natives into the Christian faith. Lay brother Luis de Escalona wanted to work among the Indians at Cicuye. Fray Juan de la Cruz also chose to stay, serving the pueblos of Tiguex.

Two African lay brothers named Lucas and Sebastián chose to go with Padilla. Some accounts say that as boys, both men had been trained at a Mexico monastery by the priest. But Jaramillo claims Sebastián, a married man with children, had been his slave and that Lucas was a Spanish slave as well. In addition, Padilla took along a free Latino black, who eventually became a Franciscan friar. Andrés del Campo, a Portuguese soldier turned church layman, also opted to join Padilla.[20]

Because the friars had their Franciscan provincial's permission to work among the Indians, Coronado had no choice but to agree that they could remain. He willingly assisted the churchmen in preparing for their journey, providing Padilla with the six Quiviran guides who had served him upon his return. He assigned a soldier to escort Escalona to Cicuye, but he rejected Padilla's request for soldiers to remain as protection for him and those accompanying him.

The stories of the three friars provide testimony to the dedication and courage of the Franciscans, who accepted great hardship and risked their lives in seeking to Christianize native peoples. Still, there is no evidence that the friars had offered any serious opposition to Coronado's excesses with the Pueblo Indians. Fray Escalona is believed to have resided in a cave at Cicuye, and Fray de la Cruz remained to work among the Tiguex pueblos. Both men fade out of recorded history with glimmerings that, after Coronado departed, they were killed by the Indians they were seeking to convert. Padilla's ultimate fate is more certain, however.

During the spring of 1542, Padilla's party headed back to Quivira with some sheep, mules, and a horse ridden by Campo. All others were on foot in the missionary mode of the day. Pack mules and Campo's horse carried the food supplies, camp necessities, church vestments, trinkets to give to the Indians, and other goods.

While the details of Padilla's missionary venture are sketchy at best, historians have pieced together a general account. It is believed that the friar stopped first at Tabiás, where Sopete lived and Coronado had planted his memorial cross. This was possibly the same cross as the one Mota Padilla tells us Fray Padilla erected.

When Coronado made known his plans to return to Mexico, Padilla declared that he would not desert the cross he had erected at Quivira, even if it cost him his life. On his return to Quivira, the priest found that the place where the cross had been erected had been swept clean as he had charged the Indians to do. Rejoicing, he knelt by the cross and performed the offices of *padre maestro* (spiritual father) and apostle to the village.[21]

After working at Quivira for a time—one account says Padilla was there for two years—the friar decided to make a sojourn to the north to expand his Christian teaching. His small party had not gone far, only from the Arkansas River to the region of present Herington, Kansas, it is believed, when tragedy struck. A band of Indian warriors blocked their path, brandishing lances, battleaxes, and arrow-cocked bows as they prepared to attack. Some historians believe these Indians were ancestors of the Kaw Indians, known later to have occupied northeastern Kansas.[22] Like other tribes of the region, this band of Plains Indians was a sedentary, buffalo-hunting people who, history has shown, had not an ounce of precious metal.

Jaramillo claims to have heard that the six Quivira guides killed Padilla for the church vestments.[23] Other accounts say it was after only one day's journey that a hostile band of Indians blocked the path of Padilla's small retinue: "Perceiving the evil intentions of those barbarians, he [Padilla] told the Portuguese that as he was mounted he should flee, taking under his protection the laymen and lads, who could thus run and escape. This they did, as they could find no other way of defending themselves, and the blessed father, kneeling down, offered up his life."[24]

After the Indians were gone, Lucas and Sebastián went back and buried Padilla, covering his grave with rocks. They then hurried to overtake Campo.[25] For five years following, Campo wandered southward from Kansas across western Oklahoma and western Texas, crossing the Rio Grande in the vicinity of Eagle Pass, Texas, and thence to Pánuco (now Ciudad Madero), Mexico, on the Gulf of Mexico. Lucas and Sebastián eventually escaped as well, following their own adventures in returning south to New Spain.[26]

ABBREVIATION KEY

F/F-*DOCS* = Flint and Flint, eds., trans., annots., *Documents of the Coronado Expedition, 1539–1542*

H/R-*NCE* = Hammond and Rey, eds., *Narratives of the Coronado Expedition, 1540–1542*

W-*CE* = Winship, *The Coronado Expedition, 1540–1542*

NOTES

1. "Castañeda's Narrative," F/F-*DOCS*, 425–426. See also W-*CE*, 288; H/R-*NCE*, 267.

2. "Castañeda's Narrative," F/F-*DOCS*, 412. See also W-*CE*, 242; H/R-*NCE*, 243. De Soto had died earlier and the party, fearing that his death could lead the Indians to attack, buried him in a hollowed-out, sand-weighted log in the Mississippi River.

3. "Castañeda's Narrative," F/F-*DOCS*, 412–413. See also W-*CE*, 247; H/R-*NCE*, 243.

4. "Castañeda's Narrative," F/F-*DOCS*, 413. See also W-*CE*, 247; H/R-*NCE*, 245.

5. "Castañeda's Narrative," F/F-*DOCS*, 424–425. See also W-*CE*, 284; H/R-*NCE*, 265. Castañeda wrote: "God was pleased to have these discoveries left to other people and to have us, who went there, be content with saying that we were the first who reconnoitered [Quivria] and received news of [the settlements beyond]." "Castañeda's Narrative," F/F-*DOCS*, 424. See also W-*CE*, 283–284; H/R-*NCE*, 264.

6. "Castañeda's Narrative," F/F-*DOCS*, 425. See also W-*CE*, 287; H/R-*NCE*, 65–66.

7. "Castañeda's Narrative," F/F-*DOCS*, 425–426. See also W-*CE*, 287–289; H/R-*NCE*, 266–268.

8. "Coronado to King, October 20, 1451," F/F-*DOCS*, 321. See also W-*CE*, 369; H/R-*NCE*, 189.

9. "Castañeda's Narrative," F/F-*DOCS*, 426. See also W-*CE*, 288–289; H/R-*NCE*, 267.

10. "Historical Introduction," W-*CE*, 90.

11. "Castañeda's Narrative," F/F-*DOCS*, 425. See also W-*CE*, 288; H/R-*NCE*, 286–287.

12. "Contreras's Testimony," in Flint, *Great Cruelties*, 110.

13. Ibid., 82.

14. "Castañeda's Narrative," F/F-*DOCS*, 425. See also W-*CE*, 284; H/R-*NCE*, 265.

15. "Castañeda's Narrative," F/F-*DOCS*, 413–414. See also W-*CE*, 248; H/R-*NCE*, 245.

16. *Relación del Suceso*, F/F-*DOCS*, 501–502. See also W-*CE*, 360; H/R-*NCE*, 293.

17. "Castañeda's Narrative," F/F-*DOCS*, 425. See also W-*CE*, 288; H/R-*NCE*, 266.

18. "Francisca de Hozes's Testimony," in Flint, *Great Cruelties*, 54–55.

19. Ibid., 61.

20. "Jaramillo's Narrative," F/F-*DOCS*, 517. See also W-*CE*, 382; H/R-*NCE*, 306.

21. Day, "Mota Padilla," 107–108.

22. Bolton, *Coronado*, 339–341.

23. "Jaramillo's Narrative," F/F-*DOCS*, 517–518. See also W-*CE*, 382; H/R-*NCE*, 306–307.

24. Day, "Mota Padilla," 108.

25. Bolton, *Coronado*, 340–341.

26. Day, "Mota Padilla," 107–108.

10

End of the Conquest

*The general traveled along, everywhere leaving people who
refused to follow him. He reached [the Ciudad de] Mexico with
fewer than a hundred men to give Viceroy don Antonio de
Mendoza a report. He was not well received.*

Castañeda[1]

Shortly after Friar Juan Padilla's party departed from Tiguex in April,
Coronado started his army and colonists on their return to Mexico. He was
still suffering from his head injury, and at times he was carried on a litter
between two mules. His once grand expedition to Tierra Nueva was similarly
dysfunctional, its morale broken by failure, by the resentment of those who
felt the vaunted treasures had been overlooked at Quivira, and by sullen disdain among many for the man they had once adored as a noble leader. The
return march was westward to Hawikuh and back down the route of the original march across the *despoblado* to Chichilticale and on south to Culiacán.

Even before they reached Culiacán, Coronado's expedition had begun
to fall apart. Pedro de Castañeda felt that in essence the military simply
disintegrated as a result of Coronado's failing authority. Many of the men,
most of whom had sacrificed their all by taking part in the expedition,
began establishing new lives at Culiacán.

Juan Suarez de Peralta told how as a young boy he witnessed Coronado's return to Mexico City, where he kissed Antonio de Mendoza's hand. The viceroy received his captain general sadly but without rancor, even though he had suffered greatly in both his expectations and the loss of the 50,000 gold pesos he had borrowed to invest in the Tierra Nueva expedition. Mendoza could only be relieved that he had not led the expedition himself, as he had once considered doing.[2]

As news of the expedition's failure spread, many other Spanish investors were similarly dismayed, having lost personal fortunes in the expedition through their financial support and contribution of resources and slaves. Coronado's followers, many of whom had stopped to rest at Compostela and elsewhere, straggled in to Mexico City for many days following, "all of them worn out with their toils, clothed in the skins of animals, and showing the marks of their misfortunes and sufferings."[3]

During his two-year absence, Coronado had officially remained the governor of Nueva Galicia, drawing his full salary even as acting governor Cristóbal de Oñate presided. After resting in Mexico City for a time, he returned to the province, taking up residence at Guadalajara. There he resumed his duties as governor, dealing still with Indian insurrections, handling civil disputes, and seeing to the building of bridges across alligator-infested streams that endangered transportation. More than one person had suddenly disappeared while trying to ford a Mexican waterway.[4]

But his Quivira expedition had not been forgotten, especially by those who blamed him for not continuing on to Harahey and seeking the gold that was surely there. Letters of complaint against Coronado and accusations of his mistreating Indians at Cibola and Tiguex reached the king and the Council of the Indies. The complaints were disturbing enough that in September 1543 orders were issued for an investigation. Lorenzo de Tejada, a judge of the Audiencia of New Spain, was commissioned to head an investigation of the Coronado Expedition and conduct an inquiry of its participants. During 1544, testimony was taken from fourteen witnesses in Mexico City and Guadalajara. In the main, they were people who had personal ties to Coronado.[5]

The witnesses included the outspoken Francisca de Hozes and her husband, two men who had served as constables and billeting officers on the expedition, Coronado's chief groom, his chief of artillery, a squire of his household, two captains of his military (one of which was his lieutenant governor's nephew, Juan de Zaldívar), and several other participants who had served with either the main expedition or the advance guard.[6]

In questioning these witnesses, Tejada was principally interested in hearing whether Coronado was responsible for the various pueblo uprisings and by whose orders the pueblos were burned, the various brutalities committed against the Indians, and why the Turk was murdered. In addition, and very important: Was the *Requerimiento* properly read to the Indians?[7]

Señora de Hozes was the first to be interviewed. When asked if she had witnessed the setting of dogs on Indians, she replied that she had. Although she did not actually see Coronado give the order, she was certain he had done so "because the general saw to it that his captains and troops were obedient and subject to his command."[8]

Her husband, Alonso Sánchez, whose testimony was taken separately, made the same charge, saying that though he had not witnessed the act, it was common knowledge in camp that Coronado gave the order. The dogging, after all, had taken place at the door of Coronado's quarters. Sánchez testified further that he had seen several posts where Indians had been tied up and burned. In one pueblo "the Indians who had been captured alive were stabbed and lanced and dogs set on many others."[9]

Juan Gómez de Paradinas said likewise that while the burning of the Indians was done by Captain López de Cárdenas, he believed it had been ordered by Coronado, as had the killing of the Turk—though he did not know for certain.[10] Domingo Martin, a soldier, agreed that the general had ordered the dogging, saying "no one would dare do such a thing without his order and consent." He did not know, however, who ordered the Indians to be burned and, "to put fear in the rest, [to] cut off their hands."[11]

Juan de Contreras, Coronado's head groom, was asked what cruelty and outrages had been committed against the Indians captured alive at Tiguex. Without hesitation, he told how the general had sent him hurrying to tell Cárdenas not to execute the prisoners until the Turk and Sopete could be brought forth to witness the execution so they could tell other Indians about it. He further described how some of the Indians had been tied to a post and dry willow canes placed around them to be set afire. When the other Indians being held in a nearby tent saw this, they revolted. Coronado's men then rushed forward with swords and lances and killed them all. Contreras felt certain that the execution had been ordered by Coronado.[12]

Much the same was said by Rodrigo Ximón, who put the number burned to death at twenty or thirty and added that the others were lanced or stabbed to death until "no one remained alive."[13] He, too, believed Coronado had ordered the executions, "since he came there soon afterwards and because he kept the people obedient and subject to his command, so that no one would dare to have carried out the execution without his order."[14]

In his testimony, cavalryman Cristóbal de Escobar was clearly sympathetic to Coronado, but even he stated that he believed the general had ordered the dogging of 150 Indians. He freely admitted to the murders; the ravaging of Indian villages; the rape of Indian women; and the looting of food, clothing, and firewood the natives desperately needed through the bitterly cold winter. But, as with the others, his testimony contained no hint of remorse in observing that the Spaniards themselves would have died of cold and hunger "if it had not been for the supplies and wood that they got from the pueblos."[15]

Juan Troyano was a professional soldier and a retainer of Viceroy Antonio de Mendoza, who provided him with the financial support needed to accompany the Coronado Expedition.[16] On his return to Mexico from Tierra Nueva, Troyano had brought a native woman with him. Though he recited the expedition's many brutalities without any apparent emotion, he spoke to the damaging effects such excesses had on pacification of the Indian population:

> The witness said that [the Indians] of the other pueblo to which [the Spaniards] had laid siege knew and saw the cruelty with which [the Spaniards] had treated [the Indians] of the [first] pueblo and that [the Spaniards] had not kept the promise of safety they had given. As a result, they never were willing to yield and come forth in peace, although they were summoned repeatedly by Francisco Vázquez. [The Indians] said that [the Spaniards] were dishonest people and did not respect the truth. They said that although [the Spaniards] might give their word and guarantee, they would not hold to it, just as they failed to do with their comrades and neighbors.[17]

Rodrigo de Frías, a member of the advance party to Cibola, spoke favorably of Coronado, as had others. He said that on the march to Cibola, the general had been kind to the Indians he met on the way, and they had all come out in peace. He blamed the Tiguex uprising on the killing of the Spaniards' horses by the Indians and said he was not present when the

Indians were burned at the stake and captives were killed. But, like the others, Frías insisted that "no one would have committed the burnings and unleashing of dogs, which he has mentioned and that he heard were carried out, without the general's order and permission."[18]

Melchior Pérez, the son of the governor of Nueva Galicia preceding Coronado, served as chief constable under Captain Juan de Zaldívar. He had been present at Tiguex when the Indians made signs that they wanted peace if they were guaranteed safety and would not be punished. When Cárdenas issued the promise by making the sign of the cross, Pérez had suspected treachery and expressed caution. Cárdenas replied that he had made the sign incorrectly and continued on with the killings. Pérez did not know if Coronado had ordered the burnings at the stake.[19]

Pedro de Ledesma, a member of Coronado's household, had gone ahead with the advance party to Cibola. He testified to the dogging incidents and added a baffling, hard-to-believe twist to the burning at the stake of the Indians, whom he numbered at twenty to twenty-five. The fire, he said, had eroded away the rope binding one of the Indians: "Burned on one side, he [the Indian] took up a stick from among the firewood with which they were burning him and attacked [the Spaniards] who were around him, giving them four or five blows. Then he freely returned to the fire, where he finished burning."[20]

Juan de Zaldívar, a nephew of Cristóbal de Oñate, had served under then-governor Coronado in Nueva Galicia prior to the expedition and was very wealthy.[21] He had also made the trip north to Tierra Nueva with Melchior Díaz to investigate the stories of Friar Marcos de Niza and later served as one of the ten captains with Coronado's expedition.

Ill and wounded during the battle at Tiguex, Zaldívar had not been present at the burning of the Indians. However, he stoutly insisted that Coronado had not ordered the action and laid the blame on Cárdenas. He added that when he recovered and returned to the field, "he saw burned human bones at the place where the burning had been done."[22]

Alonso Álvarez, standard bearer for the expedition and Coronado's personal page, was specific in his testimony that Coronado did indeed order the Indian punishments. He felt certain that the general had done so with Bigotes because he saw Coronado leave his quarters and go to those of Hernando de Alvarado. Shortly afterward, the soldier saw the dogs set on the Indian leader. After the dogging, Bigotes was brought to Coronado's quarters badly maimed and still wearing his iron collar. There, a surgeon treated the many bites on his legs and arms. Alvarez also said that Coronado ordered the burning and destruction of Indian pueblos and that it was by the general's orders that several Indians were killed by the dogs and other pueblo men's hands and noses were cut off.[23]

Coronado was tried in court, but the trial was not as we know one today. Witnesses for both the prosecution and the defense were presented, but none were cross-examined. The expedition leader was permitted to have his say in an interview conducted by Tejada at Guadalajara on September 3, 1544. Coronado gave his testimony under oath "in legal form, by God, Santa María, and a representation of the holy cross, on which he placed his right hand."[24]

Coronado promised to tell and declare the truth about everything he might know. It is difficult to believe that he did so. Certainly he did not tell the whole truth, as he volunteered virtually nothing about the expedition's proven cruelties and mayhem. Even if the testimonies of witnesses friendly to him are accepted, Coronado's testimony was a litany of untruths.

He was asked if, after the Cibola pueblo had been entered, he or any of his captains or men-at-arms committed any cruelties or outrages or caused any deaths among Indians found inside. Coronado answered an emphatic "no." He went on to say that because the Indians had rendered themselves obedient, he had treated the women and children with kindness. He had offered to let them remain in the pueblo and promised that the Spaniards would nurse their wounded and not molest their property.[25]

Coronado was asked if he knew that while gathering clothing, hides, and provisions from a pueblo home, one of his officers (Villegas) had grabbed an Indian woman by force and had sexual relations with her. Even though he had conducted an (insufficient) inquiry into the matter, Coronado answered that he had known nothing about it until he returned to Mexico.[26]

Coronado also insisted that he had not ordered the burning of pueblos at Tiguex and never knew which captain was responsible for doing so. He did not remember if he had ordered the torching. He further declared that "he himself did not order any Indian burned or set upon by dogs nor does he know that any such thing was done."[27]

Regarding the dogs, he said that after his men let some Indian prisoners loose, a dog had run after them and bitten them, and he was certain that no one had purposely unleashed the dogs on the Indians. Coronado explained away the dog attack on Bigotes in the same manner, saying that a dog wandering loose had bitten the Cicuye chief. Further, he had seen only one bite on Bigotes.[28]

When asked if he was aware that Captain García López de Cárdenas had ordered forty or fifty Indians tied to posts and burned to death, Coronado answered that "he was never aware that, in the vicinity of the besieged pueblo, don García López ordered any Indians burned."[29] He did not recall any such thing ever coming to his notice.

In addition to his own testimony, with the help of an attorney, Coronado secured testimony from four additional witnesses: expedition horseman Lorenzo Alvarez, Captain Diego López, soldier Luis de Figueredo, and Captain Pedro de Tovar. Apparently these men were carefully selected, for they all denied that their captain general had committed any transgressions and swore to his diligence on several key points of defense. They declared that Coronado had not personally committed any outrages against the Indians, that he had had the *Requerimiento* read whenever Indians were confronted, that he conferred with the Franciscan friars prior to conducting war, that he never made slaves of the Indians, and that the Turk had been executed only after he had committed treasonable acts.[30]

In February 1545, Coronado was assigned to house arrest in Mexico City while the case against him was being considered. During the next month, royal official Cristóbal de Benavente charged Coronado with six specific instances of criminal malfeasance or negligence: his execution of Indians at Chiametla, appointment of the odious Diego de Alcaráz at San Gerónimo, his brutal warring methods at Cibola, the inhumane treatment of Bigotes and Cacique, the secretive murder of the Turk, and his failure to colonize Tierra Nueva.[31]

Notably, these charges do not include the burning at the stake of Indians at Arenal. Other lesser matters, though, were still under scrutiny. Several horses and other gifts had been given to Coronado by friends and admirers. This raised the attending question as to whether these matters involved the acceptance of bribes on Coronado's part. In two cases regarding horses, he was fined. Accusations that he gambled in his own house and had relations with a married woman also surfaced and failed.[32]

Coronado was investigated on two of the matters. On the charge of abuse of Indians, he was exonerated. By ruling of the court on the issue of misconduct as governor of Nueva Galicia, however, Coronado was fined and had several *encomiendas* taken from him. These punishments were appealed, however. Eventually, the *encomiendas* were returned, and Coronado was exonerated on all charges.[33]

His exact date of birth was unknown (evidently, it was during or about 1511), but it is thought that the captain general of the Coronado Expedition was near his forty-third birthday when he died on September 22, 1554. Richard Flint speculates that he succumbed to a communicable disease that prevailed at the time and claimed the lives of a number of his contemporaries.[34]

Charges had likewise been filed in Spain on January 7, 1546, against López de Cárdenas, Coronado's onetime *maestre de campo*, who had been in command at Arenal and oversaw the burning of the natives there. In 1549 he was found guilty of cruelty to the Indians of Tierra Nueva. His sentence was merely banishment from the Indies (America) for ten years, a year's military service at a North African outpost, and a fine of 200 ducas. Appeals to the king brought a change in the place of military service and reduction of the fine.[35] This tepid punishment was the only penalty imposed on any member of the Coronado Expedition.[36]

Among the many salient observations made by Richard Flint are that the investigation of the Tierra Nueva expedition was heavily weighted in favor of Coronado; that, even so, it is clear that the Coronado Expedition exercised severe cruelties upon the Pueblo Indians, employing torture, butchery, disfiguration, and other terrorist acts to control Indian populations by fear and force; and that, despite the many conquistador excesses, activists in the Spanish government, priests of the Catholic Church, and other private citizens led the fight for human rights for native inhabitants of the New World.[37]

Truthful examination of the demeaning facets of the Coronado Expedition is not to deny Coronado credit for his resolve, stamina, and personal sacrifice in exploring and discovering much of the American Southwest. His role in the annals of American history remains intact, though regrettably tarnished by his excessive actions against native inhabitants.

Even more regrettably, the details of his experiences in Tierra Nueva would lie buried for many years in archives in Mexico and Spain. As a result, his miscalculations of treasures to be found, mis-dealings with natives of the New World, and misfortunes were destined to be repeated by other Spaniards. During the remainder of the sixteenth century, Spanish adventurers continued to lead intrusions northward from Mexico into present New Mexico, including the *entrada* of Juan de Oñate, whose colonizing efforts would be laced with many of the same faults and failures as those of the Coronado Expedition.

Richard Flint cites the observation of historian Janet Lecompte that Coronado's expedition became "all but forgotten," even as its effects lingered. He notes as well Bolton's observation that the geographic knowledge obtained by the expedition was also quickly forgotten.[38]

Certainly, it is true that Spanish intrusions into North America during the succeeding years reflected little awareness of or benefit from Coronado's experience. Even with ancestral connections in family history (Cristóbal de Oñate and two brothers of the Zaldívar family), Don Juan de Oñate would follow a similar path in pursing a wanton historical fantasy into what is now the United States.

ABBREVIATION KEY

F/F-*DOCS* = Flint and Flint, eds., trans., annots., *Documents of the Coronado Expedition, 1539–1542*

H/R-*NCE* = Hammond and Rey, eds., *Narratives of the Coronado Expedition, 1540–1542*

W-*CE* = Winship, *The Coronado Expedition, 1540–1542*

NOTES

1. "Castañeda's Narrative," F/F-*DOCS*, 430. See also W-*CE*, 299; H/R-*NCE*, 275.

2. "Historical Introduction," W-*CE*, 92, citing Juan Suarez de Peralta, *Tratado del Descubrimiento de las Yndias y su Conquista.*

3. Ibid.

4. Bolton, *Coronado*, 366.

5. Flint, *Great Cruelties*, 8, 31.

6. The witnesses were Francisca de Hozes and her husband, Alonso Sánchez, ibid., 54–74; Juan Gómez de Paradinas, Coronado's chief constable and billeting officer, ibid., 75–87; Domingo Martin, an expedition member, ibid., 88–106; Juan de Contreras, Coronado's chief groom, ibid., 107–125; Rodrigo Ximón, an expedition member, ibid., 126–140; Cristóbal de Escobar, an expedition member, ibid., 141–160; Captain Juan Troyano, Coronado's chief of artillery, ibid., 161–188; Rodrigo de Frías, member of the advance guard, ibid., 189–205; Melchior Pérez, who also served for a time as chief constable and billeting officer for the expedition, ibid., 206–229; Pedro de Ledesma, a member of Coronado's

household, ibid., 230–249; Juan de Zaldívar, a captain in the expedition and nephew of Cristóbal de Oñate, ibid., 250–269; Coronado himself, ibid., 270–311; and Alonso Álvarez, expedition standard bearer, ibid., 312–324.

7. "Lorenzo de Tejada's Testimony," in Flint, *Great Cruelties*, 36.

8. "Testimonies of Francisca de Hozes and Alonso Sánchez," in Flint, *Great Cruelties*, 60.

9. Ibid., 64.

10. "Juan Gómez's Testimony," in Flint, *Great Cruelties*, 81.

11. "Domingo Martin's Testimony," in Flint, *Great Cruelties*, 95–96.

12. "Contreras's Testimony," in Flint, *Great Cruelties*, 113–114.

13. "Rodrigo Ximón's Testimony," in Flint, *Great Cruelties*, 131.

14. Ibid., 132.

15. "Cristóbal de Escobar's Testimony," in Flint, *Great Cruelties*, 144–151.

16. "Troyano's Testimony," in Flint, *Great Cruelties*, 161.

17. Ibid., 175.

18. "Rodrigo de Frías's Testimony," in Flint, *Great Cruelties*, 196.

19. "Melchior Pérez's Testimony," in Flint, *Great Cruelties*, 216–217.

20. "Pedro de Ledesma's Testimony," in Flint, *Great Cruelties*, 240.

21. This Juan de Zaldívar was the brother of Vicente de Zaldívar whose grandsons Juan de Zaldívar and Vincente de Zaldívar were prominent participants in the Juan de Oñate Expedition five decades later. See "Oñate Genealogy Diagram," in Simmons, *The Last Conquistador*, 33.

22. "Zaldívar's Testimony," in Flint, *Great Cruelties*, 250–252.

23. "Alonso Alvarez's Testimony," in Flint, *Great Cruelties*, 315–319.

24. "Coronado's Sworn Statement," in Flint, *Great Cruelties*, 277.

25. Ibid., 281.

26. Ibid., 287.

27. Ibid., 289–290.

28. Ibid., 285, 291.

29. Ibid., 292.

30. "Defense Offered by Coronado," in Flint, *Great Cruelties*, 345.

31. "Accusations against Coronado," in Flint, *Great Cruelties*, 326–327; Bolton, *Coronado*, 380.

32. Bolton, *Coronado*, 374–375.

33. "A Final and Definite Decision," in Flint, *Great Cruelties*, 457–458.

34. "The Nominal Target, Coronado," in Flint, *Great Cruelties*, 271, 276.

35. "Defense Offered by Coronado," in Flint, *Great Cruelties*, 339.

36. "The Maestre de Campo Held Responsible," in Flint, *Great Cruelties*, 336–339.

37. "Results and Repercussions," in Flint, *Great Cruelties*, 537–540.

38. Ibid., 534–535.

Part 2

Post-Coronado Incursions

Written history does not know, and this book cannot say, what actually happened to Captains Francisco Leyva de Bonilla and Antonio Gutiérrez de Humaña. These two men defied Spanish law and, on their own, plunged ahead into Tierra Nueva in 1593, five years before Oñate reached Nueva Mexico. Did Gutiérrez murder Leyva, as the Indian guides reported? And, as the Escanjaques told Oñate when he arrived at Quivira in 1601, was Gutiérrez crippled by a prairie fire set by the Rayado Indians and still held captive? Oñate made no attempt to learn for certain or even to try to know if his fellow Spaniard was alive, so we do not know.

It seems almost certain that the captains' true fates will never be learned unless by chance some startling new evidence emerges. Almost surely, artifacts from Oñate's battle with the Escanjaques are still rusting away somewhere beneath the Kansas soil. As discussed in appendix E, who knows whether the engraved message Coronado left behind in 1541, if it were carved in stone, may still be awaiting the glory of modern "true" discovery (see The Sword and the Stone, appendix E).

11

For Slaves and Souls

The friars replied that they did not want to go, but wished to stay [in New Mexico] in order to preach the holy gospel to these heathen people.

Hernán (Hernando) Gallegos[1]

The remains of Francisco Vázquez de Coronado, as were those of his family members later, were interred at the Church of Santo Domingo in Mexico City. As time passed, participants in his grand *entrada* to Tierra Nueva would fade away and with them memories of the event. A brief account of the Coronado Expedition by Francisco López de Gómara, *Historia de las Indías*, was published in Spain in 1552 and reprinted several times. But while it is generally an accurate account, the book failed to reveal the harsh details of the adventure to descendant Spaniards in Mexico.[2]

Still, the vast, slightly known realm claimed by Spain north of Mexico beckoned for further exploration. Coronado had explored it in part, but he had not convincingly disproved the bewitching potential of golden treasures to be found. The discoveries of Hernando Cortés and Francisco Pizarro and the persistent myths of cities of gold in the north still glittered in the minds of ambitious men, giving impetus to further exploration on behalf of the Spanish Empire and Christianity.

There were other incentives for men to push north, among them the procurement of Indian slaves and a reverse objective: saving Indian souls by converting them to Christianity. In addition to many unrecorded sorties northward in pursuit of Indians who marauded cattle ranches or for the purpose of capturing Indian slaves, several organized Spanish incursions occurred into Tierra Nueva following Coronado's 1540–1542 expedition. They included the Chamuscado-Rodríguez entry in 1581, the Espejo entry of 1582, the illegal Gaspar Castaño de Sosa entry in 1590, the Morlete party that rode north to arrest Castaño in 1591, and the illegal Leyva-Humaña entry in 1593.

In 1573 the Spanish Crown issued the "Comprehensive Orders for New Discoveries," mandating that Catholic missionaries would bear primary responsibility for such intrusions and that only licensed parties would be permitted to conduct them. Illegal entries, it was threatened, would suffer "pain of death and loss of all their property."[3]

The motivations for these state-church ventures were various: the spreading of Christian teachings among the heathen Indians, the extension of the Spanish Empire through colonization, the innate curiosity that propels adventurous men toward the unknown, and always the hope of finding an advanced native society with vast riches. As with Coronado, all of these efforts would come to dismal, if not fatal, ends. Still, the myth of golden treasures lived on.

In June 1581, Fray Agustín Rodríguez, escorted by Captain Francisco Sánchez Chamuscado and nine soldiers, set out from Santa Bárbara, Mexico, to spread the gospel and light of civilization among a tribe of Indians who lived to the north. Rodríguez had been intrigued by a story told by a captive Indian of a settlement to the north that grew cotton and made blankets and clothing. These people, the Indian said, raised corn, beans, and melons. Publication of Alvar Núñez Cabeza de Vaca's odyssey further inspired the expedition.[4]

Joining Fray Rodríguez on the journey were Frays Francisco López and Juan de Santa María, from the monastery of New Spain in Mexico City.[5] Also, there were nineteen Indian servants who herded the expedition's 90 horses and 600 head of stock. In addition to providing protection for the friars, Chamuscado carried a commission to make a "discovery"— a word the Spanish government preferred in lieu of "conquest."

By fall, the party had advanced northward up the Rio Grande to the San Felipe area between present Albuquerque and Santa Fe, the area in which Coronado had quartered at Alcanfor pueblo. From there, Chamuscado made explorations in various directions, taking possession of the land for the Spanish Crown. One of his adventures of particular interest was his visit as far east as the Canadian River to investigate stories of a strange animal that existed in great numbers on the "Plains of the Cattle."[6] An expedition member described the witnessing of the buffalo, as Hernando de Alvarado with Coronado's expedition had done forty years earlier:

> They are as large as the cattle of New Spain, hump-backed and woolly, with short, black horns and big heads. The bulls have beards like he-goats. They are fairly swift and run like pigs. They are so large that when seen in the midst of a plain they resemble ships at sea or carts on land. According to our estimate and that of the men who discovered them, the bulls must weigh more than forty arrobas each when three years old. Their meat is delicious and to our taste as palatable as that of our beef cattle.[7]

Prior to the buffalo excursion, one of the friars, Juan de Santa María, had announced that he was leaving the expedition to return to Mexico. It was said that he was eager to spread the word of finding a large Indian society, offering great potential to the church. Chamuscado ordered him not to go. But much to the dismay of the others, he declared that "he intended to go to Mexico City and that no one was going to stop him."[8]

When it was seen that the determined fray was leaving, Chamuscado called a meeting of the expedition and demanded a new pledge of allegiance from everyone.[9] Hernán (Hernando) Gallegos, who chronicled the discovery march, told of Santa María's fate as he trod southward by himself along a route east of the Sandia and Manzano Mountains: "When the natives saw that the friar was leaving, they became alarmed, believing he was going to bring more Christians in order to put them out of their homes; so they asked us by signs where he was going, all alone. We tried to dissuade them from their wicked thoughts, but, as they were Indians, this did not prevent them from doing evil. They followed the friar and killed him after two or three days of travel. We knew nothing of this until we returned from our trip to the buffalo."[10]

Fearful that the Indians also intended to kill the remainder of the expedition, Chamuscado turned back toward Mexico. At their request, he left Friars Rodríguez and López at the pueblo of Puaray (north of present Albuquerque) to continue their missionary work. The officer attempted to dissuade them, but they were determined to stay: "His Grace gave the friars good reason why they should leave the region with him, since they could not reap any harvest there at the moment without an interpreter. To these entreaties the friars replied that they did not want to go, but wished to stay in order to preach the holy gospel to these heathen people."[11]

Chamuscado became ill during his return trip and died shortly before his party reached Santa Bárbara on April 18.[12] It was left to the soldier Gallegos to record the expedition and excite the Mexican frontier about the northern pueblo cities with tales of two- and three-story houses built of stone where people wore cotton clothing and leather shoes and raised crops and fowl for food, where vast herds of buffalo on the adjacent plains provided the natives with an abundance of meat, and where the land was filled with good salt-producing lakes as well as prospects of high-grade silver mines.[13]

But was even this everything? Gallegos admitted that there were many places they had been unable to visit. Other expedition members told of hearing stories of a large lake with many towns where people "rode in canoes bearing large, bronze-colored balls in the prows."[14] Those in Mexico who heard such tales were left to imagine that surely a "great new kingdom" to the north lay waiting to be discovered and exploited.

One of those who heard these stories of marvel was a prominent rancher in northern Mexico, Antonio de Espejo. Antonio had once killed an Indian who worked for him and in 1581 was charged with complicity in another killing committed by his brother Pedro. Pedro was found guilty, but Antonio suffered only a fine, which he avoided paying by hiding out on the Chihuahua frontier. He was there when the Chamuscado party returned.[15]

When they learned that Friar Santa María had been killed and the two other friars had remained at Puaray, members of the Franciscan order became greatly concerned for their safety. Espejo, eager to seek out mining and other potential, stepped forward with an offer to finance and lead a mission to rescue Friars Rodríguez and López. The Franciscans eagerly accepted his offer. They were shocked, however, when they were told by an Indian servant in the Chamuscado party that the pueblos had revolted and the two friars had been murdered.

Testimony to this fact was given by Hernando Barrado, a Chamuscado soldier. After his return to Mexico, Barrado met his former Indian servant, who had stayed in Puaray with the two Franciscans. The servant said the Indians had killed López and that he had witnessed the friar's burial. In great fear for their own safety, the servant and two others tried to escape. Even as they fled the pueblo, they heard a great commotion which meant, they felt certain, that the Indians had killed Friar Rodríguez and the Indian boys serving him.[16]

Espejo, still determined to make a great discovery, remained undeterred. He again declared his determination to lead a small group north to investigate. Anxious to know the truth about the friars' fate, the Franciscans again accepted. As soon as an official permit had been obtained, Espejo gathered together fourteen soldiers and several Indian servants. Well supplied with arms and provisions and over 100 horses and pack mules, on November 10, 1582, Espejo and his small band of soldiers, accompanied by Friar Bernardino Beltrán, rode out of San Bartolomé, Mexico, headed for the pueblos of Tierra Nueva.

The group followed the Conchos River to the Rio Grande where, at a small village called San Bernardino, they recruited Juan Cantor, an Indian interpreter. They were exhilarated to hear from other Indians that Friars Rodríguez and López were still alive.[17]

Following the general course of the Rio Grande, the party marched upriver, visiting Indian pueblos along the way. After resting for a week at the site of present El Paso, they pushed north past the present site of Elephant Butte Dam and from there to the Piro Indian country south of present Albuquerque. Here, the story of the fate of the two friars at Puaray was again reversed and decided conclusively—Espejo's party was informed that the priests had indeed been killed by the Tigua Indians, who were in revolt.[18]

Much alarmed at this news and well aware of their small number, the men discussed building a temporary fortress from which they could reconnoiter the surrounding countryside. Instead, during February 1583 Espejo led two of the soldiers and a few of his Indian allies on a brief exploratory tour to the region beyond the Manzano Mountains. Afterward, they rejoined the others and marched on for two days to Puaray.

Their arrival frightened the Tigua Indians, who fled into the mountains. While waiting there for the inhabitants to return, Espejo's party replenished its food supply at the Tigua village. The Spaniards also enjoyed turkeys and other foodstuffs brought to them by friendly Indians residing farther to the north. In response to their invitation, Espejo led his small expedition up the Rio Grande four leagues to the pueblos of some friendly Indians before heading up the Jémez River to the pueblo of Zia. From there he turned south past the Zuni Mountains, visiting the famous mesa city of Acoma and Inscription Rock on the march to Zuni. At Zuni the Spaniards were received with great hospitality.

Exploring southward, Espejo visited several pueblos, including one that had been attacked and destroyed by Coronado. Near the pueblos, the Spaniards found crosses Coronado had erected forty-three years earlier. They also came upon three Christian Indians Coronado had brought to the land from New Spain. Once their memory of the Spanish language was somewhat revived, the three told of hearing tales of a large lake with many towns sixty days' journey inland (eastward). The people there wore cotton clothes along with gold bracelets and earrings. The Indians had given Coronado "many ores," they said, but the Spaniards had lacked the equipment to smelt them. Coronado's expedition, the three recalled somewhat erroneously, had traveled in that direction for twelve days from the Zuni pueblos before using up all of its water and turning back.[19]

After taking possession of these villages, Espejo took four men and plunged westward into what is now Arizona looking for mines he had been told were there. Going as far as present Jerome, Arizona, he was disappointed to learn that the lodes were mostly copper with only slight traces of silver.[20]

Father Bernardino and several others became discouraged upon learning from the three Indians that Coronado had failed to find either gold or silver at the Arizona site. They expressed their wish to return to Mexico.[21] After some debate they were permitted to leave, and Espejo led the remaining eight soldiers and Indian servants back to Acoma. There, an incident occurred when one of the soldiers attempted to recapture a woman servant who had fled to an Indian village. The Indians put up a strong resistance, and the Spaniard failed to get the woman back.

A more intense conflict occurred when the party returned to Puaray. Most residents of the village had fled when the Spaniards arrived, though some remained on the rooftops and mocked them. Espejo withdrew his forces, leaving men at a corner of the pueblo where they could not be seen. They were thus able to capture sixteen people when they ventured out. Espejo then initiated brutal reprisals against the pueblo captives to instill fear and dread among the surviving Indians: "We put them in an *estufa* [large room]. And as the pueblo was large and the majority had hidden themselves there, we set fire to the big pueblo of Puala, where we thought some were burned to death because of the cries they uttered. We at once took out the prisoners, two at a time, and lined them up against some cottonwoods close to the pueblo of Puala, where they were garroted and shot many times until they were dead. Sixteen were executed, not counting those who burned to death."[22] The slaughter succeeded. Word of it spread, and the natives from surrounding pueblos brought the Spaniards turkeys and other gifts and bowed to them in subservience.

From Puaray, Espejo swung eastward, hoping to find mines that would give him an exciting discovery to report. Mostly, however, he found more pueblos and large herds of buffalo. The group also met a band of Indians—apparently a Plains tribe—who brought them fish, prickly pears, and buffalo hides. Near the site of present Fort Davis, Texas, the party turned west to the Pecos River and followed it back to Mexico, arriving home on September 20, 1583.

Espejo issued a widely read report that described good pueblos, a healthy Indian populace with attractive women, wooded mountains, good pasturelands, and—most important—rich mining prospects.[23] Espejo's report reached the archbishop in Mexico City. The bishop was so impressed that he sent a copy of the report to the Spanish Council of the Indies, which governed New Spain, and another to King Philip II.

As a result, the Crown issued a *cedula* (decree) instructing the viceroy "to make a contract with some suitable person for the conquest of the new lands in accordance with the laws and regulations for colonization."[24] The much-sought-after award would ultimately be given to Don Juan de Oñate. But before that happened, other ambitious Spaniards in New Spain would undertake more illegal excursions to Tierra Nueva.

NOTES

1. "Fathers López and Rodríguez Remain at Puaray," in Hammond, *Rediscovery of New Mexico*, 125 (emphasis added).

2. Day, "Gómara on the Coronado Expedition," 348; "Testimony of Gallegos," in Hammond, *Rediscovery of New Mexico,* 77n3.

3. Weber, *Spanish Frontier*, 78–79.

4. Expedition member Hernán Gallegos testified that his expedition was guided by information in Cabeza de Vaca's book *Relación*, which was first printed

at Zamora, Spain, in 1542 and reprinted at Valladolid in 1555. "Testimony of Gallegos," in Hammond, *Rediscovery of New Mexico*, 134.

5. "Testimony of Gallegos," in Hammond, *Rediscovery of New Mexico*, 69.

6. "Introduction," in Hammond, *Rediscovery of New Mexico*, 14.

7. "Testimony of Gallegos," in Hammond, *Rediscovery of New Mexico*, 91.

8. "Departure of Fray Juan de Santa María," in Hammond, *Rediscovery of New Mexico,* 121.

9. Ibid.

10. Ibid., 95–96.

11. "Fathers López and Rodríguez Remain at Puaray," in Hammond, *Rediscovery of New Mexico*, 125.

12. "Introduction," in Hammond, *Rediscovery of New Mexico*, 14.

13. "Testimony of Gallegos," in Hammond, *Rediscovery of New Mexico*, 137–138.

14. "Discovery of New Mexico by Nine Men," in Hammond, *Rediscovery of New Mexico*, 142–143.

15. "Introduction," in Hammond, *Rediscovery of New Mexico*, 15–28.

16. "Testimony of Gallegos," in Hammond, *Rediscovery of New Mexico*, 139–140.

17. "Introduction," in Hammond, *Rediscovery of New Mexico*, 20.

18. Ibid., 22.

19. "Report of Antonio de Espejo," in Hammond, *Rediscovery of New Mexico*, 225. It appears that the three Indians remembered the Turk's exaggerations about golden treasures at Quivira but not the details of Coronado's expedition.

20. "Introduction," in Hammond, *Rediscovery of New Mexico*, 25.

21. Ibid. Though Espejo does not say so directly, this event reveals that the expectation of discovering a treasure trove had been a strong incentive for members of the expedition.

22. "Luxán's Account of the Espejo Expedition," in Hammond, *Rediscovery of New Mexico*, 204.

23. "Report of Antonio de Espejo," in Hammond, *Rediscovery of New Mexico*, 230–231.

24. "Introduction," in Hammond, *Rediscovery of New Mexico*, 28, citing AGI, *Audiencía de México*, legajo 1064.

12

Renegade Conquistadors

So great was the hardship endured before we reached water that only those of our people who witnessed the ordeal will believe how much we suffered.

Captain Castaño de Sosa [1]

Even as Antonio de Espejo was exploring in present New Mexico, King Philip II had issued his decree authorizing the viceroy in Mexico to search for the proper person to lead a colonization effort into Tierra Nueva. It was mandatory that the person have his own wealth to finance the venture. The Spanish Crown was far from having any interest in backing such excursions, as historian Stafford Poole states: "Royal finances in Spain throughout the sixteenth century were precarious at best, but during the forty-two year reign of Philip II the crown lurched from one fiscal crisis to another."[2]

In November 1584, Espejo made a substantial offer to lead another expedition to settle New Mexico, to include 24 Franciscan friars; 400 men, 100 with their wives and children; 4 army captains and 100 soldiers; 1,000 mares and "the necessary number of stallions"; 4,000 cows and bulls; 800 horses; 50 pack animals laden with provisions; 1,000 sheep, male and female; 50 boxes of iron objects; dried beef from 500 cows; a supply of iron bars; and bellows and pipes for metal work and tools.[3]

The selection of members for an official expedition came slowly. Espejo's offer was still pending in 1586 when he died in Havana on his way to Spain. Death thus likely denied him the honor of becoming the conqueror of New Mexico, and the opportunity was left open to other men of ambition.[4]

Even as the viceroy was considering possible candidates for an approved colonization effort, other, illegal intrusions into the north were being conducted. The call of New Spain's northern frontier was simply too strong for some Spanish men to resist. One such person was Gaspar Castaño de Sosa, lieutenant governor of Nuevo León province on the northeastern frontier. An aggressive, tough-minded man, he had been involved in founding several cities in the province, as well as in developing silver mining. But things had not gone well. The mines were not producing enough, settlement was stagnant, and the governor of the province, Luis de Carbajal, had been arrested on charges of heresy—that is, his refusal to obey the viceroy's order to abandon the lucrative enterprise of Indian slave trading.

Carbajal and others had found that the scattered tribes to the north offered an abundant supply of slave labor for Mexico's *rancherías* and mines. Raiding parties ventured beyond the Rio Grande, often capturing 800 to 1,000 hapless victims—both male and female—to sell in Mexico. Though Indian slavery had been expressly forbidden by the Spanish Colonization Law in 1573, northern Mexico was frontier country where legalities were often ignored and infractions seldom punished. But Carbajal's violations had been too severe to ignore, and he was arrested and jailed. Even from prison, he appointed Castaño de Sosa as his lieutenant to carry on the nefarious trade.[5]

With the province's economy suffering badly, the tales of great potential wealth to the north told by the Chamuscado and Espejo parties were heard loud and clear by the ambitious and energetic Castaño. He began recruiting a colony to lead to the new country. Word of his plan reached the viceroy in Mexico City, and Captain Juan Morlete was dispatched to visit Castaño and order him not to leave for Tierra Nueva without official authorization. Further, he was to abstain from his Indian slave activities.

Castaño considered going to Mexico City himself to plead his case, but in the end he sent four men led by army captains Francisco Salgado and Manuel de Mederos to Mexico City to make his plea. Then, ignoring the orders Morlete had delivered, he plunged full speed ahead with his plans.[6]

On July 27, 1590, Castaño set out from the village of Almadén (Monclova today) at the lead of his colony of soldiers, settlers with their families, and oxen-drawn carts—perhaps the first wheeled conveyances to enter the present United States.[7] He moved slowly in expectation of the return of Salgado, Mederos, and the others. A member of the expedition (likely secretary Andrés Perez Verlanga) was assigned the task of recording the march. He produced a report entitled "Castaño de Sosa's *Memoria*" that was later published.[8]

The *Memoria* tells us that while the colony was in camp for several days at the Rio de los Nadadores, Indians raided its horse herd. Castaño pursued them with twelve soldiers, recovering the animals and catching three of the thieves at the foot of a mountain. As a dire warning to other Indians in the region, he ordered two of the culprits hanged. The third, who was very young, was spared and given to a soldier as a servant.[9]

The emissaries to Mexico City had still not returned when the group reached the Rio Grande at the site of present Ciudad Acuña opposite Del Rio, Texas, on September 9.[10] Castaño went into camp for nearly a month and waited for word from the viceroy, keeping his men occupied searching for mines and making raids to capture slaves. Finally, on October 1, Castaño resumed his march, crossing the Rio Grande and pushing northwestward into Texas.

The wandering march across the extremely rugged, rock-studded Texas Big Bend country was far from easy. Not only was the expedition beset by a severe water shortage and riverbanks often so precipitous the caravan could not descend them, but the food supply was dwindling as a result of the longer-than-anticipated journey. Castaño, who had grown weak from ill health, ordered that only a small ration of wheat or corn be issued to each of the 170 people per week. Finally, a member donated one of his oxen to the cause. It was quickly slaughtered, providing a distribution of a pound and half of meat per person. But as the scorching-hot days passed, the complaints against Castaño grew louder.[11]

A scouting party sent out by Castaño to capture Indian guides was waylaid at an Indian pueblo, suffering some men wounded and the loss of guns and equipment. Castaño responded with a larger force, attacking the village and killing several Indians. He also captured two tribesmen to be used as guides. Meanwhile, the troubles and hardships of the march continued, as the expedition's diarist noted:

> Twenty-five dozen horseshoes were worn out on the mountains here, since there was no way to travel save on horseback. Many horses wore out their shoes in two or three days, incredible as it may seem, and a large number of the animals became lame. So great was the hardship endured before we reached water that only those of our people who witnessed the ordeal will believe how much we suffered. If the discovery of this route were to be paid for in money, it would take an enormous sum.[12]

The strain on expedition members continued to increase. Juan Pérez de los Rios, who had donated the oxen, became disheartened and pleaded tearfully with Castaño to turn back for the sake of his wife and children. He accused Castaño of leading him astray.[13] Many other members issued heartfelt complaints as well. Pedro Flores suffered an attack of melancholia, becoming physically exhausted and incoherent. Eventually, he simply disappeared—horse, saddle, harquebus, armor, and all.[14]

The expedition continued northward up the Pecos into present New Mexico, passing the sites of Fort Sumner and Santa Rosa. Somewhere in the vicinity of the latter, a party sent to capture Indian guides was attacked by the inhabitants of a pueblo they were visiting. The Spaniards escaped with the loss of five harquebuses, eleven swords, nine sets of horse armor, plus clothing and bedding.[15]

The militant pueblo proved to be Pecos, the Cicuye of Coronado's day where a half century earlier Bigotes and Cacique had resided. According to Spanish accounts, Castaño made every effort to deal peacefully with the Indians, but their hostility eventually forced him to attack. Several Indians were killed before the Spaniards won victory, and they found that the goods the Indians had captured were almost totally smashed or otherwise ruined. Eventually, peace was made, though during the night the entire village fled from their homes—despite high winds, driving snow, and such bitter cold that the rivers had frozen over.[16]

At Pecos as well as a number of other pueblos, Castaño performed the Spanish ritual of conquest, erecting a large cross accompanied by the sounding of trumpets and firing of harquebuses. Thereafter, he explained the ritual's purpose to the mystified and frightened natives, demanding their pledge of allegiance to the king of a far-off place called Spain. He then appointed a governor, *alcalde*, and *alguacil* for the pueblo.[17]

Leaving the large portion of his expedition in camp at a place called Uraca, Castaño led a detachment of soldiers westward beyond the Sangre de Cristo Mountains to the Rio Grande valley. There he again conducted his ritual of conquest at various pueblo towns. He also took time to scout out potential mining sites, usually from places where the Indians already gathered ores. In one village he found an abundance of turquoise, including an armband made of rich stones that one man was wearing. The man suspiciously refused to allow Castaño to inspect the armlet too closely. On another occasion, the Spaniards encountered an Indian captain who carried a silver chalice bowl.[18]

It is believed that Castaño's detachment went as far north as Taos. It and the other villages proved to be friendly, with the residents compliantly giving the men some of their corn, beans, and other foodstuffs. Taking these supplies, Castaño and his men returned to the colony camp, which was in a state of near starvation. After resting briefly, he again set the entire expedition in motion in early March 1591, leading it on to the pueblo of Santo Domingo north of present Albuquerque.

It was here that Castaño learned of a plot by some soldiers to assassinate him. One man in particular was considered the ringleader. Castaño ordered that he be garroted, but pleas from the entire expedition persuaded him to pardon the man. Suspecting that the natives were becoming restless, Castaño led a small group of mounted soldiers on a visit to several of the pueblos between present Albuquerque and Santa Fe, making a show of kindness and friendship. While traveling between the pueblos, he was met by three of his men from the main camp. They reported that Captain Morlete and fifty men had arrived from Mexico City to see him.[19]

These were not the emissaries he had expected. The news was foreboding, and Castaño galloped ahead to meet Morlete. The two men embraced, whereupon Morlete pulled forth a document, a royal decree signed by the new viceroy of Mexico, Don Luis de Velasco. It called for the arrest of Castaño and his men and an end to his expedition.[20] Though Castaño submitted meekly, he may have often regretted doing so.

Perhaps the new viceroy was seeking to establish his authority, or perhaps Morlete had a vindictive nature. Whatever the reason, leg irons with heavy chains were placed on Castaño, and he bore them throughout the long, slow ride to Mexico City. There he was placed on trial and found guilty of illegally raising troops, invading lands held by peaceful Indians, and leading an expedition to New Mexico without authorization. He was sentenced to six years of exile in the Philippine Islands. While there, he was killed aboard ship during a revolt by Chinese galley slaves. Following his death, the Council of the Indies in Spain heard his case on appeal and revoked his sentence.[21]

Yet another illegal incursion, the farthest-reaching and also the most mysterious, occurred prior to the great colonizing effort of Juan de Oñate. This expedition was led by Captains Francisco Leyva de Bonilla and Antonio Gutiérrez de Humaña in 1593.[22] These officers, it seems, had learned nothing from Castaño's experience. Or perhaps they simply became so fascinated by the lure of golden treasurers that they were willing to risk arrest and imprisonment.

The expedition developed from an effort by the governor of Nueva Vizcaya province to curtail the raiding of cattle ranches by Indian renegades on Mexico's northern frontier. Captain Leyva was assigned the task with a command of soldiers. Though little is known about the specific orders or the size of their force, Leyva and Humaña apparently had heard tales from the Coronado era regarding the supposed gold in Quivira and were set upon searching for it. The two officers began making plans for a discovery expedition into Tierra Nueva.

When it was learned that the officers were recruiting members for an expedition, the governor dispatched Captain Pedro de Cazorla to order them to desist. If they did not, Cazorla warned, they would be declared traitors to the king and be severely punished. Leyva and Humaña ignored the order and continued with their plans. Some of their men refused to join the expedition but they recruited others, including some Indian slaves. Soon they had marched northward, and for the next five years no one in New Spain would know what had become of them.

Many Spaniards wondered what had happened to the Leyva-Humaña excursion. Had the two illegal conquistadors found the vaunted treasures of the north that so many sought? Could they still be living in the place called Quivira in golden luxury? Or had they and their party been destroyed by Indians?

It would take the expedition of Juan de Oñate and a lowly Indian slave to provide at least some of the answers.

NOTES

1. "Castaño de Sosa's *Memoria*," in Hammond, *Rediscovery of New Mexico*, 255.

2. Poole, *Juan de Ovando*, 162.

3. "Espejo's Offer," in Hammond, *Rediscovery of New Mexico,* 238–239.

4. Ibid., 238n1.

5. "Viceroy Villamanrique to His Successor," in Hammond, *Rediscovery of New Mexico*, 296–297.

6. "Introduction," in Hammond, *Rediscovery of New Mexico*, 30.

7. Weber, *Spanish Frontier*, 80.

8. "Castaño de Sosa's *Memoria*," in Hammond, *Rediscovery of New Mexico*, 245n2.

9. Ibid., 246.

10. Ibid., 249.

11. Ibid., 252–253.

12. Ibid., 255.

13. Ibid., 252–253.

14. Ibid., 269.

15. Ibid., 266–267.

16. Ibid., 269–279.

17. Ibid., 281.

18. Ibid., 285, 294.

19. Ibid., 294.

20. "Instructions to Captain Juan Morlete," in Hammond, *Rediscovery of New Mexico*, 298–301.

21. "Introduction," in Hammond, *Rediscovery of New Mexico*, 48.

22. Ibid., 48–50.

Part 3

The Oñate Expedition

In 1605, one of the last of the Spanish conquistadors, Don Juan de Oñate, left posterity a personal note inscribed around an Indian petroglyph on the great cliff rock known today as El Morro in western New Mexico. In Spanish it reads: "Paso por aqui el adelantado don juan de onate del descubrimiento de la mar del sur a 16 de April de 1605." As translated into English: "There passed this way the Adelantado Don Juan de Oñate from the discovery of the South Sea, on the 16th of April, 1605."[1]

No photographs record the presence of Spanish conquistadors actually in the American Southwest. But we do have the phantasmal image of mounted Spaniards, their long lances aslant skyward, riding in line across a remote cliff in Cañon del Muerto (Canyon of Death) in Arizona (figure 13.1).[2]

The image was likely placed there centuries ago by an Indian who actually witnessed such a procession. It could well be that this tapestry

FIGURE 13.1. *Pictograph of conquistadors on march in Cañon del Muerto, Arizona (Arizona State Museum, University of Arizona, Helga Teiwes, photographer)*

of the past portrays Oñate and his men riding by on their way to find the "South Sea." Thus we today are provided with a glimpse of history through the eyes of a witness of the past, almost as though the native artist had turned from his work and said to us, "See, people of tomorrow, who once came here."

NOTES

1. Weber, *Spanish Frontier*, 82–83; courtesy, the Vargas Project, University of New Mexico. The inscription can be seen at the El Morro National Monument in New Mexico.

2. The pictograph from the Arizona State Museum, photographed by Helga Teiwes, is in ibid., 27.

13

Contract with Destiny

The governor took the royal cedula in his hands, kissed it, placed it on his head, and rendered obedience with the respect due to an order from his king and natural lord.

Antonio Negrette[1]

In 1595, Don Juan de Oñate y Salazar had everything he had ever wanted in life—almost. He was very wealthy; he had a palatial home near Zacatecas, a solid military reputation as an Indian fighter, a proud Basque heritage, and a sound social and political position in Mexico stemming from the families of both his father and his mother as well as that of his wife. Also, it was very important to him that he had a young son who would carry the Oñate name into the future.

What he did not yet have was the very special, exalted stature that came with being a renowned Spanish conquistador.

With his fiftieth birthday approaching, Don Juan knew his days of Indian fighting were behind him. With each passing year he would become less and less saddle-hardened, and soon time would have passed him by. When his wife, the beautiful Doña Isabel de Tolosa, died, his life had become empty. His Basque blood and heritage called upon him even more than before to make a truly grand achievement in life. He had long been aware of the *cedula* King Philip II had issued in 1583 calling for the conquest of New Mexico, and he also knew about the failures to do so that had taken place since then. It would be a crowning achievement to succeed where others—Coronado, Francisco Sánchez Chamuscado, Agustín Rodríguez, Hernán Gallegos, Antonio de Espejo—had not. Now, with his wife gone, it had become possible for him to accept a challenge that would take him far from hearth and home for months, perhaps years.

It has been suggested that Don Juan may have first become interested in leading an expedition to New Mexico as early as 1592.[2] The date of Doña Isabel's death and the circumstances thereof are not known. We know only that in 1595, Viceroy Luis de Velasco wrote to his successor, the Count of Monterrey, explaining why he had chosen Oñate to lead an expedition to New Mexico: "Since Don Juan de Oñate had become a widower and was free to negotiate in regard to this project, I chose him."[3]

Thus, when the opportunity to lead a new colonizing *entrada* into Nueva Mexico arose and with it the potential reward of becoming the *adelantado* of a new Spanish province, Don Juan leaped at the opportunity. Added to this was the prospect of making a grand discovery equal to that of Cortés.

The Spanish spirit in the sixteenth century boasted a tradition and a penchant for soldiering and adventure. Spaniards commonly sought their fortunes from the back of a horse. As soldier-explorers, they plunged brashly into the distant and perilous corners of the New World to extend Spain's empire. Historian David J. Weber has explained that even wealthy Spaniards in the sixteenth century were strangely willing to forgo the comforts and security of home and family and ride off to conquer distant lands: "These military chieftains [the conquistadors] risked their own capital, knowing that success would bring titles of nobility, land, broad governmental powers over the conquered domain, and the right to part of the spoils of war. Under this arrangement, the rewards for the adelantado could be considerable."[4]

Don Juan de Oñate was born in the central Mexico mining town of Zacatecas, northwest of Mexico City, around 1552. He was the second- or third-oldest son of Cristóbal de Oñate and his wife, the former Catalina de Salazar. It appears that he may have been one of twin sons among five boys and two girls. His twin was Don Alonso, who eventually became procurator general of the mines of New Spain. The other siblings were Fernando, the eldest son; Luis, the youngest; and the girls, Ana and María, in between.[5]

Both his father, Cristóbal, and his uncle, Juan de Oñate, had served with Nuño de Guzmán in the bloody conquest of Nueva Galicia. Juan later fled to Peru to escape arrest for atrocities committed against native Indians. Cristóbal had discovered the famous silver mines of Zacatecas, amassed a considerable family fortune, and served as lieutenant governor of Nueva Galicia and as governor during Coronado's two years in Tierra Nueva.

Don Juan's life as a youth shifted between Zacatecas and Mexico City, permitting him to experience both the rough milieu of the frontier silver-mining camp and the urbaneness of the Mexican capital. Born to wealth as he was, he was probably tutored as a boy in his family home at Pánuco, near Zacatecas, and in the town's parochial church.[6] His letters as an adult indicate that he was well versed in the arts and the sciences of the period.

It is equally clear that Don Juan was fully steeped in the Basque heritage his father had brought with him from Spain and nurtured in the colonial hierarchy of early Mexico. Independent, self-reliant, strong-willed, adventurous, and passionate about family, the Basques were an aristocratic people who saw themselves as apart from and well above "normal" society. Their strong feelings of superiority aroused the resentment of other Spaniards and in their New World conquest prompted a callous contempt for native populations.

> With or without the *reconquista* [Spain's moral crusade to spread Spanish culture and Catholicism to pagans in all parts of the Americas], Spaniards of the early sixteenth century [much the same as the English and Americans who followed] would have believed that Providence sided with them. They knew that persons radically unlike themselves, who neither held Christian beliefs nor lived like Christians, were inferior human beings, perhaps even bestial, deserving of slavery or whatever other ills might befall them.[7]

Don Juan was initiated into military activity at an early age. His father, who had helped crush the Indian rebellion during the bloody Mixon War, often led expeditions against the fearsome Chichimeca Indians, who regularly ambushed caravans carrying ores and supplies between Mexico City and Zacatecas. Don Juan is said to have participated in these sorties even before he reached puberty.[8] In a 1623 statement regarding his services to the Crown, Oñate said that from the time he was old enough to bear arms, he fought against the Chichimeca and Guachile Indians of Mexico.[9]

Like his father, he was late to take a wife. The exact date of his marriage to heiress Doña Isabel de Tolosa Cortés Montezuma is unknown. She was the great-granddaughter of Moctezuma and the granddaughter of Hernando Cortés and Isabel Montezuma. Gaspár de Villagrá described her as "a lady of most surpassing beauty."[10]

Undoubtedly, the wedding was a huge social event. It is reckoned to have taken place during the late 1580s, when Oñate would have been well into his thirties. His first child, a son whose long formal name is simplified as Cristóbal de Oñate, is thought to have been born in 1590[11] (see appendix B).

Following his marriage, Oñate worked and exploited the silver mines of Sombrerette, San Martin, and Aviño, all of which had been discovered by Doña Isabel's father. He claimed, too, that he helped discover the mines at San Luis, Chicu, and Charcas and "conquered them, entirely at his own cost."[12] Through his silver operations, he won government favor because of his sizable contribution of revenues to the Royal Treasury.

Despite all of the failed entries into Tierra Nueva, both the legends of treasures there and the Spanish Crown's determination to colonize the vast lands and Christianize the people remained alive. These objectives simmered in the minds of state and church officials as well as those of individual Spaniards. Encouraged by the reports from Chamuscado and Espejo, in 1583 King Philip II issued a *cedula* giving the viceroy of New Spain, Don Luis de Velasco, authorization to find a suitable person to pacify (conquer) and colonize the lands that had become known as Tierra Nueva. But it was required that this be done according to Spain's 1573 "Comprehensive Orders for New Discoveries."[13]

Velasco first considered two other very wealthy men from New Spain, Don Juan Bautista de Lomas y Colmenares and Don Francisco de Urdiñola. But these candidates became so engrossed in charging one another with crimes and making outlandish demands in their efforts to head the New Mexico colonization that their chances were negated. During 1594 Velasco turned to Oñate. Three years earlier the viceroy had chosen Oñate to organize a government and civic community for the new mining center of San Luís Potosí. The viceroy had been very pleased with Oñate's performance there and was well aware that he met the first and most important requirement for the New Mexico venture—he could finance much of it himself.[14]

But that was not Oñate's only advantage. His soldiering and mining experience was also important, as was his Indian-fighting background. There would be Indians to conquer and, it was hoped, silver and gold mines to find and operate for the colony's financial success.

As mentioned, Oñate leaped at Velasco's invitation to apply, and on September 21, 1595, in Mexico City, he signed a formal contract with the viceroy. By it, Oñate was obligated to organize a large group of soldiers and colonists and lead them to Tierra Nueva, provide for their subsistence largely at his own expense, pacify the native inhabitants, and establish a settlement for the Crown. In doing so, he would be rewarded with the title of captain general of his expedition as well as *adelantado* of the new lands.[15]

In typical Basque form, Oñate looked to his extended family for logistic and military leadership. His brothers, particularly Don Alonzo, would remain in Mexico to provide legal help, raise funds, and procure supplies. Distant cousins Cristóbal, Juan, and Vicente de Zaldívar—sons of the elder Vicente de Zaldívar whose brother, Juan de Zaldívar, had served with Coronado—would likewise play major roles.

Cristóbal remained behind in Mexico in a support capacity, while Juan was assigned the role of *maestre de campo* of the expedition and Vicente assumed the duties of *sargento mayor* and recruiting officer. Both were determined hidalgos (noblemen) who would play critical roles in Oñate's expedition in the days ahead.[16] A muster roll for the expedition in January 1598 provides a brief description: "*Maese de Campo* Juan de Zaldívar, son of Vicente de Zaldívar, a native of the city of Zacatecas, well built, chestnut-colored beard, 28 years of age . . . and Sargento Mayor Vicente de Zaldívar, son of Vicente de Zaldívar, native of Zacatecas, medium sized, chestnut-colored beard, 25 years of age."[17]

Fate would soon deal a tragic blow to elder brother Juan, but Vicente would prove to be a determined and zealous soldier for Oñate. Hearings conducted relative to Vicente's many services justly present a heroic picture of him and his actions in Oñate's behalf. Eventually, however, he would be found guilty of offenses that included murdering a fellow officer, excessively punishing natives who had surrendered in battle, bringing captives to New Spain and selling them as slaves, having his soldiers flayed, conducting scandalous associations with army women, and ordering the execution of a colony deserter and a fellow captain who sought to return to New Spain against Oñate's wishes.[18]

Oñate began recruiting soldiers and colonists in the plazas of Mexico City, Zacatecas, and other Mexican towns where jobless men were plentiful. Recruiters would arrive at a town plaza, attracting crowds with their drums and fifes and colorful silk standard, virtually like a town fair. Eloquent orations were delivered, issuing grand promises of the rewards and adventure awaiting the impoverished villagers in the new land.[19] Soon, Oñate had the beginnings of an army and a colony.

But disasters and troubles large and small hindered his grand quest. The records are not clear, but sometime prior to January 27, 1598, Doña Isabel died,[20] leaving Don Juan with a young son and a female child who, it appears, was only recently born. Then, before Oñate could get fully organized and ready to march, Velasco was replaced by a new viceroy, Don Gaspar de Zúñiga y Acevedo, known otherwise as the Count of Monterrey.

Though suspicions of Don Juan were raised by the rejected candidates and others, Monterrey permitted the contract made under Velasco to stand. The new viceroy did, however, modify the pact because of accusations that Oñate had shown he was not an effective leader by squandering his family's wealth and falling deeply into debt.

Oñate would no longer have permission beyond the outset to recruit soldiers and colonists. He would not be permitted to appoint officials in New Mexico or set their salaries. He was not permitted to evade the authority of New Spain, reporting instead directly to the Spanish Council of the Indies. He was denied the authority to determine the amount of tributes Indians would pay. His ability to grant *encomiendas* was subject to an accounting and regulation; it was required that his colonists must serve five years to become hidalgos; and his request to have his New Mexico colony supplied by ships twice annually was denied—which, as had been proven during Coronado's expedition, was virtually impossible anyway.[21]

But this was only the beginning of Oñate's troubles. After receiving his contract, he and his men had worked arduously to recruit more colonists and soldiers for his expedition and to purchase the stock and equipment his contract required him to furnish. By the summer of 1596, even as final approval from King Philip was still anxiously awaited, the expedition had come together enough that it began to move slowly out of Zacatecas northward to the mines of Casco.

Then, orders arrived from the king sternly commanding that the expedition's contract be placed on hold. Under threat of death if he disobeyed, Oñate was not to proceed farther. Also, an inspection of the expedition to see if Oñate was living up to his contract would be conducted by the man who was to deliver the king's *cedula*, Don Lope de Ulloa y Lemos. It would later be learned that enemies of Oñate were working against him in Spain and that an appealing new candidate had emerged. This new competitor was Don Pedro Ponce de León, who had a solid reputation and many friends in Spanish political circles.

Eventually, Ponce de León's competition failed because of his bad health and financial troubles. During April 1597 the king reinstated Oñate's original contract.[22]

The king's *cedula* was dated May 8, 1596, and the Count of Monterrey issued confirmation at Mexico City on August 12. Ulloa announced the news to Oñate in his tent on the Nazas River near Santa Bárbara on September 9. The order was a devastating blow to Oñate, but he had no choice but to obey: "The governor took the royal cedula in his hands, kissed it, placed it on his head, and rendered obedience with the respect due to an order from his king and natural lord."[23]

But Oñate faced a difficult situation. Delays to his expedition meant depletion of provisions, loss of stock, desertion of soldiers and colonists, and potential failure of the entire enterprise. Villagrá, who served under Oñate and penned a poetic history of this first effort to colonize New Mexico, described the ruinous effects of these delays: "Don Juan sadly saw all his plans shattered, his army dwindling away, his priests ready to leave, his soldiers impatient at the many promises made, then only to be broken. The children of the colonists wandered about the camp like loose cattle ... Matters reached such a stage that there was not a single soldier who did not do as he pleased, taking what he chose of the stores, and leaving, saying, 'This is mine.' The camp was on the very verge of destruction."[24]

According to Villagrá, the avalanche of disintegration was halted in part by Doña Eufemia, wife of Oñate's lieutenant governor Francisco de Sosa Peñalosa, who issued a defiant challenge to the nearly deserted camp: "Tell me, O, noble soldiers, where is that courage which you so professed when you enlisted in this noble cause?"[25]

But there was far more to it than that. Well hidden behind Villagrá's picture of triumphant virtue, another image—an opposite one—emerges from the musty records in Mexican archives. Oñate did not give up politely or nobly. Despite the king's stern and threatening command not to proceed farther and even with his vow to accept the command, he was determined not to sit idly by and let his hopes and ambitions disintegrate.

Historian George P. Hammond's discovery of documents in the archives at Guadalajara, Mexico, brought to light an entirely new view of Oñate's actions during his period of restraint at the Casco mines. These documents bear evidence of atrocities committed on Oñate's orders in the cause of perpetuating the expedition. "In particular," Hammond wrote, "Oñate was charged with sending his soldiers and captains to round up and seize whatever oxen, horses, equipment, or Indians they could find."[26]

The charges issued against Oñate stemmed from a raid on the estate of Don Juan Bautista de Lomas conducted soon after Ulloa arrived in Oñate's camp with the king's ultimatum. Lomas, wealthy owner of the mines of Nuestra Señora de las Nieves near Zacatecas, had been a principal competitor of Oñate's to conduct the *entrada* into New Mexico. Early on the morning of October 14, 1596, a captain and six soldiers from Oñate's expedition invaded the estate's fields, where Indian servants were burning wood to produce the charcoal used in extracting silver from mined ore. The invaders wore coats of mail and were armed with harquebuses and hooked knives.[27]

Several Indian workers testified similarly to Lomas's complaint: that Oñate's men rounded up and took whatever oxen, horses, clothing, and equipment they could find. The soldiers threatened to kill Lomas's workers when they attempted to interfere. Worse still, Oñate's men abducted the wives and children of Indians on the estate, threw them on horses, and carried them off.

Lomas had forewarned Juan de Artiaga, foreman of the charcoal fields, that Oñate might be sending soldiers to take by force the material and people he needed to fill his quota for the expedition. He advised Artiaga to place extra guards over the oxen and cattle. Bad blood existed between the two very wealthy, influential mine operators. Even before Oñate had secured the contract for colonizing New Mexico, Lomas had sought an injunction against Oñate for any injury the latter might cause him. The injunction had been issued in March, ordering Oñate to keep his men away from Lomas's property.[28]

But this injunction failed to deter the expedition leader. Artiaga told that Oñate's soldiers had arrived at the ranch and asked for something to eat. He provided them with food, after which one of the soldiers took him aside and said that Oñate had declared that he could have any single Indian women he could capture:

> He [Artiaga] replied that he did not have any on that rancho, that all were married. But in answer to this he was told, "Although they may be married, I must have them." While things were in this pass, two others of the soldiers went to the house of Gabriel, the carpenter, the one on horse and the other on foot. He who went on foot seized a boy, son of Gabriel, named Melchor, and put him on the [back of the horse] which the other soldier was riding. The boy began to shout, calling his father and mother. In response to this, his father came, seized him by the arm and pulled him to the ground. The soldier who was on foot went to Gabriel, the Indian, threw him to the ground and struck him in the face with his fist, from which he got a nosebleed. The boy took to flight, two soldiers going after him, one with a hooked knife, the other pointing a gun. The one with the knife struck him with it, struggled with him on the ground, seized and bound him and placed him on the back of a horse belonging to the soldier with the gun. They then seized an Indian woman named Clara, married to an Indian named Juan Martin, and a soldier who was on foot put her on the back of Hinojos' horse, at his order. Before they had her mount, Clara came to this witness, wishing to be helped by him. But the soldier who was on foot took hold of the woman and both together fell to the ground. Then, as the soldier got up, he struck the woman a violent blow and asked her where she had her clothing . . . Afterward, they went to the house of Bonifacio, an Indian married to Maria, and took her by force, striking him in the face; the said Indian woman, crying out, called to this witness to protect and defend her. But, in spite of the resistance put up by the Indian woman, they mounted her on the back of the horse on which the chief [of the soldiers] was riding.[29]

Though Lomas pressed his claims in court and before the Audiencia of Nueva Galicia province, no action was taken against Oñate. "Since two powerful influences were at work in this case," a Mexican historian concluded, "the one [Oñate] more than the other, the Guadalajara tribunal washed its hands of the affair."[30]

ABBREVIATION KEY

H/R-*DJO* = Hammond and Rey, eds., *Don Juan de Oñate*

NOTES

1. "The Ulloa Inspection," H/R-*DJO* 1: 115.

2. "Introduction," H/R-*DJO* 1: 5.

3. "Velasco to His Successor," H/R-*DJO* 1: 76. The report is undated, but we can assume it was in late 1595 because we know the Count of Monterrey arrived in Mexico in September 1595; "Introduction," H/R-*DJO* 1: 9. When examined closely, Velasco's statement seems to imply that the death of Oñate's wife had occurred recently.

4. Weber, *Spanish Frontier*, 23.

5. Simmons, *Last Conquistador*, 34–35.

6. Ibid., 32–35.

7. Weber, *Spanish Frontier*, 21.

8. Simmons, *Last Conquistador*, 36–37.

9. "Services of Don Juan de Oñate," H/R-*DJO* 2: 1146.

10. Villagrá, *History of New Mexico*, 58. See also 60n12.

11. Simmons, *Last Conquistador*, 45.

12. "Services of Don Juan de Oñate," H/R-*DJO* 2: 1146.

13. Weber, *Spanish Frontier*, 78–79.

14. Simmons, *Last Conquistador*, 42–47.

15. Ibid., 3, 58.

16. Ibid., 58.

17. "The Salazar Inspection," H/R-*DJO* 1: 289.

18. "Oñate's Conviction," H/R-*DJO* 2: 1114–1115.

19. Simmons, *Last Conquistador*, 59.

20. "Juan Guerra de Resa's Bond," H/R-*DJO* 1: 378–379.

21. Ibid., 1: 10.

22. Ibid., 1: 11–12.

23. "The Ulloa Inspection," H/R-*DJO* 1: 115.

24. Villagrá, *History of New Mexico*, 90.

25. Ibid., 91.

26. Hammond, "Oñate a Marauder?" 252. Lawyers know that virtually nothing is deniable, but the testimony recounted in Hammond's article would be persuasive to most juries. The question mark in Hammond's title is polite but questionable. Though too often ignored, the implications of Hammond's find hold significant relevance as to Oñate's guilt relating to charges issued against him in future actions.

27. Ibid., 253.

28. Ibid., 269.

29. Ibid., 260–261.

30. Ibid., 269.

14
Cavalcade of Conquest

*The entire army was drawn up in formation, and in the presence
of the multitude the governor solemnly took possession of the
newly discovered land.*

Villagrá[1]

Lope de Ulloa y Lemos and his staff arrived at the mines at Casco and
began their inspection and inventory of the expedition on December 9,
1596. Don Juan de Oñate opened the event by presenting a large amount
of steel and iron rods and plate, which he promised to make into goods.
He followed with an assortment of plowshares, hoes, axes, saws, augers,
chisels, adzes, blacksmith's tools, and numerous small items such as pulleys, hocking blades, knives, padlocks, hammers, scissors, needles, mirrors,
and trade items that included glass beads, bells, tin images, fans, necklaces,
whistles, thimbles, and rings.[2]

Even more reflective of Oñate's personal wealth were the fifty-three
well-broken horses, all carrying his brand, and the twelve saddles—one
embroidered with blue velvet trappings, another decked with a caparison
cloak of crimson and gold straps, and others of green velvet, black trimmed
in gold, or brown cordovan. Added to these items were cavalry shields,

leather jackets, swords, daggers, harquebuses, lances, horse armor made of buckskin hide, barrels of gunpowder, a bronze *culvern* (fieldpiece), and Oñate's twenty-four carts with iron-rimmed wheels plus nineteen others belonging to his captains and soldiers and six more furnished by the Franciscan friars. Two days later the governor presented the group with nearly 200 head of oxen to pull the carts, 6 animals per cart. Oñate had been advised that where he was going, oxen would serve better than mules.[3]

At the end of January, Don Juan announced that he had no more to offer at the mines but said he could contribute further at Santa Bárbara, twenty-eight leagues to the south. Leaving the expedition at Casco, the governor escorted the inspection commissary to Santa Bárbara, where he presented them with 4,632 horseshoes and 137,338 extra horseshoe nails, Michoacán frieze, sackcloth, flour, beans, wheat, corn, lead for ammunition, 1,012 goats, 4,439 sheep and rams, nearly 1,900 head of cattle, 2 state carriages with 4 mules each, plus 9 more carts, 20 barrels of mercury, 154 colts, and 30 mules and jackasses.[4]

Returning to Casco, Oñate made preparations to parade his officers, soldiers, and the entire expedition in review. The grand event took place on February 17, 1597, with Oñate proudly leading the procession. Don Juan wore a coat of mail and a helmet with a beaver armor over his throat and lower face. Cuisses of mail covered his thighs, and he carried both a sword and a harquebus. His prancing steed wore a blanket of buckskin and bull-hide armor. In the mounted cortege that followed were Oñate's two secretaries, a chamberlain (household attendant), a chief waiter, two lords of the bed chamber, four pages, and a servant—all but the latter in full armor and all well armed.[5]

Behind this group were Juan de Zaldívar and his three pages, Vicente de Zaldívar and his page, and twelve army captains or substitutes therefor. Each was mounted, armed, and armored. Behind these men came a long line of other officers and soldiers, all likewise in armor and carrying their weapons, their horses draped with bull-hide protection. Some were accompanied by their servants. At the rear of this group (or so he was listed) was Oñate's boyish son, Don Cristóbal, also decked out with armor for both himself and his horse. The commissary had wanted to place him beside his father, but Oñate had insisted that the boy be included among the soldiers.[6]

During the year the expedition was stalled at the Casco mines, Oñate learned that a "quarrelsome and turbulent" person named Andrés Martín

Palomo was gathering people in the San Bartolomé valley for an unauthorized *entrada* into New Mexico. This was in direct competition with, and a threat to, Oñate's plans. Vicente was dispatched, undoubtedly with some soldiers, to "arrest and punish" Martín. The *sargento mayor* complied, making a painful ride across uninhabited land during freezing weather. He arrested Martín and duly enacted the punishment—which was death, most likely by decapitation.[7]

An itinerary recording the march states that when the expedition finally departed from Casco for Santa Bárbara on August 1, 1596, it included eighty-three carts and wagons. The record also tells that at a stop along the trail the oxen were unyoked "and more than five thousand head of livestock of all kinds drank, and later two thousand more head of cattle and mares that were following behind."[8]

The inspection and review were not the final acts before full approval. During this time a number of the officers and colonists still disposing of their estates had been absent. New members were recruited, but the long wait had driven morale very low and men were deserting. No one could tell how many members there were.

Matters improved somewhat when five Franciscan priests and a lay brother under Father Rodrigo Durán joined the expedition, with Ulloa's permission, as it moved slowly northward to Santa Bárbara and beyond.[9] Another member of Oñate's group was an Indian woman Gaspar Castaño de Sosa had brought back from San Cristóbal pueblo in 1590. Unfortunately, she had forgotten her native tongue.[10]

Despite the presence of the priests, conditions and morale continued to deteriorate. In defiance of the expedition's military regimen, a group of soldiers conspired to desert and strike out on their own to New Mexico. Learning of the plot, Oñate sent Vicente de Zaldívar to arrest the men. This was done, then, in the Draconian mien so common to the conquistadors, Oñate had the leader of the group beheaded.

It may have been this incident that caused Father Durán to withdraw from the expedition with all the priests except Oñate's cousin, Fray Cristóbal de Salazar, and Fray Alonso Márquez.[11] The departing friars were replaced on March 3 at the San Pedro River by a new group of ten priests and lay brothers headed by Fray Alonso Martínez.[12]

Ulloa continued with the expedition, with plans to conduct another inspection down the line. But as he was preparing to do so, he received orders appointing him commander of a Spanish fleet headed for the

Philippine Islands. A replacement inspector, Juan de Frías Salazar, arrived with his staff. Salazar, a retired army officer, proved much more difficult to deal with than Ulloa, demanding that Oñate adequately fulfill his contract in terms of goods supplied and the number of soldiers.[13]

Suspecting that if the inspection were held in Santa Bárbara Oñate might try to slip non-members into the count, Salazar insisted that the expedition continue on to the San Gerónimo River. There, Salazar conducted a second inspection for over a month, through January 26, 1598.[14] The expedition's wheeled conveyances presented an interesting advance from Coronado's time. The conveyances included a large number of mule- or ox-drawn carts, many with iron-rimmed wheels. Most of them belonged to Oñate, his *maestre de campo*, captains, and soldiers. The Franciscan friars had six carts that had been furnished by the king, each with six mules.

In the valley of San Bartolomé near Santa Bárbara, Oñate also purchased two large, well-equipped carriages pulled by four mules. These were likely for the women and children accompanying their husbands and fathers on the long journey. By the time the expedition camped on the San Gerónimo River, one of the coaches had broken down and was being repaired.[15]

In addition to itemizing Oñate's contribution, Salazar interviewed ninety-two members of the expedition, recording their names, number of family members, servants, and the livestock, arms, and equipment they brought with them. These colonists of varying economic levels had brought everything they had—coats of mail, helmets, beavers, mailed gloves, shields, horses, horse armor, saddles, bridles, harnesses, milk cows, oxen, mules, donkeys, goats, carts, harquebuses, handguns, lances, halberds, swords, daggers, hooked blades, clothes, spurs, spare horseshoes, kettles, pans, ladles, picks, hammers, saws, adzes, horse-shoeing tools, tongs, hoes, branding irons, needles, and other items deemed necessary for the march, potential battles, or creating a colony in the new land.[16]

Only thirteen members said they had tents, though others may have had them depending upon each man's interpretation of the order to list "arms and equipment," which some took to mean only "military equipment." Some listings were more detailed. The long list of items taken by Captain Alonso de Quesada included a bed, two blankets, a bedspread, a hundred cakes of soap, numerous personal items including "three pairs of garters," and "seven books, religious and non-religious."[17] Captain Juan

Gutiérrez Bocanegra, pre-assigned as commander of a fortress to be built in New Mexico, listed among his belongings "one chain with [iron] collars."[18] This item would be put to much use among the New Mexico pueblos.

While Coronado's expedition had traced the Pacific coastline west of the Sierra Madre chain into present Arizona, Oñate's march, which started in Santa Bárbara, followed a route east of the mountains paralleling the routes taken by the Rodríguez-Chamucado and Espejo expeditions into New Mexico. From the San Gerónimo, Oñate moved north to the Conchos River. There, with all of the army and colony assembled for mass on the banks of the river on February 7, 1598, the much disliked Salazar curtly issued his permission for the expedition to proceed. He then mounted his horse and led his staff to the south.[19]

Greatly relieved that Salazar was finally gone, Oñate and his people could at long last move on to Tierra Nueva at their own speed. Leaving the Conchos at Santa Bárbara, Oñate struck due north across the Chihuahuan Desert to the Rio del Norte (Rio Grande). There, on April 20, 1598, near present El Paso, the group crossed into what is now the United States. Ten days up the Rio Grande the expedition halted again, this time to conduct a special ceremony of conquest.

From Villagrá's account, it is clear that Oñate saw the event as having enormous historical significance. He ordered all officials, captains, soldiers, and others of the expedition to wear their finest clothes to honor and celebrate the act of laying claim to the land. Not doing so would mean forfeiting the grants and favors bestowed by the king.[20] With the entire army drawn up in formation along with all the colony members and friars, Oñate pontificated at great length, declaring that he had come to "demand and take possession of my kingdoms" in the name of the Holy Trinity and our "most Christian king, Don Philip."[21]

Thereafter, Oñate fixed the Spanish royal standard and King Philip's coat of arms in place at the site. These items were blessed, trumpets were sounded, harquebuses were fired in salute, and an official "act of possession" was signed by witnesses and authenticated with the high seal of office. All present then conducted a great celebration, and that afternoon a farce written by Captain Marcos Farfán de los Godos was presented, depicting the Catholic priests arriving in New Mexico and being reverently received by the natives, who begged on bended knee to be baptized. Though Villagrá does not say as much, a keg of wine was likely opened for everyone as the army celebrated "with great joy and mirth."[22]

As the expedition moved up the Rio Grande, it began to encounter lingering evidence of previous *entradas*. On May 4 it "passed the ruts made by the ten carts that [Gaspar] Castaño [de Sosa] and [Juan] Morlete took out from New Mexico," verified by Captain Juan de Vitoria who had been with the party in 1591. On May 11 the group camped at the place where Morlete had hanged the Indian horse thieves.[23] By now the expedition was suffering greatly for lack of water, and its supply of food and other provisions had become so exhausted that it was creating great distress. A child died and was buried on May 17, and four days later sixty-year-old Pedro Robledo also died.[24] "We were in such extreme need that the governor found it necessary to send men ahead to the first pueblos with eighty pack animals to bring maize for our relief. They brought back the animals, all loaded, although it was against the wishes of the natives and to their grief."[25]

Leaving the struggling wagon train behind, Oñate pushed ahead with an advance party of horsemen, arriving at the pueblo of Puaray on June 27. It was here that in 1582 Frays Agustín Rodríguez and Francisco López of the Chamuscado party had been murdered and thereby martyred. Ultimately, Oñate's initial march would take him to the pueblos above present Albuquerque, where the injured Coronado had spent the winter of 1541–1542 in great misery. Today, the route Oñate followed through Mexico is known as the Camino Real.

To secure maize and other food for his hungry expedition, Oñate sent men to other pueblos—settlements that had been well known to Coronado: San Ildefonso, Jémez, Zia, Taos, Pecos, and others where in a previous generation bearded strangers wearing metal had arrived on horseback wielding deadly weapons and demanding the natives' goods.

During mid-June Oñate, the Zaldívars, and Father Salazar set out with a small force for Santo Domingo to search for two men named Tomás and Cristóbal, who had been mentioned to them by a native. It turned out that the pair had been Christian Indians who had come to Santo Domingo with Castaño de Sosa in 1590 and remained to take up wives and a life among the Pueblo Indians. Because both men spoke both Spanish and the dialect of the pueblos, when found they were seized and taken back to be used as interpreters.[26]

One of the most striking connections to past *entradas* was the medal spotted dangling about the neck of a minor chieftain at the pueblo of Jémez. On close examination it was found to have once belonged to either the murdered Fray Rodríguez or Fray López. The chieftain gave it up in trade for a hawk's bell, saving the Spaniards from having to take it by force.[27]

It was not until August 19 that the expedition's carts and live-stock arrived at the pueblo of San Juan (also known as San Juan de los Caballeros) in the Tiguex village complex on the Rio Grande north of present Santa Fe. There, on the same river where Coronado had once win-tered, Oñate established his headquarters.

In taking over the pueblos, the Spaniards cut doors and windows in the structures as they saw fit. Soon, the soldiers began digging an irriga-tion ditch; and on September 23, after the expedition was consolidated at San Juan, erection of the Church of Saint John the Baptist began. Its construction took only two weeks. A great celebration was held to dedi-cate the structure on September 8. Following a sermon by Father Salazar, the entire camp joined in a sham battle representing attacking Moors, mounted and wielding shields and lances, as well as defending Christians on foot armed with harquebuses. Undoubtedly in repeat of Spanish his-tory, the Christians won.[28]

The fête's gala, boisterous atmosphere was followed by dark events in the days to come.

ABBREVIATION KEY

H/R-*DJO* = Hammond and Rey, eds., *Don Juan de Oñate*

NOTES

1. Villagrá, *History of New Mexico*, 130.
2. "The Ulloa Inspection," H/R-*DJO* 1: 130–136.
3. Ibid., 136–139.
4. Ibid., 140–147.
5. Ibid., 150.
6. Ibid., 150–160.
7. "Zaldívar Inquiry," H/R-*DJO* 2: 811–812, 818, 825, 831–832; "Memorial on the Discovery of New Mexico," H/R-*DJO* 2: 946; "Oñate's Conviction," H/R-*DJO* 2: 1110, 1114.
8. "Itinerary of the Expedition," H/R-*DJO* 1: 313.
9. Simmons, *Last Conquistador*, 71–72.
10. "Itinerary of the Expedition," H/R-*DJO* 1: 321.
11. Simmons, *Last Conquistador*, 84.

12. "Itinerary of the Expedition," H/R-*DJO* 1: 311; Simmons, *Last Conquistador*, 93.

13. Simmons, *Last Conquistador*, 87.

14. "Itinerary of the Expedition," H/R-*DJO* 1: 311.

15. "The Ulloa Inspection," H/R-*DJO* 1: 146, 226.

16. "The Salazar Inspection," H/R-*DJO* 1: 215–282.

17. Ibid., 252–253.

18. Ibid., 238–239.

19. Simmons, *Last Conquistador*, 90.

20. "Velasco to Viceroy, March 22, 1601," H/R-*DJO* 2: 611.

21. Villagrá, *History of New Mexico*, 131.

22. Ibid., 130.

23. "Itinerary of the Expedition," H/R-*DJO* 1: 315–316.

24. Ibid.

25. "Velasco to Viceroy, March 22, 1601," H/R-*DJO* 2: 609.

26. Simmons, *Last Conquistador*, 106–107.

27. "Itinerary of the Expedition," H/R-*DJO* 1: 322.

28. Ibid., 323.

15

The Devil's Doing

*Oñate sought the ancient land
From whence the Aztec came,
A new Mexico at hand
Wherein to win his fame.*

Villagrá[1]

As it had been for the Coronado Expedition, New Mexico quickly proved a harsh and difficult land for the Spaniards who came north with Oñate. Their provisions had been exhausted well before they reached the pueblo settlements in the fall of 1598. The expedition arrived not only destitute of food but poorly supplied with clothes and bedding to protect them through the extremely cold and snowy winter. The Spaniards spent long months shivering near whatever fires they could manage. They described it as "*ocho meses de invierno y quarto de inferno*" (eight months of winter and four in hell).[2] In a letter to the viceroy, Captain Don Luis de Velasco described the situation more fully:

> The cold is so intense that the rivers freeze over, and it snows most of the time during the winter, which lasts eight long months. After this there follows heat so oppressive that it rivals burning fire. It has driven us from our houses [the Indian pueblos they had taken over]

and forced us to sleep outdoors. The country breeds an infinite number of mice, bedbugs, and other vermin. We burn no lights at night [candles or oil lamps, presumably] for lack of means. To keep warm in the winter, we have to go four or five leagues [ten or more miles] for firewood, and none is to be obtained except from cottonwood trees along the river.[3]

The suffering Spaniards did not realize that they were caught in a unique worldwide phenomenon known today as the Little Ice Age. In Europe at this same time, the ice flows had advanced as far south as the Mediterranean, freezing animals and food supplies even into the summer months. No climate records exist for North America, but there can be little question that it was affected as well. Oñate's colony of Spaniards, coming from the warmer clime of central Mexico, were not provisioned or clothed for even a mild winter.

In Oñate's efforts to feed the colony of 500 settlers and soldiers and their families, it became a regular practice to send men—two or three at a time—out in all directions to wrest meager food supplies away from Indian families whose crops had been severely stunted by drought. The men returned with their pack animals and carts loaded with maize, beans, melons, and other items of subsistence taken forcibly from the pueblo natives, who were in dire need themselves.

The Spanish Crown had made it perfectly clear that Oñate's principal mandate in establishing a colony in New Mexico was to Christianize the Indian natives there. Further, the appointment the viceroy of New Spain had issued to Oñate carried specific instructions regarding his colonization efforts. Under all circumstances, the viceroy ordered, Oñate was to see that his soldiers and settlers treated the Indians well: "They must humor and regale them so that they come in peace and not in war. They must not harm or annoy them nor set them a bad example. This is very important for the success of such an important undertaking."[4] This wisdom was unlikely to be followed by the cold, hungry colonists.

One of Oñate's first acts when he arrived in New Mexico was to assign the Franciscan friars to various pueblos in the region: Fray Francisco de Zamora to Picuríes and Taos; Fray Francisco de San Miguel to Pecos; Fray Juan de Rozas to San Felipe, Santo Domingo, and other places; Fray Alonso de Lugo to Jémez; Fray Andrés Corchado to Acoma, Zuni, and the Hopi villages; and Frays Cristóbal de Salazar, Juan de San Buenaventura, Pedro de Vergara, and Alonso Martínez to San Juan.[5]

Yet either out of the desperation of his situation or because he simply did not connect purpose and deed, Oñate did nearly everything he could to alienate the native population that was normally agreeable and peaceful. He commandeered Indian homes for himself and his people, forcing the natives to find new shelters. He looted their vital food and clothing, leaving them to suffer the bitter cold of winter in dire hunger. His army's horses were allowed to invade Indian maize fields, devouring the food supply and stalks that were the natives' winter fuel. He permitted—or at the least bore responsibility for—abuse of Indian women by his soldiers, and at times he acted with brutal force against Indian offenders who reacted to the despotism exercised by him and his men.

Because of this, Oñate would endure an ongoing conflict with the native population that was closely reminiscent of Coronado's tenure in New Mexico. At the heart of the conflict was the Spanish system of demanding tributes from the natives with almost total disregard for the effects that system had on them. Velasco spoke about the matter in his letter to the viceroy:

> As we had run short of food so far back, when we reached the said pueblos, we had to support ourselves by taking as much as we could from each one. Because of this and other annoyances, the Indians fear us so much that, on seeing us approach from afar, they flee to the mountains with their women and children, abandoning their homes, and so we take whatever we wish from them . . . The feelings of the natives against supplying it cannot be exaggerated, for I give your lordship my word that they weep and cry out as if they and all their descendants were being killed.[6]

Fray Zamora gave additional testimony to the practice: "They [Oñate's men] took away from them [the natives of the land] by force all the food they had gathered for many years, without leaving them any for the support of themselves and their children, robbed them of the scanty clothing they had to protect themselves, their women and children, and took many other valuables from their homes, causing the natives much harm and wounding their feelings."[7] "The fact is," Fray Francisco de San Miguel swore under oath, "that in order to induce the Indians to furnish corn for food, it has been necessary to torture the chieftains, even to hanging and killing them."[8] Fray Lope Izquierdo cited an instance whereupon Captain Diego de Zubía, in an effort to get food from an Indian, tortured the man with such "exquisite pain" that he finally revealed where he had buried mud-sealed ollas with a small amount of maize.[9]

Moreover, a severe summer drought had caused the pueblos' corn crops to dry up and shrivel in the fields. The harvest had been so small, Velasco said, that when Oñate's men rode off with their carts of stolen corn, Indian women would follow for miles picking up the kernels that fell on the ground.[10]

One woman who was weak from starvation, Fray Izquierdo testified, entered a colonist's home with her young son and pleaded for food. In exchange, she offered to accept baptism for herself and her eight-year-old son. She was fed and given medicine, but as she and her child were being baptized by the priest, they both died.[11] Izquierdo continued: "This matter has come to such a point that it is well known to the friars and settlers, and especially to this witness, that many natives have starved and are starving to death, since there was absolutely no food in some pueblos. The country's only products are some fruits and roots, with which the people occasionally alleviate their hunger, and ground charcoal and ground cornstalks, which the people eat without even waiting for the ears to develop."[12]

Yet another issue that deepened the natives' distrust and hatred of the Spaniards was the treatment of Indian women. Fray Zamora declared, "I know for certain that the soldiers have violated them often along the roads."[13] When he instructed the Indians to become Christians, they asked why they should become Christians when it was Christians who caused them so much harm.[14]

Oñate had other troubles to deal with as well. The long, trying march from Mexico had been difficult, spawning the seeds of rebellion among certain members of the expedition. The severe, uncompromising discipline Oñate exercised had further inflamed the discontent. Velasco spoke about the matter in a letter to the viceroy: "Although he began to use his authority and power then [upon taking possession of New Mexico], and though some did not like it, no one dared say a word, for he was not on good relations with everyone. Up to this day, he has always treated us so badly and with such severity that there is no one who does not fear death at any moment."[15]

This last statement was no exaggeration. When Oñate discovered that an attempt to organize a desertion among the expedition was under way, he ordered the arrests of two captains and a soldier considered the ringleaders. Without the formality of a trial, he sentenced the trio to death by strangulation. Only after pleas had been made by the friars and army officers did Oñate relent and spare the men.[16] In his report to the viceroy on the matter, Oñate wrote:

> And the devil, who has always tried to prevent the great loss that he would suffer through our coming, resorted to one of his usual tricks with the mutiny of more than forty-five soldiers and officers, who in anger at not finding bars of silver on the ground right away and resentful *because I did not allow them to abuse the natives either in their persons or property*, became dissatisfied with the land, or rather with me. They tried to band together and escape to New Spain, or so they said, but their intention, as became clear later, was rather to take slaves and clothing, and to commit other outrages. I seized two captains and a soldier, who were said to be responsible, and was ready to garrote them, but, having ascertained that their offense was not so great, and considering my situation and the insistent requests of the friars and of the entire army, I gave up the idea of punishing them and closed the matter with the punishment already inflicted.[17]

The expedition's journal reveals little of the affair, noting obliquely only that "on the 20th [of August 1598] the worthlessness of some soldiers who organized a conspiracy was evident. The 21st was the day of merciful punishment. It was the occasion of the famous sermon of tears, and of universal peace."[18]

As mentioned, when the friars and many in the army pleaded that he show the three men mercy, Oñate relented. He needed three fighting men much more than he needed more disaffection among his colonists.[19]

Two days later, construction of the Church of San Juan Bautista began at San Juan. But the insurrection was far from dead. On September 12, only four days after the church was dedicated, four soldiers from the expedition deserted, stealing some horses and making a dash to escape back to Mexico. The miscreants were the brothers Juan and Marias Rodríguez and two natives of Portugal, Manuel Portugués and Juan González. When informed of their flight, Oñate dispatched Captain Gaspar de Villagrá (figure 15.1), Captain Gerónimo Márquez, and three soldiers to overtake the four.[20] He ordered that, once they had been arrested, the deserters were to be executed on the spot.

It was a long, fourteen-day chase, but Villagrá and his party eventually caught up with the four men on the San Pedro River in Mexico. Lured by Villagrá's promise that they would not be executed, the deserters surrendered; but once they had done so, Villagrá reneged on his promise.

FIGURE 15.1. *Gaspar de Villagrá, Oñate captain*

The Rodríguez brothers were allowed to escape, Villagrá letting them go, it was said, "for special reasons."[21] But the Portuguese were immediately condemned to death.

Though they begged to be taken to a priest for confession, Villagrá refused. The unfortunate men were beheaded, probably under Villagrá's sword. Each man's right hand was cut off and packed in salt to take back for Oñate to display before others who might be tempted to desert the colony.[22] Villagrá's story does not end there; he would encounter his own deadly peril as he made his way back to New Mexico.

Meanwhile, as he was awaiting Villagrá's return during September 1598, Oñate dispatched Sargento Mayor Vicente de Zaldívar to visit the eastern prairie to find buffalo.[23] Not only was meat badly needed for his struggling New Mexico colony, but Oñate also viewed the massive herds of "cattle" (buffalo) on the prairies east of the New Mexico pueblos as a "discovery" he could announce.

The conquistador buffalo-hunting sojourn to the Texas Panhandle was reminiscent of similar ventures by Alvarado sixty years earlier and later by Chamuscado. Fortunately, an excellent account of Vicente's effort was made and testified to by participants.[24]

Vicente led the expedition of sixty officers and men to find the buffalo. Also accompanying the expedition were Fray San Miguel; lay brother Juan de Dios, who could interpret the language of the Pecos Indians; and Jusepe Gutiérrez, an Indian native of Culhuacán, Mexico. Setting out from San Juan on September 20, 1598, Vicente's party marched eastward to the Gallinas River near present Las Vegas, New Mexico.

The water was low in the river, and "by the aid of a single hook"[25] the men caught 500 fish—mainly catfish (*bagres*)—that night and many more the next day. They also met four Vaquero Apache Indians. Vicente presented them with food and small gifts. After this, many other Indians came forward from their hiding places in friendship, responding to the Spaniards with gifts of *pinole* (ground roasted corn). As the hunting party moved eastward, it encountered still more Apaches.

The Spaniards were intrigued by the Apaches' use of large droves of shaggy dogs for conveyance, since the Indians had no horses at the time. Holding the dogs' heads between their legs, the Indian women harnessed them on both sides with tent poles that dragged behind, travois-like, carrying the tents and loads of foodstuffs that weighed up to 100 pounds. The dog trailed obediently along with the tribespeople as they moved from site to site.

Below present Tucumcari, the party encountered its first buffalo, one old stray animal. Soon after, 300 more were seen watering at a small lake, and then seven leagues farther on they spotted a herd estimated at 4,000. Soon there were more. Vicente and his officers put their men to work building a corral of cottonwood logs with long wings into which the buffalo could be driven. Three days were spent constructing the enclosure that would hold, it was hoped, 10,000 buffalo.[26]

Once the corral was completed, a hunting expedition set out to the prairie, where a herd of 100,000 buffalo had been seen, with the intention of driving them into the pen. But buffalo, they found, were far different than domesticated cattle. Though the men were able to start them in the direction of the corral, the buffalo soon stampeded in such great fury that the Spaniards were totally incapable of stopping them. During their three-day effort, the Spaniards had three horses killed and many others gashed by the short, sharp horns of the buffalo.

Finally realizing that the grown buffalo could not be captured, Zaldívar and his men decided to go after the calves. The Spaniards tried dragging some of the calves by the tail and pulling others up onto their horses. Within an hour, all the calves died; not one reached camp alive. In the face of these defeats, the hunters settled for simply killing many of the animals, whose fat was found to be superior to lard and the meat better-tasting than that of cows.

"One could kill as many animals as he might wish to bring to the settlements," Vicente concluded in his report, "which must be some thirty or forty leagues distant. It will be difficult to bring them alive, unless through time and gradual crossing with our cattle we should be able to tame them."[27]

Even more significant than the buffalo, however, the expedition brought back an intriguing story the Indian guide Jusepe had told during the trip—history repeating itself, in this case regarding the 1540 experience of Alvarado and the Turk. Jusepe reported that he had traveled to the buffalo country five years earlier with the *entrada* of Antonio Gutiérrez de Humaña. He recounted that in 1592 he had been recruited by Humaña from his home village in Mexico to serve with an *entrada* to the north. Jusepe had gone with Humaña to the valley of Santa Bárbara in the state of Chihuahua, staying for a time at the pueblo of San Ildefonso. From there, Humaña's party of thirty men had marched through the country of the Pecos and Vaquero Indians, traveling slowly and reaching the buffalo country in a month.[28]

There was more to Jusepe's story, and when the occasion was right, Oñate wanted very much to hear it. But for now he had other important matters to address.

ABBREVIATION KEY

H/R-*DJO* = Hammond and Rey, eds., *Don Juan de Oñate*

NOTES

1. Villagrá, *History of New Mexico*, 38.
2. "Valverde Investigation," H/R-*DJO* 2: 656n14.
3. "Velasco to Viceroy," H/R-*DJO* 2: 610.

4. "Introduction," H/R-*DJO* 1: 66.

5. Ibid., 17–18.

6. "Velasco to Viceroy," H/R-*DJO* 2: 609–610.

7. "Desertion of the Colony," H/R-*DJO* 2: 675.

8. Ibid., 674.

9. Ibid., 680. Fray Damián Escudero had Izquierdo's testimony read to him and under oath verified that all of it was true. H/R-*DJO* 2: 682–683.

10. "Velasco to Viceroy," H/R-*DJO* 1: 610.

11. "Desertion of the Colony," H/R-*DJO* 1: 680.

12. Ibid., 679.

13. Ibid., 676.

14. Far away and centuries later, Cherokee chief Corn Tassel spoke with essentially the same Indian wisdom to treaty commissioners at Long Island, Tennessee, in 1877. "We should be better pleased," he told the white treaty makers, "with beholding the good effect of these doctrines in your own people than with hearing you talk about them"; Williams, "Tatham's Characters," 177–178.

15. "Velasco to Viceroy," H/R-*DJO* 2: 611–612.

16. Simmons, *Last Conquistador*, 116.

17. "Oñate to Viceroy," H/R-*DJO* 1: 481 (emphasis added).

18. "Itinerary of the Expedition," H/R-*DJO* 1: 323.

19. Simmons, *Last Conquistador*, 116.

20. In a letter to the viceroy, Oñate noted that he had been notified of the escape of the two brothers and suggested that they may have been punished in New Spain for their mutiny. "Oñate to Viceroy," H/R-*DJO* 1: 482.

21. Villagrá says little about the sordid affair, merely noting that "like Torquatus, who ordered that his beloved son be beheaded for disobedience of orders, we had two of them executed"; *History of New* Mexico, 150. Then, after complaining of his own misfortunes that followed and observing that "miserable is he who must bear his trials alone," Villagrá tells of "having left these unfortunate men dying upon the plains, their throats cut wide open"; ibid., 172.

22. Simmons, *Last Conquistador*, 120–121; "Itinerary of the Expedition," H/R-*DJO* 1: 324; "Oñate to Viceroy," H/R-*DJO* 1: 482.

23. "Oñate to Viceroy," H/R-*DJO* 1: 482.

24. "Discovery of the Buffalo," H/R-*DJO* 1: 398–405.

25. Ibid., 398.

26. Ibid., 401–402.

27. Ibid., 403.

28. Captain Juan de Ortega testified that the Indians were so fearful of Oñate's soldiers because when Humaña and Francisco Leyva de Bonilla had been in the area, they had taken some Indian women. "Valverde Investigation," H/R-*DJO* 2: 659.

16

Death on a High Plateau

*The Indians . . . threw so many stones, and shot so many arrows
that they forced the Spaniards to a high cliff where they killed the
maestre de campo.*

Captain Gaspar López Tabora[1]

With Villagrá chasing down the deserters and Vicente de Zaldívar away
on his buffalo hunt, Oñate became anxious to explore the land and discover its still mysterious potential. Leaving his *maestre de campo* Juan
de Zaldívar in charge at San Juan, he led a detachment of thirty-four
mounted soldiers and Fray Alonso Martínez on a swing southward along
the eastern side of the Sandia-Manzano Mountain ranges.[2] He examined
the salines that spotted the region and won the obedience of the various
pueblo towns located there.[3]

Evidently on a sudden but optimistic whim, on October 23, 1598, at
the pueblo of Puaray, he turned due west across the Rio Grande to search
for the vaunted "South Sea," which he thought was nearby—"whose trade
with Peru, New Spain, and China," he wrote, "should not be underesti-
mated . . . What I consider important in this respect is the trade in pearls,
the report of which is so reliable, as I have stated, and we have seen their

shells here with our own eyes."[4] After making this decision, Oñate sent a message back to Juan de Zaldívar at San Juan, issuing instructions for him to come forth with thirty men, pick up his trail, and join him as soon as the party returned from the buffalo country.[5]

Oñate's line of march now ran due west to Acoma, the pueblo city atop the giant rock butte where Coronado's men had been so favorably received nearly six decades earlier. Oñate was accorded the warm hospitality of the Acoma inhabitants, who provided him and his men with food and water. On October 27 the governor, accompanied by Fray Alonso Martínez and others, met at the base of the huge rock with a group of Acoma Indians led by three of their chiefs. There, through Indian interpreter Don Tomás, Oñate addressed the Indians to conduct the "Act of Obedience and Vassalage" common to Spanish conquest. He told the pueblo natives that "he had come to their country to bring them to the knowledge of God and the king our Lord, on which depended the salvation of their souls and their living securely and undisturbed in their nations, maintained in justice and order, safe in their homes, protected from their enemies, and free from all harm."[6]

To receive these rewards, it was required that they render obedience to God and the king. Oñate told the Indians further that King Philip III (Philip II had died on September 13, 1598) would look after them and defend them in peace and with justice against their enemies. The Spaniards, of course, had no capacity to do that. This absurd promise— similar to those made later by the English and Americans in dealing with Indian tribes of North America—was listened to by the chiefs who, according to Oñate, understood and discussed among themselves what he had said. Supposedly, they "replied with spontaneous signs of pleasure," indicating that they wished to become vassals of the Spanish king. As directed, the three chiefs then rose, embraced Oñate and the father commissary, and kissed their hands.[7]

How much of the ceremony the Indians actually understood and just how agreeable they really were is questionable. But they did allow Oñate to climb up the boulder-strewn passage to the top of the butte where he could observe both the pueblo atop and the tiny figures of horses and men below. Later, the Spaniards suspected that the Acomans had tried to entrap the captain general by attempting to lure him into an *estufa* (large room) and killing him. That may well have been the case.[8]

From Acoma, Oñate continued west, passing by the great towering rock known as El Morro and from there on to Zuni and Hawikuh, where Espejo was a visitor in 1583. Oñate discovered crosses Coronado had erected sixty years earlier still standing. He later wrote: "The Indians show great devotion for them and often offer them what they offer their idols, such as flour, sticks painted in various colors, and feathers of native fowls." Two Christian Indians left behind by Coronado were now dead. But their two sons, one named Gaspar and the other Alonso, remained. While the two men could speak a few words in Spanish, they understood virtually nothing in that language.[9]

Having been welcomed hospitably by the natives, Oñate remained at Hawikuh during the week preceding November 8. While there, he sent a detachment under Captain Marcos Farfán de los Godos across the present Arizona border to inspect a saline of which he had been told. Farfán was impressed with the salt works.

Meanwhile, a snowstorm struck the area, causing some of the Spaniards' horses to stray. Three soldiers were sent out to find them. By coincidence, at the great rock of El Morro they happened onto Captain Villagrá, on his way back from pursuing the four deserters. He was staggering along afoot, frozen, and near death. The officer had an unhappy tale to tell.

Eager to report to Oñate and perhaps to present him with the salted hands of the two men he had executed, Villagrá had hurried ahead of his companions. At Puaray he was told that the governor had passed through there recently and turned west to search for the South Sea. Villagrá promptly set out in pursuit at a gallop. But as he approached Acoma, he encountered an Indian ambush set up along the trail. He made it past the ambush, only to run squarely into a well-laid Indian snare—a deep hole, well covered with brush and, atop that, the fresh snow from the storm. Villagrá's horse plunged headlong into the hole and was killed, likely by sharpened stakes planted in the floor of the pit. The Spaniard survived the fall, but he was forced to leave his coat of mail, helmet, shield, harquebus, and everything else except his sword and dagger and continue on by foot.[10]

Villagrá claimed that to confuse the Indians, whom he feared would torture him if they caught him, he put his shoes on backward—a seemingly improbable accomplishment—so his footprints in the snow would look as though he were going the opposite direction. He also told a pathetic story of becoming so hungry after several days that he killed his faithful dog, which licked his hand as he did do. But with no way to make a fire and struck with shame and remorse, he could not feast on the dog.[11] The captain wandered westward through the snow for four days before, by enormous luck, he encountered the soldiers who were searching for the lost horses.[12]

Oñate, who still did not know that another tragedy—a major one— had taken place behind him at Acoma, went ahead with his explorations. While waiting at Hawikuh for his *maestre de campo* to arrive, he visited the Hopi pueblos of present Arizona and searched for the mineral deposits Espejo had seen during his visit there.

Also, Oñate sent Farfán on another mission, this time to seek a band of Indians known as the Cruzados, of whom he had been told. Farfán found them in central Arizona, and they willingly led him to their silver mines along the Verde River. The samples of ores Farfán brought back, as well as erroneous reports that the coast of the South Sea was only thirty days distant from the mines, excited the hope of important new discoveries.[13]

The fact that Juan de Zaldívar had not arrived had become an increasing concern. This worry combined with the approaching Christmas holidays persuaded Oñate to give up his South Sea quest for the present and return to San Juan. On December 12 he led his men out of Zuni and back down the trail by which he had come. The next day at El Morro, he was met by Captain Alférez Bernabé de las Casas and soldiers from San Juan. They had horrific news to report. Juan de Zaldívar had become involved in a big fight with the Indians at Acoma, and he and ten of his men had been killed.

When his brother Vicente returned from his buffalo hunt on the Canadian River, Juan, as ordered, had mounted a troop of thirty-one soldiers. Leaving Vicente in charge at San Juan, he headed south to pick up Oñate's trail. The troop arrived at the base of the Acoma mesa around 4:00 p.m. on December 1, 1598. Because there was no wood or water near the mesa and the Indians, who appeared friendly otherwise, would supply them with only a small amount, Zaldívar went into camp at a stream two leagues away. He returned to the mesa three days later with eighteen men and, leaving four men to watch the horses, climbed to the pueblo settlement atop the mesa. Their purpose was to secure provisions for their journey in exchange, it was claimed, for hatchets.[14]

The Spaniards went about with sacks, gathering flour and maize, but the supply fell short of their needs. Zaldívar ordered Captain Diego Núñez with six men to gather more goods. After a time, when the men had not returned, Zaldívar sent a man to investigate. The messenger returned to report that the Indians were refusing to give up anything and that Núñez was asking for six additional men. Zaldívar sent the men forth, but he soon heard a commotion from their direction. With the Spaniards now divided, the Indians launched an attack on the soldiers with stones, arrows, and clubs. Captain Gaspar Tabora later testified:

> This witness saw Captain Diego Núñez and his soldiers fall back toward the maese [*sic*] de campo, who at that very moment received an arrow wound in the leg, and other soldiers were killed and wounded. The Indians were so numerous, threw so many stones, and shot so many arrows that they forced the Spaniards to a high cliff where they killed the maese [*sic*] de campo, Captains Felipe de Escalante and Diego Núñez, other soldiers and two Indian servants. This witness escaped down a cliff. The Indians hurled so many stones at him that he was stunned and forced to abandon his harquebus and sword.[15]

Alférez Bernabé, who was tending the horses, heard the firing of harquebuses from above and looked up to see two soldiers preparing to jump from some high rocks. He shouted at them not to jump and fired his harquebus in an attempt to drive the Indians back. But in the end, both men jumped. One was dashed to pieces on the rocks, but the other landed on the sandy slopes that had been blown adrift against the foot of the mesa. Though badly bruised, the man was able to get up and walk away.[16] Bernabé described the melee:

> Then this witness saw that the maese [*sic*] de campo, Captains Escalante and Diego Núñez, and other soldiers were defending themselves against large numbers of Indians at the edge of the rock. Soon afterwards this witness saw the Indians brandishing the swords they had taken from the Spaniards and heard them shouting, calling him [Bernabé] a bastard murderer, *aputo temiquiz* in the Mexican language. He picked up some of the wounded men who had jumped from the rock, put them on horses, and returned to camp with them and a few Christian Indians who had escaped.[17]

Sergeant Rodrigo Zapata described that he had seen a soldier killed at Zaldívar's side and many others wounded. The Indians atop the mesa, he said, attacked en masse, men and women alike, driving the Spaniards back against some rocks and onto the ground where they beat their heads with stones.[18]

While the Spanish officers were one in claiming that they tried to treat the Indians fairly and with kindness, as the Spanish government had decreed, the testimony of an eighteen-year-old soldier, Alonso González, indicates that at the start the Spaniards may have been far more demanding and abusive than they professed. When asked by Oñate to state under oath whether Juan de Zaldívar's party had caused any harm to the Indians, González replied that all he saw was a soldier holding a turkey in his hand and an Indian woman complaining about it.[19] Food supply was not a casual issue for the Indians of Acoma. An Acoma man said he had heard that the pueblo had gone to war because a soldier demanded a turkey from a woman. Another said the fight occurred because the Spaniards had either wounded or killed an Acoma Indian.[20] Oñate's chief auditor, Ginés de Herrera Horta (Orta), who took part in the Acoma battle, testified that the Indians "killed the maese [sic] de campo and the soldiers because of the abuse of an Indian woman by a soldier who took away her blanket or fowl."[21]

Villagrá is believable in describing Oñate's reaction when he learned about the Zaldívar tragedy on his way back to San Juan. On horseback when Bernabé met him with the news, the governor dismounted, went down on both knees, and issued a heartfelt prayer. He wept and prayed during the night, but by the following morning he had composed himself.

With swollen eyes and a choked voice, he called his troops together to urge them as "soldiers of Christ" to lay aside their grief and place their trust in God. Wearing full battle array and wary of Indian ambushes or attacks, Oñate bypassed Acoma during his return to San Juan. Reaching the post without further conflict, he assembled the people together at the church, where he embraced them in sorrowful silence as the priests chanted "Te Deum Laudamus" (We Praise Thee God).[22]

Juan de Zaldívar had not only been Oñate's *maestre de campo* but was also a valuable ally in controlling both the native Indians and the rebellious-minded officers and colonists. His loss was a severe blow to Oñate. Still, the Acoma disaster was even more disturbing for its potential implications. Who knew whether this had been the opening act of a major Indian uprising, such as the vicious Mixen War Mexico had experienced.

Everyone at San Juan realized that they were alone in a remote land "surrounded by innumerable savage foes, who, if they chose to rise, might easily destroy our small force."[23]

ABBREVIATION KEY

H/R-*DJO* = Hammond and Rey, eds., *Don Juan de Oñate*

NOTES

1. "Trial of the Indians of Acoma," H/R-*DJO* 1: 435.
2. Ibid., 428.
3. "Oñate's Visit to the Salines," H/R-*DJO* 1: 393–397.
4. "Oñate to Viceroy," H/R-*DJO* 1: 486.
5. "Introduction," H/R-*DJO* 1: 19.
6. "Act of Obedience," H/R-*DJO* 1: 354.
7. Ibid., 355–356
8. Simmons, *Last Conquistador*, 126–127.
9. "Oñate's Visit to the Salines," H/R-*DJO* 1: 395.
10. Villagrá, *History of New Mexico*, 174.
11. Ibid., 174–175. Perhaps Villagrá lashed his entire shoe beneath his foot so the heel was to the front, but this would seem not only awkward but very uncomfortable in the snow.
12. Simmons, *Last Conquistador*, 130–131.
13. Ibid., 131–132.
14. "Trial of the Indians of Acoma," H/R-*DJO* 1: 433–439.
15. Ibid., 435.
16. Ibid., 438.
17. Ibid.
18. Ibid., 440–441.
19. Ibid., 448–449.
20. Ibid., 467.
21. "Valverde Investigation," H/R-*DJO* 2: 665.
22. Villagrá, *History of New Mexico*, 206.
23. Ibid.

17
Pacification of Acoma

Such as this, I surmise
Was the picture Juan de Oñate made,
As noble as Mars, for battle arrayed
As wise as Jupiter, in peace . . .
Ravage and burn and cut and scar,
The marks he left will perish not.

Villagrá[1]

The defeat of the Spaniards at Acoma presented the ominous threat that the pueblo villages might unite in a general insurrection against their Spanish intruders. With the loss of so many men, Oñate's fighting strength was precariously low, at fewer than 120 men.[2] The sense of immediate danger increased when the compliant Indians of San Juan reported a rumor that Indians from other villages were preparing to attack. Oñate posted men to defend the entrances to San Juan's central plaza, while the wives of officers were sent to the pueblo rooftops as sentinels.

The best remedy against such an uprising, Oñate concluded, would be bloody vengeance for Juan de Zaldívar's defeat. His Basque pride and reputation as a conquistador—and perhaps the lives of every Spaniard in New Mexico as well, he felt—demanded it. Acoma, the unassailable "fortress in the sky," must somehow be conquered and the Indian rebels punished—severely.

To Oñate, there was no question that the Acoma defeat must be avenged and quickly. He concluded that he was on solid legal ground to exert the punishment. His decision to act was supported, to his thinking, by the rationale that because the Acomans had taken the vow of loyalty prior to their uprising, they were traitors to the Spanish Crown. Still, Oñate realized that revenge must be achieved under Spanish law and in accommodation with the church.

The friars were agreeable. When consulted, they found sufficient moral argument to support punitive action. A written statement signed by Fray Alonso Martínez concocted a convenient logic that argued "as the purpose of war is to establish peace, then it is even justifiable to exterminate and destroy those who stand in the way of that peace."[3] This was accompanied by his plea for the protection of the innocent souls who had done no wrong and the avoidance of bloodshed and death to the extent possible.[4]

But while the priests gave their support to the reprisal against the Acomans, they were hardly prepared for the ruthlessness of the battle to follow and the ensuing punishment of the Acomans. Oñate's first move was to initiate a military strike against the Acoma pueblo. He appointed Vicente de Zaldívar, now twenty-one years of age, lieutenant governor of New Mexico province and elevated him in rank to captain general. As such, he was honored with the task of leading seventy soldiers against the seemingly impregnable fortress to avenge his brother's death. Oñate's instructions to Vicente were:

> If the Indians are entrenched and should have assembled many people and you think there is danger of losing your army in trying to storm the pueblo, you will refrain from doing so, for there would be less harm in postponing the punishment for the time being than in risking the people with you and those left here for the protection of the church of God, its ministers, and me. In this matter you must exercise the utmost care and foresight.
>
> If the people should have deserted the pueblo, you will burn it to the ground and destroy it . . . If God should be so merciful as to grant us victory, you will arrest all of the people, young and old, without sparing anyone. Inasmuch as we have declared war on them without quarter, you will punish all those of fighting age as you deem best, as a warning to everyone in this kingdom. All of those you execute you will expose to public view at the places you think most suitable, as a salutary example.[5]

194

Special preparations were made. Equipment for the horses—bridles, reins, bits, stirrups, packsaddles, harnesses, buckles, and eyelets—was carefully tended; the heavy steel breastplates for the horses were burnished and shined. Harquebuses were oiled and their springs tried, gunpowder sifted and dried in the sun, and knapsacks filled with powder and ball. A detail of twelve men was sent to the Zia pueblo, northwest of San Juan, to gather provisions for two weeks and then join the army en route to Acoma.

Villagrá, who was present, provides a description of the Spanish force as it arrived at the foot of the great *peñol* (peak) during January 1599: "Every man was clad in shining mail of double strength and of the finest steel. From their powerful shoulders hung heavy shields. Some had lances fitted with double heads, others with heads in the form of a crescent. Every detail had been carefully attended to. Even the war-horses were gaily adorned."[6]

When they arrived at Acoma, the Spaniards found that in front of them rose challenging rock cliffs, rimmed at the top by hundreds of clamoring natives who shouted angry defiance of, and disdain for, Vicente's small force. At this place of battle, both sides knew the Spaniards' horses would no longer provide the great tactical advantage they offered in the open field. The challenge that lay before Vicente—scaling the vertical cliffs of the towering rock plateau and conquering the rebellious natives who resided atop it—appeared to be a virtually impossible assignment.

Surprisingly, Vicente would prove equal to the daunting task assigned to him. As the Spanish force rode closer to the base of the rock fortress, it was greeted from the heights by a shower of arrows and rocks, accompanied by derisive taunts from Acoma warriors who—wearing coats of mail and flaunting weapons taken in their recent attack—jeered them as "scoundrels and whoremongers."[7] Villagrá told of long-haired defenders who swarmed the precipices, some wearing colorful blankets, others dressed in skins and wearing masks. Many were naked, among them women warriors with their bodies painted with black, red, and white stripes.[8]

Vicente circled the rock plateau with his horsemen three times, formulating a plan of attack and looking for the most advantageous place to make an ascent. The Spaniards found that in fortifying their stronghold, the Acomans had dug numerous pit traps at the base of the mesa to entrap Spanish horses and their riders.[9] The pits were detected and avoided, however, because Vicente and his men had been forewarned by Villagrá's experience and perhaps because the sun had melted their cover.

The Acomans, confident of the impregnability of their position, scornfully rejected Vicente's perfunctory suggestion that they surrender peacefully. With the sun ready to disappear below the western horizon, Vicente withdrew a short distance and went into camp. That night he laid his plan of attack before his men.[10]

The giant 70-acre, 367-foot-high sandstone mesa was split almost at the center by a fissure that divided it into two parts, with the Acoma pueblo occupying its southwestern half. Realizing the futility of a frontal assault up the steep face of the mesa, Vicente devised a plan whereby his main force would feign an attack at the principal entrance to the village. As the Acoma defenders were drawn to that place, he and a small group of his men would scale the plateau at a secluded crevice on the opposite, northeastern side. Villagrá listed these men as Vicente, León de Isasti, Marcos Cortés, Lorenzo de Munuera, Antonio Hernández, Juan Velarde, Cristóbal Sánchez, Cristóbal López, Hernán Martín, Juan Cordero, Pablo de Aguilar, and himself.[11]

Before dawn, Vicente led the eleven chosen men to a hiding place at the back side of the mesa from which they could scale the rock walls. At the first light of day, the main army broke camp and made a trumpet-blaring approach to the main entrance. The ruse was successful, drawing the horde of Acoma warriors to the main entrance while Vicente's party worked their way unobserved to the top. They handed their weapons up to those above as they moved from one holding point to another.

The twelve men managed to reach the top of the mesa before they were discovered. The Acomans spied them then and rushed forward, shouting battle war cries. The Indians leaped the narrow-but-deep chasm that split the huge rock, and fierce hand-to-hand combat followed. The Indians held the advantage of numbers, but the Spanish swords, knives, harque-buses, and armor were too much to overcome. Vicente and his men were able to hold their position as more troops climbed up to join the fight.

A large timber was hauled up the cliff side and used by some of the Spaniards to cross the chasm. Thinking they would need it farther on, they took the timber up behind them. But they were soon attacked by a large number of warriors with spiked clubs. The seldom modest Villagrá later described how he rushed forward, leaped across the crevice, and replaced the timber, permitting the remaining Spaniards to join their comrades.[12]

Two cannons were hauled up the rock by rope. Once put into action, these weapons wreaked death upon the Acomans and, by the third day of fighting, so overwhelmed the Indians that the sword-wielding Spanish soldiers were able to slash and slaughter them unmercifully. Many of the natives fought to the death, but others yielded and came forward to make peace offerings of blankets and fowl to the Spaniards. Vicente rejected the overtures. He ordered that the Indians be arrested and imprisoned in rooms of the pueblo:[13]

> To do this he had them seized and placed in some *estufas* where these Indians fortified themselves in their prisons and broke away through many tunnels and mines concealed in the *estufas* and which opened out into adjoining houses. The Indians ran from house to house and killed each other without sparing their children, however small, or their wives. In view of this situation, the lieutenant governor [Vicente] ordered the battle to proceed without quarter, setting fire to all of the houses and even the provisions.[14]

Ginés de Herrera Horta testified:

> Then he [Vicente] ordered them [the Indians] taken out one by one, and an Indian he had along stabbed them to death and hurled them down the rock. When other Indian men and women, who had taken shelter in other *estufas*, saw what was going on, they fortified themselves and refused to come out. In view of this the *sargento mayor* ordered that wood be brought and fires started and from the smoke many Indian men, women, and children suffocated. This witness was told that some were even burned alive.[15]

As Oñate had instructed, the Spaniards ravaged the settlement, torching and destroying the shelters along with food supplies. More than 500 survivors were taken captive. While several soldiers were wounded, miraculously, only 1 was killed, and that was by "friendly" fire.[16] After their village had been torched, the Acoma captives were marched east to the Rio Grande and north up the river to the pueblo of Santo Domingo, where they were again imprisoned.

Oñate arrived there during early February 1599 to conduct a formal trial of the prisoners. He took testimony from officers and soldiers who had been involved in both clashes with the Acomans and from six Acomans themselves. Captain Alonso Gómez was appointed defense attorney for the Indians. He asked them through an interpreter if they had any pleas to offer or witnesses to bring forth in their behalf. They replied that they did not; their only defense, they said, was the fact that they were not guilty or not present when the Spaniards were killed. "For this reason and from what was learned in the testimony that your lordship took from some of the Indians," Gómez contended in a plea to Oñate, "you should acquit them, set them free, allow them to go wherever they wish, and order that they be compensated for the expenses resulting from their arrest."[17]

He knew, as did everyone else, that none of this would happen. On February 12 Oñate declared the trial closed and ordered that his sentence be read. His punishment was nothing short of horrendous. All Acoma males over age twenty-five were to have one of their feet cut off. Thereafter, they would serve twenty years of servitude. Two Indians from the province of Moqui who fought with the Acomans would have one hand cut off, then be set free to return home and tell of their punishment.[18] The gory sentences were duly carried out during the remaining days of February 1599 at Santo Domingo and other pueblos nearby.

All women over age twelve would be held to twenty years of slave servitude. Children under twelve were shown some mercy, as Oñate saw it. The girls were placed under the charge of Fray Alonso Martínez, who could distribute them throughout New Mexico monasteries as he wished. Some were sent to Mexico convents, never to see their homes again. The boys were turned over to Sargento Major Zaldívar for distribution among Spanish captains and soldiers as slaves for twenty years.

Oñate ordered that the elder Acoma men and women were to be "freed"; that is, they were given over to the Querecho Apaches, whose pueblos they were not permitted to leave. Despite these draconian sentences, many of the Acoma people soon slipped away from their bondage and returned to the mesa. Eventually, they would rebuild their pueblo village atop the great rock plateau.[19]

ABBREVIATION KEY

H/R-*DJO* = Hammond and Rey, eds., *Don Juan de Oñate*

NOTES

1. Villagrá, *History of New Mexico*, 38–39.
2. "Introduction," H/R-*DJO* 1: 19–20.

3. Villagrá, *History of New Mexico*, 208–209.

4. Ibid., 209.

5. "Trial of the Indians of Acoma," H/R-*DJO* 1: 458–459. One wonders why Oñate, carrying as he did the rank of captain general of his army before bestowing it on Vicente, did not—like another duke of Alba, who conquered Flanders, or marquis of Santa Cruz, who fought the Moors—assume personal leadership of this military operation that was so critical to all of Spain's ambitions in New Mexico. Villagrá said that though the general wished to lead the troops in person, he did not do so because of protests by the priests and the people; *History of New Mexico*, 209. Coronado, remember, undertook personal leadership against the Cibolans with dire results. But there is a political rationale to consider as well: because the possibility of taking Acoma was under considerable doubt, Don Juan must have known that he could bear personal blame for a defeat if he were in command on the ground. By passing his commanding rank to Vicente, he could avoid the blame for a defeat yet garner credit for a great victory (as Villagrá presented to him in verse; see the beginning of this chapter). Later, in fact, in considering what he called the "great cruelty" at Acoma, Viceroy Monterrey reasoned that the Audiencia could not proceed against Oñate because he had not been present at the battle; "Viceroy to the King," H/R-*DJO* 1: 502–503.

6. Villagrá, *History of New Mexico*, 219–220.

7. "Trial of the Indians of Acoma," H/R-*DJO* 1: 460.

8. Villagrá, *History of New Mexico*, 222.

9. "Trial of the Indians of Acoma," H/R-*DJO* 1: 460.

10 Villagrá, *History of New Mexico*, 231–232.

11. Ibid., 233.

12. Ibid., 243; Simmons, *Last Conquistador*, 143.

13. *Estufa* is the anthropological term for the Hopi *kiva*. Kivas—social-religious strutures common in the Pueblos—were used primarily by men. One Spaniard described the *estufa* as "a cave . . . plastered and whitewashed on the inside and [with] a roof over it"; H/R-*DJO* 2: 635. Another said the Indians stayed in *estufas* during cold weather; ibid., 660.

14. "Introduction," H/R-*DJO* 1: 462.

15. "Valverde Investigation," H/R-*DJO* 2: 649.

16. Simmons, *Last Conquistador*, 143.

17. "Trial of the Indians of Acoma," H/R-*DJO* 1: 469.

18. Ibid., 477.

19. Simmons, *Last Conquistador*, 146. Yet another condemnation of Oñate would be issued. It was charged that following the Acoma battle he seized the horses, military arms, and clothing of the men who had died at Acoma, as well as elsewhere, and had them sold, the proceeds of which were sent to Zaldívar. No accounting of this was ever made. "Oñate's Conviction," H/R-*DJO* 2: 1111.

18

To Sail a Scuttled Ship

Beyond the Great Settlements there are, according to reports, people who are very white and blonde, who live and dress well, after our custom, who use garments of cloth, and who have a yellow metal which resembles gold.

Don Juan de Oñate[1]

With the Acoma affair settled to his satisfaction, Oñate could now turn to other matters. In his report on the buffalo, Vicente had mentioned that during his visit to the prairies, campfire ashes and horse dung had been found that, so Jusepe said—though it may be hard to believe—had been left behind by the Antonio Gutiérrez de Humaña and Francisco Leyva de Bonilla *entrada* eight years earlier. The Indian had also told of reaching a great settlement on the buffalo prairie, so large that they had traveled through it for two days.

This was especially interesting to Oñate. Viceroy Monterrey had issued an order that Humaña and Leyva be found and arrested, and now, according to Jusepe's story, it appeared that Humaña would be charged with murder. Even more impelling, the officer's absence of several years raised an important issue. If Humaña had indeed found the golden treasures he sought, would it not be Oñate's duty to wrest them from him for the Crown? The governor wanted to hear the Indian's story directly. On February 16, 1599, with the help of interpreter Juan de Caso Barahona, Oñate personally interviewed Jusepe at San Juan.[2]

Jusepe told Oñate that the houses of the "Great Settlement," as it became known to the Spaniards, were built on stake frames with straw roofs and on narrow streets. In some places between the houses there were fields of maize, calabashes, and beans:

> After traveling for fifteen days more by short marches, they [the Spaniards] reached two large rivers, and beyond them many populous rancherías. Farther on in a plain they came to a very large settlement which must have extended for ten leagues, because they traveled through it for two days, and it must have been two leagues wide, more or less. One of the two rivers they crossed earlier flowed through this pueblo . . . The natives were very numerous but received the Spaniards peacefully and furnished them abundant supplies of food. These Indians obtained their subsistence from the buffalo.
>
> On leaving this pueblo and proceeding on north, after three days' travel the soldiers came upon such a multitude of buffalo that the plain—which was level, for there are no mountains—was so covered with them that they were startled and amazed at the sight. Continuing farther on they did not find any more Indian rancherías, but found always more buffalo . . . Near a large river some ten days from the said Great Pueblo there were also numerous plum and walnut trees and some white sapotes. The climate here was more temperate. This river was about one-fourth of a league wide, deep and sluggish. They did not dare to cross it.[3]

Three days beyond the Great Settlement, the two officers had quarreled. Leyva threatened to give Humaña a sound beating with a stick. Humaña remained alone in his tent all morning and afternoon writing, evidently brooding over the argument and threat before sending a soldier to call Leyva forth. Leyva was dressed in a shirt and breeches. Before he reached the tent, Humaña went out to meet him. He drew a butcher knife from his pocket and stabbed Leyva twice, killing him. Humaña had him buried at once, afterward showing the Spanish soldiers some papers Jusepe did not understand.

When they witnessed this murder, five Indians with the party ran away to the Great River (the Arkansas perhaps) and headed back toward New Mexico. On the prairies, however, some of the group became separated and lost. Only Jusepe and a companion are known to have made it to an Indian ranchería. There the companion was killed by the Indians, but Jusepe escaped to another Indian encampment, where he was taken captive and held for a year. Eventually, some Spanish traders came to conduct trade with the Indians. Jusepe managed to join the traders and escape with them to San Juan Bautista, where Vicente de Zaldívar had recruited him for the buffalo expedition.[4]

The mystery of Humaña's fate revived the ever-lingering myth of a city of golden treasure and with it intriguing questions. Had the officer found the city? Was he living among lavish wealth that should be reported to the king? Or had some other dark event occurred in which Humaña had also been killed? Such haunting possibilities gave Oñate even further reason to lead an expedition to the buffalo plains. Though Jusepe had not mentioned such during his recorded interview, Oñate later reported: "Beyond the Great Settlements there are, according to reports, people who are very white and blond, who live and dress well, after our custom, who use garments of cloth, and who have a yellow metal which resembles gold. This could not be verified, as the Indians who told about it pointed to the color of the tassels of the cords they saw us wearing. Captain Humaña reached these settlements and presumably is living among them."[5]

While one member of the *entrada* later testified that gold was the principal reason Oñate decided to launch the expedition to find the Great Settlement,[6] the governor was inspired in part by yet another great hope. He might possibly learn more about the mythical "Strait of Anián" passage across North America to the North Sea, a potential direct trade route to the Far East, which Spaniards and others of that day supposed existed. That in itself would please the Spanish crown immensely.[7]

"According to reports," Oñate wrote, "ships could be built and could be sailed between the North and the South Seas."[8] To conduct such an expedition, Oñate realized, he would need more men, equipment, and supplies. To obtain them, on March 2, 1599, he wrote a lengthy report and letter of request to Viceroy Monterrey.[9] He entrusted the letter to Captains Villagrá, Marcos Farfán de los Godos, and Juan Pinero, along with his cousin Friar Salazar (who died on the way), to deliver to the viceroy in Mexico City. They took with them several captive children from Acoma to be turned over to the church.

In his letter, Oñate told of the journey to Tiguex, how he had suppressed a rebellion led by two captains and a soldier but generously had not had them garroted, how he had sent Villagrá after the four horse thieves, how Vicente had found the buffalo, and how Juan de Zaldívar had been killed at Acoma. Of Vicente's bloody Acoma conquest he said only, "As a warning to the others, I razed and burned their pueblo."[10]

He told also of the first mass conducted in the new church and how he had discovered and inspected the various provinces in New Mexico. From there, he launched into lavish praise of New Mexico's potential in terms of its salines, great abundance of ores (yet to be found), vast offering of buffalo wool and skins, and the rich foods yielded from other natural resources. Not to be overlooked were the enormous rewards New Mexico's vassalage and tributes would provide to the king. The South Sea, he assured the viceroy, was close at hand, offering a wealth of pearls as well as trade opportunities "with Peru, New Spain [Mexico], and China."[11]

> It would be an endless story to attempt to describe in detail each one of the many things that are found there. All I can say is that with God's help I am going to see them all [the provinces] and give more pacified worlds, new and conquered, to his majesty, greater than the good Marquis [Cortés] gave him, despite his having done so much, if your lordship but gives me the succor, favor, and aid that I expect from such a hand . . . In order that your lordship may be inclined to grant them to me, I beg you to take into consideration the great increase of the royal crown and his majesty's revenues and their future expansion from such numerous and diverse sources.[12]

Oñate concluded with a request for six small artillery pieces and powder along with all the help possible, particularly married men, who were the "solid rock on which to build a lasting new nation."[13] Separately, he asked for stamping irons with which to mark the silver he hoped to be sending back one day. He also asked to be sent two skilled Indians who could teach their crafts to other Indians.

Don Juan said he intended to remain in New Mexico permanently, declaring that he had "scuttled his ships." He requested that permission be granted for his daughter, Mariquita, and any other of his relatives who so wished to join him.[14]

Oñate's promise to outdo Cortés revealed the great hopes aroused by Jusepe's story of a city of gold. That venture, however, would have to wait until help arrived from Mexico. In the meantime, he would have his men explore the local provinces for the silver lodes he hoped to find. And he would send Vicente out with a small party to make another attempt to reach the South Sea.

Vicente and twenty-five men set off from San Gabriel on the new mission of discovery in mid-July 1599. The party rode south to the pueblo of Abó, where they hoped to obtain provisions and tortillas for the trip. But the resident Jumano Indians refused to supply them. From Abó, Vicente turned west into present Arizona. The party's bad luck continued when the mountainous country severely bruised their horses' hooves. The animals became so crippled and exhausted that the Spaniards were forced to abandon them. Leaving the horses and nine of their party to guard them at a pueblo known as Topia, the remainder of the group pushed ahead on foot. Unable to find food at the small rancherías they encountered, the Spaniards were forced to sustain themselves by eating small berries produced by mesquite. When they discovered that Indians had laid an ambush for them in a grove of trees ahead, they gave up the quest and returned to San Gabriel, having spent over three months on the trail.[15]

The official approval of newly installed viceroy Don Gaspar de Zúñiga y Acevedo, the Count of Monterrey, was required for Oñate's relief expedition. But it was Oñate's kinsman, Juan Guerra de Resa, who financed the cost of recruiting colonists and fighting men, as well as the purchase of supplies and equipment to be sent to New Mexico. Because of the magnitude of the operation, the government decreed that an official inspection and detailed accounting of the expedition be made.

The many facets of the expedition—the colonists, army recruits, animals, armament, equipment, and supplies—were accumulated at Santa Bárbara, Mexico, during the summer of 1600. Finally, early in the afternoon of August 28, 1600, the inspection began. A group of New Spain officials headed by Commissaries General Captain Juan de Gordejuela Ybarguen and Captain Juan de Sotelo Cisneros took their seats at a table beneath a brush arbor in the valley of San Bartolomé near Santa Bárbara. Nearby was the expedition's encampment.[16]

When he had first arrived at Santa Bárbara in May, Gordejuela interviewed an Indian servant of Oñate's who had recently escaped back to Mexico. The man gave an account of the desperate conditions of the New Mexico venture, stressing the need for cattle for food and other provisions. Gordejuela was sympathetic to Oñate's needs. Knowing that Fray Alonso de la Oliva was at Santa Bárbara waiting for soldiers to escort him to New Mexico, the inspector contacted Guerra de Resa.

Guerra held the title of lieutenant general and captain general of New Mexico, even though he had never crossed the Rio Grande. He and

Gordejuela had sent a small supplement of horses, armor, powder, munitions, and other supplies ahead of the main expedition to New Mexico with Fray Alonso and a party of seven soldiers.[17]

Monterrey had ordered the current assembly for the purpose of inspecting and making an inventory of the soldiers and other persons, cattle, provisions, arms, munitions, and everything else provided to Oñate. A certified muster roll was required; for this, in nothing less than a royal pageant, the military units came forth in formation—each man mounted and fully armed with harquebuses—to be reviewed by the commissaries.

At the lead was Guerra, staff of office in hand, looking very much the conquistador on his prancing mount, though he would remain in Mexico. He was accompanied by a page mounted on a horse draped with buckskin armor.[18]

Next came Captain Alférez Bernabé de las Casas, commander of the reinforcement army. The black-bearded, thirty-year-old soldier from the Canary Islands was a veteran of the Acoma battle. Both he and his horse were fully armored. Captain las Casas and his *maestre de campo*, Captain Gerónimo Márquez, swore by God and made the sign of the cross to testify that their arms were their own and that with such they would serve their majesty in New Mexico. The company of thirty-two men was reviewed by passing in formation before the commissaries. As they did so, the recruits fired their harquebuses and bronze pieces before being ordered to halt and rest in formation while a muster roll was taken and the oath of loyalty and service was rendered by all.

Captain Gaspar de Villagrá, now listed as procurator general of the reinforcements, followed with seventeen recruits. The veteran of New Mexico conquests joined his company in swearing that he would return to New Mexico to serve his majesty under the royal banner, obey the orders of his superiors, and not turn back under any circumstances. His vow was far from sincere, however, for evidently he had had enough of Oñate's conquest crusade.

Soon after the inspection, Villagrá took refuge in San Bartolomé's Convent of Saint Francis, where he could not be arrested, and announced that he refused to return to New Mexico. He was not alone. Captains Farfán and Juan Pinero likewise failed to return with the expedition.[19] These desertions foretold a growing mutiny among the members of Oñate's colony and army who were still in New Mexico.

On August 30, Captain Juan de Ortega, fully decked for battle, presented his company. The red-bearded, twenty-seven-year-old native of Los Angeles, Mexico, and his seventeen recruits were ordered to march about the camp, firing their harquebuses as they went. This done, they then lined up before the commissary party. They all made vows of service before God and the cross, swearing that they were going on the expedition on their own free will and would not turn back.

That same day, the commissaries and notary Hernán Sanchez paid a visit to the expedition camp to make a final inspection and to catalog "all the women, whether Spanish or Indian, married or single, free or slave" on the muster roll.[20] Captain las Casas had them assembled. Their count numbered five wives, two unmarried sisters-in-law, nine daughters, four sons, a mulatto servant, a ten-year-old Indian slave girl, and an unmarried woman servant who was a Mexican native. Record was made as well of the seventeen or so Indian women, married and unmarried, who would accompany the expedition and, separately, of those brought illegally by the officers and soldiers.[21]

Isabel de Olvera, a mulatto woman, petitioned to accompany the expedition and presented her credentials as a free woman "unbound by marriage or slavery." By doing so, she said, she hoped to escape the advances of soldiers during the long journey. Las Casas also sought approval for a mulatto male servant to accompany the expedition. A slave brand scarred the man's face.[22]

Recruitment of soldiers continued even after the inspection, with officers appointed by the viceroy. Delayed briefly by a dispute over what authority the inspectors held over the expedition, the relief column got under way during early September 1600. In total, eighty additional men, as well as six Franciscan friars, would be added to Oñate's New Mexico army and colony. Also, the expedition would deliver 700 head of cattle and 20 mares.[23]

After a march of nearly four months, the relief expedition arrived at San Gabriel on December 24. It was greeted by much rejoicing and made a gala Christmas celebration possible.[24] But once the euphoria was over and the new members saw the colony's sorry condition, they were soon complaining loudly that they had been misled by the letters and reports they had received. They claimed they had been defrauded into selling their estates and forsaking their comfortable lives in Mexico.[25]

As part of the relief expedition, the viceroy had included a number of men he had appointed as captains in Oñate's army. This action by the viceroy infuriated Oñate, who felt such authority rested with himself. He threatened to deny the appointments. When he received the official letter of appointments, he issued a proclamation requiring each of the men to present his royal patent before a judge.

In one instance a newly appointed officer, who was ill, informed Oñate through a friend that the viceroy had commissioned him orally. "Tell him," Oñate replied bitterly, "to wipe his rear with his patents."[26] The remark eventually reached Viceroy Monterrey.

Despite the provisions the relief expedition brought, both the New Mexico colony and Oñate's army fell into dire straits during the winter of 1600–1601. Deep despair reigned throughout the San Gabriel camp. Now, no one dreamed of finding golden treasures. No great discoveries had been made, and the land itself—in sharp contrast to the glowing assessment Don Juan had given the viceroy—appeared distressingly sterile and unpromising. The lack of fuel and clothing and the inadequacy of the pueblo housing exacerbated the snow-blinding, bone-chilling weather. The supply of cattle and sheep had been seriously depleted. Seldom was there meat for the table; only the never-ending diet of hard dried corn or tortillas appeared at mealtime. It was even worse for the Indians. Frays Francisco de San Miguel and Francisco de Sosa Peñalosa described the situation at San Gabriel:

> We find ourselves in extreme need of food and see the natives starving to death, eating whatever filth there is in the fields, even the twigs from the trees, dirt, coal, and ashes. This witness knows that many of them have died of hunger. There has been and there is hunger in the camp, and no possible way to relieve it, because there is no ripe corn anywhere in the land, and the cornfields are in the worst condition that they have ever been. If we stay any longer, the natives and all of us here will perish of hunger, cold, and nakedness. This witness has clothed some Spaniards and relieved them with many things, in view of their dire needs and the poverty of the country. For some days he [Oñate] has been trying to hold back many who want to leave, taking the few horses there are at present in the camp.[27]

Expedition members later testified on the issue. Captain Alonso Sánchez painfully recalled that when he saw the royal standard raised at Zacatecas, he had sold all his goods and lands—including a cattle ranch on which he had 1,000 calves—to join Oñate's expedition and serve the king. He had brought his wife and two married daughters with him to

New Mexico, also three unmarried daughters and two sons who were soldiers. After serving in virtually all of Oñate's *entradas*, he was now certain
there was no gold or silver in the land: "For this reason and because of the
extreme sterility of the land, his family has suffered much privation, being
without clothes for the inclement climate of the country—at times frost
and snow and at other times infernal heat." Sánchez pleaded to be permitted to leave the country, even "with only his bare back and in poverty."[28]

The situation was hard for everyone to bear, but it was particularly
difficult for men with wives and children. Some looked back agonizingly
at the comfortable estates in Mexico they had forfeited and property
they had lost in joining the expedition. Many now felt they had been
sorely misled in doing so. Moreover, they had come to live in fear of
Oñate's oppressive, iron-handed rule over them. Not surprisingly, colonists, soldiers, and even the friars yearned mightily to leave and return to
Mexico—with or without Oñate's permission. To Don Juan, the matter
reeked of treason.

ABBREVIATION KEY

H/R-*DJO* = Hammond and Rey, eds., *Don Juan de Oñate*

NOTES

1. "True Report Based on Oñate's Letters," H/R-*DJO* 2: 621.
2. "Account Given by an Indian," H/R-*DJO* 1: 416–419.
3. Ibid., 417.
4. Ibid., 416–419.
5. "True Report Based on Oñate's Letters," H/R-*DJO* 2: 621. See also
"Zaldívar Inquiry," H/R-*DJO* 2: 785. Five members of the *entrada* testified that
Jusepe told of "quantities of gold" at Quivira; "Memorial on the Discovery of New
Mexico," H/R-*DJO* 2: 943.
6. "Memorial on the Discovery of New Mexico," H/R-*DJO* 2: 940.
7. Simmons, *Last Conquistador*, 11.
8. "True Report Based on Oñate's Letters," H/R-*DJO* 2: 621.
9. Ibid., 1: 480–488.
10. Ibid., 485.
11. Ibid., 486.
12. Ibid., 485–486.
13. Ibid., 487.
14. Ibid.

15. "Introduction," H/R-*DJO* 1: 22; "True Report Based on Oñate's Letters," H/R-*DJO* 2: 620–621; "Valverde Investigation," H/R-*DJO* 2: 640–641.

16. "Gordejuela Inspection," H/R-*DJO* 1: 514–518.

17. Ibid., 578.

18. Ibid., 549.

19. Ibid., 576; "Oñate to Viceroy, March 2, 1599," H/R-*DJO* 1: 488; Simmons, *Last Conquistador*, 155.

20. "Gordejuela Inspection," H/R-*DJO* 1: 557.

21. Ibid., 557–565.

22. Ibid., 559–561.

23. "Discussion and Proposal," H/R-*DJO* 2: 906n5, 907.

24. "Introduction," H/R-*DJO* 1: 24.

25. "Valverde Investigation," H/R-*DJO* 2: 656.

26. "Velasco to Viceroy, March 22, 1601," H/R-*DJO* 2: 617; "Valverde Investigation," H/R-*DJO* 2: 657.

27. "Desertion of the Colony," H/R-*DJO* 2: 674.

28. Ibid., 684.

19

So Bloody the Sword

The sargento mayor [Vicente], with seventy men, waged war against them [the Jumanos] by fire and sword, killed more than nine hundred Indians, burned and leveled their pueblo.

Captain Luis de Velasco[1]

The records are vague, but sometime after he wrote his letter to Viceroy Monterrey from San Juan de los Caballeros on March 2, 1599, and prior to July 28, 1600, Oñate moved his capital to the pueblo of San Gabriel.[2] He had wanted to establish a town at San Juan with an *alcalde mayor*, but his Spanish colonists were weary of the privations they were enduring. They refused, fearing that founding a town would cause them to remain in New Mexico even longer. Many of them wanted desperately to return to Mexico.[3]

But Oñate did move his colony headquarters across the Rio Grande to a pueblo opposite the mouth of the Chama River. The pueblo, which became designated San Juan Bautista, contained 400 Indian homes. Oñate took over the pueblo, forcing the Indian occupants out so his people could adapt the abode to their pleasure by inserting doors and windows. The confiscated quarters were far from satisfactory, however, as one Spaniard testified later: "The people leave their houses to sleep in their small vegetable gardens in order to escape the unbearable plague of bedbugs. Furthermore, there are an infinite number of field mice, which breed a species of lice, the pain from whose sting lasts for almost twenty-four hours."[4]

The only fuel for fires was green cottonwood. It smoked so intensely that when it was burned inside the pueblo rooms it made people's eyes burn and brought the women and children to tears. Yet at nighttime there was little else but candles for lighting the rooms. One person later testified that he had never heard a single person say he lived there of his own free will, only through force and compulsion.

Despite the rampant discontent within his colony and all his disappointments in making discoveries, Don Juan was very serious about colonizing New Mexico. During the spring of 1601, as he organized his Quivira expedition, he exercised gory punishments against anyone who attempted to leave the New Mexico colony and return to Mexico. Men who did so suffered Oñate's wrath to the extreme.

Two notorious cases involved army captains. Both men—Captain Pablo de Aguilar, of Acoma fame, and Captain Alonso de Sosa Albornoz—had contributed much to the expedition, both materially in animals and armament and by dent of service. After his return from New Mexico several years later, Oñate, like Coronado, would be brought to trial on numerous charges relating to their deaths and other events that occurred under his command. Much of the testimony taken in that trial exists today. Though some historians hold less certain views of Oñate's guilt in the deaths of these two men sometime prior to March 1601,[5] the records as seen here provide strong evidence regarding Oñate's complicity.

Aguilar, a thirty-six-year-old native of Ecija, Spain, had enlisted with Oñate's *entrada* from Mexico City. He left behind his wife, Doña Ana Clara Contreras, described as an "honorable and distinguished woman."[6] A man of good stature who had a chestnut-colored beard, Aguilar contributed a cart, sixteen oxen, and sixteen horses to the expedition in addition to his armor, arms, and other equipment. According to Captain Luis de Velasco, Aguilar was a truthful, well-liked, and honorable man. During the march to New Mexico, Oñate had called on him several times to reconnoiter the trail and Indian villages ahead.

On the original march up the Rio Grande from Mexico, Oñate had carefully instructed Aguilar to go on ahead and scout out any Indian village he might find but, important lest the inhabitants should flee with their foodstuffs, he was to avoid detection if at all possible. Under no circumstances was he to enter the village. When Aguilar returned and reported that he had indeed entered a village, Oñate was infuriated, so much so that he ordered that Aguilar be put to death by strangulation. Only the appeals of other officers, men, and friars had persuaded him otherwise.[7]

Aguilar again put himself at the mercy of Oñate's wrath when he was one of the two officers involved in the attempted desertion during August 1598. Again, Oñate nearly had him garroted. Once more the officer's life was saved by the tearful pleas of the clergy and the army. Aguilar rode with Vicente de Zaldívar's party to the Texas Panhandle prairies to hunt buffalo. He also served as the captain of cavalry at the second battle of Acoma, one of the men who bravely scaled the back wall with Vicente to first engage the Indians there.[8]

But Aguilar was far from happy with his service in New Mexico. Undoubtedly like others, he was totally disillusioned by the hard duty and lack of rewards. He greatly missed his wife and yearned to be with her. He had left her all alone in Mexico City, he said, without means of support. Oñate sent him an Indian woman as a concubine, but that was not enough. Aguilar went to Oñate and pleaded, as he had before, for permission to return to Mexico. Surprisingly, this time Oñate was friendly and agreed to give him a written permit to do so when his secretary had been summoned.

The events that followed are somewhat confused in the two existing accounts: one given by Captain Velasco, who claimed he was at the scene, and another presented in the charges preferred against Oñate during his trial. Both accounts agree, however, that Oñate invited Aguilar to his house after having issued him a permit to leave, greeted him affably, and ushered him into a room where two servants—an African and an Indian—were waiting with butcher knives. The account in the formal charges read:

> Don Juan walked in behind him, seized a loaded and primed gun, which he himself had placed behind the door, turned the wheel, [and] shouted, "Death to the traitor, stab him." Immediately the said negro [*sic*] and Indian attacked and began to slash the victim. As they were unable to harm him because of his heavy buckskin coat, Don Juan de Oñate took a sword from one of the accomplices, and while the Indian and negro pushed the victim over a bed, Don Juan thrust the sword

between his legs and drove it clear to his chest. Then he raised the skirt of the man's coat and told them to stab him there, and the negro and the Indian stabbed him again.[9]

For his part, Oñate stated that Aguilar was still enough alive to plead for a priest to whom he could make a final confession. Velasco wrote: "Captain Aguilar was already breathless and in convulsions, his teeth set, his eyes staring at the governor. They cut off his head, not satisfied with the many wounds, each one mortal, that covered his body."[10]

Nine witnesses eventually attested to this charge against Oñate, seven of whom were challenged on grounds only that they themselves had been prosecuted for rebellion. Oñate answered the Aguilar charge by claiming that after he had twice pardoned Aguilar from sentences of death, the officer mutinied again, fleeing one night with five soldiers and a woman with whom he lived in concubinage. Don Juan claimed he then had Aguilar seized and, after sentencing him to death, ordered him beheaded. Perhaps most damaging to Oñate's case was his admission that he had been present during Aguilar's arrest and murder. He acknowledged that he had had Aguilar arrested by others but insisted that he "took no other part in the affair [other] than to seize an harquebus for his defense and to make sure that justice was carried out in proper manner."[11]

Six other men were charged as Oñate's accomplices in Aguilar's death: Captain Alonso Núñez de Ynojosa, Captain Domingo de Lizama, Captain Juan de Salas, Captain Dionisio de Bañuelos, Oñate's Indian servant Agustín, and African servant Luis Bautista. Captain Cristóbal de Herrera was listed in the complaint but not charged.[12]

The murder of Captain Alonso de Sosa Albornoz, as told by Velasco, was equally treacherous and sordid. When he enlisted with Oñate, Sosa was described as a native of Mexico, forty-eight years of age, of dark complexion with graying hair. His contribution to the expedition was considerable: 35 horses, 23 colts, 65 oxen, 80 tame milk cows, 30 steers, 7 carts, 500 sheep, and 80 goats in addition to armor, weapons, tools, and horse equipment.[13] At the time of the delayed second inspection, he claimed that an equal amount had been used up, stolen, or lost. Further, his commitment to Oñate's expedition had been complete in that he had brought his wife and five children along to New Mexico.[14]

Not long after Aguilar's murder, Sosa went to Oñate to ask permission to take his family back to Mexico, saying he was unable to provide for them otherwise. Oñate granted the request, and Sosa began loading his carts preparatory to receiving orders to leave. During this time, a relative of Sosa's (Captain Francisco de Sosa Peñalosa perhaps)[15] made a complaint against Vicente de Zaldívar, who he claimed had entered his house without invitation. The relative said Vicente was trying to dishonor his family (by seducing his wife?) and requested permission to take his family back to Mexico as well.[16]

While both Sosa families were waiting to leave, Oñate issued orders for all captains and soldiers, with no exceptions, to go out and round up the army's horses. Don Alonso was among those who obeyed the order, only to meet with disaster. Vicente and some allies were waiting for him in ambush. Velasco described Sosa's murder: "When he had gone two leagues from the camp, he was attacked in a ravine by the sargento mayor [Vicente] and some of his followers. They stabbed him to death, without giving him an opportunity to confess. After they had murdered him, they covered his body with stones so that it could not be found. No one dared to look for it. His widow was left with a large number of children ... The relatives of Captain Sosa did not again ask for permission to leave."[17]

Oñate was charged with ordering Sosa's killing "after granting him security and without giving him time to confess, and without any reasons to justify his action." The charge was rendered on the testimony of twelve witnesses. Ten of the witnesses were challenged by Oñate, once again solely on the basis that they were his mortal enemies whom he had sentenced to death for deserting the army. Oñate also claimed that Sosa's punishment was necessary to avoid trouble, disturbances, and uprisings by friends and relatives, who threatened great harm.[18]

Captain Domingo de Lizama, Captain Juan de Salas, Captain Alonso Gómez, mestizo Francisco de Vido, mestizo slave Juan, and African Luis Bautista were charged as accomplices in Sosa's murder.[19] No other explanation of his death was offered.

Oñate was also implicated in the earlier murder in Mexico of Captain Julián de Resa. Both Resa and his killer, Captain Juan Ruiz, had been listed in the Ulloa inspection conducted at San Bartolomé as joining the expedition with their personal armor and horse. Ruiz not only killed Resa, but he also cut off his head.[20]

With his New Mexican colony sliding into severe disarray, the governor was sorely in need of a worthy—and wealth-providing—new discovery. Great discontent as well as fear flourished among army officers, soldiers, priests, and impoverished settlers alike, threatening the success of the principality that was Spain's initial entry into North America. Even as Oñate recruited men and prepared for a new, large expedition, a major rebellion was developing around him.

Oñate's punitive actions against the Indians had also heightened serious fears among the San Juan colonists that a native uprising might result. A sordid affair with the Jumano Indians to the south at Abó was of special concern.

Don Juan had been incensed upon learning that the Jumano Indians at Abó had refused to supply Vicente on his South Sea venture. Deciding that the Indians must be punished, in the spring of 1601 he personally led a large force to the village and demanded a tribute of blankets. The Jumanos furnished a dozen or more, saying they had no more to give. Oñate withdrew his men to a watering hole for the night, but the next morning he returned to the pueblo with an Indian interpreter who could speak the Jumano tongue. Through the interpreter, Don Juan informed the Jumanos that he was going to punish them for their insolence.

He ordered his soldiers to torch some of the Indian homes and then to fire a volley from their harquebuses. Several Jumanos were killed, and others were wounded. Oñate decided that two men who had shown some resistance were too warlike, and he had them hanged. After this was done, Oñate ordered his interpreter to deliver a message to the Jumanos. The man did so, but a soldier persuaded the governor that the interpreter was saying something against the Spaniards. Oñate had the interpreter hanged.[21]

Following this, a command under Vicente fought yet another battle with the tribe. This, too, proved to be a bloody affair, though it is less well documented than the Acoma fight. Testimonies by Spanish soldiers state that trouble originated when five soldiers who were deserting to Mexico passed through the pueblo of Abó. Through no provocation on their part, the men claimed, they were attacked and two were killed. The Spaniards had apparently forgotten that Oñate had ravaged the Jumano settlements, but the Jumanos had not.

At the time, Oñate was preparing for his expedition to Quivira, on which he would take a sizable force of the Spanish garrison. Word of the killing of the two soldiers spread through the Spanish colony at San Gabriel, creating great consternation that the Jumanos would rise up and attack them while the soldiers were gone. The colonists, priests, and others implored Oñate to punish the Jumanos before he left. Still nervous about the Acoma uprising, men with wives and children insisted that unless the Jumanos were put down, they could not be asked to stay and risk having their families killed.[22]

During a mass meeting of everyone in the camp, Oñate assigned Vicente to lead a force to Abó. When the Jumanos learned of the impending attack, they consolidated their forces at another pueblo known as Agualagu. By most Spanish accounts, Vicente approached the Indians with repeated offers of peace and vows that a just arrangement would be made. But the Jumanos had heard of the Acomans' fate and well remembered Oñate's visit. Their warriors, estimated at more than 800 by Captain Gerónimo Márquez, attacked Vicente's vanguard with bows and arrows and stones until he and his men were finally forced to withdraw.[23]

Instead of a frontal assault, Vicente and his officers chose to lay siege to the pueblo. For five days and nights, the Spaniards managed to keep the Indians contained. The soldiers torched the pueblo, driving some of the natives from the village. Vicente's men attacked with lance and sword. He was at the forefront of the battle and was wounded so severely that he could no longer ride a horse. The fight that had begun on Monday finally came to an end on Saturday when the Spaniards entered the pueblo and took 400 of the Indians captive. The Jumanos were instructed that they should live peacefully and not kill Spaniards. Vicente generously gave each of his soldiers a male Indian for a servant. They were taken to San Gabriel, but many soon escaped their bondage and fled. Velasco wrote of the bloody affair: "Equally cruel [as the Acoma incident] was the war recently waged against another pueblo, this one belonging to the Jumanos. It was caused by similar attempts to take their food and blankets. The sargento mayor [Vicente], with seventy men . . . killed more than nine hundred Indians, burned and leveled their pueblo, and took more than two hundred prisoners, who ran away a few days later."[24]

Fray Lope Izquierdo, a member of the 1600 relief expedition and one of those who eventually abandoned the New Mexico colony, declared under oath that a great number of Indians had been killed by soldiers who were taking their maize and that "there was no other cause for the wars against the people of Acoma and the Jumanas. This does not include other natives that I could tell about who were killed in this search for food, against all justification and Christian piety."[25]

His testimony was supported in full by Frays Gastón de Peralta and Damián Escudero.[26] Loyal colonists rebutted it, however, saying that the natives had been the aggressors in both instances. They claimed that the Indians had started the hostilities and killed Spaniards without justification.[27]

Soon after the Jumano fight, the wounded Vicente led his men back up the Rio Grande to join Oñate, who had departed on his expedition to find the Great Settlement. The general was anxious to learn Humaña's whereabouts and, with luck, to make a grand, astounding discovery. Like many of his colonists and captains, he had invested greatly in his effort to colonize New Mexico. The enormous rewards of finding a city of gold would be of immense value to that effort.

ABBREVIATION KEY

H/R-*DJO* = Hammond and Rey, eds., *Don Juan de Oñate*

NOTES

1. "Velasco to Viceroy, March 22, 1601," H/R-*DJO* 2: 615.

2. Diego de Zubía, Alférez Leonís Tremiño de Bañuelos, and Fray Francisco de San Miguel gave their testimony at San Gabriel during the period July 28–31, 1600; "Zaldívar Inquiry," H/R-*DJO* 2: 816, 823, 830.

3. "Valverde Investigation," H/R-*DJO* 2: 652, 656.

4. Ibid., 656.

5. The published records do not designate the date on which either murder took place. This time frame is based in part on Velasco's report of Aguilar's murder in his letter to the viceroy on March 22, 1601; "Velasco to Viceroy," H/R-*DJO* 2: 612. Also, it is known that Aguilar served on Oñate's Council of War in the Acoma trials held through January 1599. Because the account of Aguilar's murder tells that he wore a heavy coat at the time, that event must have occurred during winter.

6. "Oñate Charges Reviewed," H/R-*DJO* 2: 1130.

7. Simmons, *Last Conquistador*, 102.

8. "Discovery of the Buffalo," H/R-*DJO* 1: 398; "Trial of the Indians of Acoma," H/R-*DJO* 1: 459.

9. "Oñate Charges Reviewed," H/R-*DJO* 2: 1130.

10. "Velasco to Viceroy, March 22, 1601," H/R-*DJO* 2: 612.

11. "Oñate Charges Reviewed," H/R-*DJO* 2: 1132. The argument made in Oñate's favor by Simmons (*Last Conquistador*, 159) that Velasco—himself a mutineer and critic of Oñate—provided the sole account of Aguilar's death is debatable. The official charges against Oñate, taken from nine witnesses, provide

numerous details of the gory deed not mentioned by Velasco. Of the nine witnesses, seven were challenged by Oñate on the grounds that they were mutineers and traitors—which means, of course, that two of them were not challenged. Though Hammond and Rey did not record the witnesses' testimony, the official charge clearly reflects the accounts they gave of Aguilar's death. There is no corroboration whatever of Oñate's rebuttal that Aguilar fled with five soldiers and a woman one night before he was arrested, sentenced, and beheaded. In fact, Oñate's answer to the charges is put to question by the fact that, after his death, an inventory of Aguilar's belongings revealed a license Don Juan had signed for his return to Mexico. The existence of the license indicates that Aguilar was killed after receiving the permit; thus he had no reason to have been "fleeing," as Oñate claimed; "Oñate Charges Reviewed," H/R-*DJO* 2: 1131.

12. H/R-*DJO* 2: 1118–1124.

13. "Salazar Inspection," H/R-*DJO* 1: 240–241.

14. "The Ulloa Inspection," H/R-*DJO* 1: 165; "Salazar Inspection," H/R-*DJO* 1: 240–241, 290.

15. "The Ulloa Inspection," H/R-*DJO* 1: 165.

16. "Velasco to Viceroy, March 22, 1601," H/R-*DJO* 2: 612–613. Perhaps Vicente had acted "romantically." He was later charged with and exonerated of associating "in an immoral and dishonorable way with women of the army, which resulted in great scandal and offense to its captains and soldiers"; "Oñate's Conviction," H/R-*DJO* 2: 1114.

17. "Velasco to Viceroy, March 22, 1601," H/R-*DJO* 2: 613.

18. "Oñate Charges Reviewed," H/R-*DJO* 2: 1132.

19. Ibid., 1118–1124.

20. "The Ulloa Inspection," H/R-*DJO* 1: 161–162; "Oñate's Conviction," H/R-*DJO* 2: 1110. Resa's death may have occurred before the Salazar inspection, which does not list him as a member of the expedition.

21. "Valverde Investigation," H/R-*DJO* 2: 650–651; "Report of Loyal Colonists," H/R-*DJO* 2: 704–705.

22. "Zaldívar Inquiry," H/R-*DJO* 2: 795.

23. Ibid., 705, 795–796, 802–803, 806–807.

24. "Velasco to Viceroy, March 22, 1604," H/R-*DJO* 2: 615.

25. "Desertion of the Colony," H/R-*DJO* 2: 679.

26. Ibid., 682–683.

27. Ibid., 723, 727.

20

Rediscovering Quivira

They [the Rayados] began to make threats and to give indications they wanted to fight, waving their arms, pulling the strings of their bows, and throwing dirt into the air.

Captain Juan Gutiérrez Bocanegra[1]

There is no mention in the Spanish records that the Oñate Expedition was advantaged by accounts of the Coronado Expedition sixty years earlier. In taking a direct course from San Gabriel eastward to the Canadian River, Oñate avoided the hazard of becoming lost on the prairies of the Texas Panhandle. He was possibly aided by Indians, including Jusepe, who were interviewed earlier regarding the interior country beyond New Mexico. Even as the expedition was still in the field in October 1601, Sergeant Alonso de la Vega, who had accompanied the march for fifty leagues until he fell ill and returned, testified at San Gabriel that prior to Oñate's departure some natives had been interviewed through an interpreter. They told of large pueblos in the interior and had drawn "lines on the ground and pointed in the direction of the road followed by the governor."[2]

Oñate embarked on his Quivira quest from his San Gabriel head-quarters at the mouth of the Chama River, north of Albuquerque, on

June 23, 1601. The expedition consisted of "more than seventy picked and well-equipped men, more than seven hundred horses and mules, six carts drawn by mules and two by oxen bringing four pieces of artillery, and sufficient servants to transport the necessary baggage."[3] Prominent among the other members were Vicente de Zaldívar as the *maestro de campo*; Oñate's son, Don Cristóbal, now about fifteen years of age; two Franciscan friars, priest Francisco de Velasco and lay brother Fray Pedro de Vergara; and the Indian guide Jusepe. Vicente later complained that half of the men Oñate took with him were more of a hindrance than a help.[4]

The expedition also included a herd of cattle for feeding the members. This sizable impediment naturally restricted the party's rate of travel, which is suggested as averaging three or four leagues a day—coinciding with how often they generally found water.[5] With plodding oxen, cattle, a spare horse remuda, and those making the journey on foot, the expedition could hardly have moved with much speed. Eventually, the cattle were consumed by the army and replaced for food by buffalo found in enormous herds on the ravine-slashed plains of the Texas Panhandle. But the hunting, slaughtering, and butchering of buffalo was time-consuming and further impeded the *entrada*'s advance.[6]

As with the Coronado Expedition, uncertainty has long existed concerning the route of Oñate's march across the regions of present Texas, Oklahoma, and Kansas in 1601. Despite the studied efforts of historians, anthropologists, and archaeologists, neither his route in total nor his final destination has been determined satisfactorily. Some scholars have concluded that Oñate's visit to the Escanjaque and Rayado (Wichita) villages occurred in present Oklahoma, while others think it took place at various locations in Kansas. This study offers yet another theory of Oñate's route and final destination for consideration (see appendix C).

A map prepared by cartographer Enrico Martínez in 1602 depicts Oñate's route in terms of the known landmarks of the time (figure 20.1). In drawing the map, Martínez was guided from memory by Juan Rodríguez, a Portuguese mariner experienced in sea navigation who had been a member of the Castaño de Sosa Expedition in 1590 and made the journey to Quivira with Oñate. The Martínez map is said to be the oldest surviving map to show the interior of Tierra Nueva with any accuracy.[7] Because of its geographic disproportion and the difficulty it presents in relating its place references beyond the Canadian River to those of today, however, the map leaves much to interpretation.

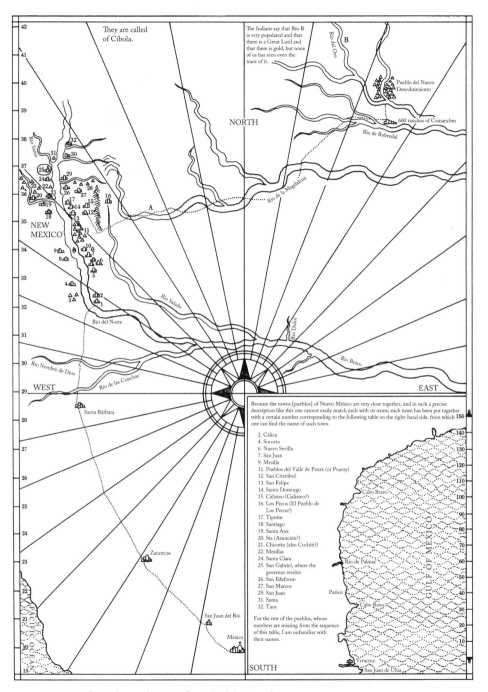

FIGURE 20.1. *Oñate's march, 1602 (map by Martínez)*

By any reasoning of the *entrada*'s route, it appears certain that the map does not include all of the streams the *entrada* is said to have followed or crossed. But while the map is perplexing in its lack of specific data, it is most valuable in establishing general directions. Early map makers were limited in their knowledge of native sites and of the full extent and course of rivers the exploring parties saw only in small segments as they crossed over them.

But the travelers of that day—especially a mariner such as Rodríguez—knew their compass directions well enough and had a credible idea of distances, measured in leagues.[8] Although we are uncertain what the map tells us about the streams it does or does not depict, we do know that the map's course along the Canadian River is valid and that beyond the Canadian the overall directional indications of the map agree very closely with participant accounts.

There is no indication that Oñate followed Coronado's practice of assigning a man to count the steps or paces of each day's march, to accurately measure in leagues the distance marched. Thus, distances given in Oñate's official report on the expedition were evidently reasoned estimates, possibly made according to the length of time the *entrada* marched each day.[9] Because early village sites, rivers, and other landmarks in New Mexico proper in 1601 were better defined than those elsewhere in North America, the first portion of Oñate's march is far more firmly determined than the portion on the prairies to the east.

From San Gabriel, Oñate moved south along the Rio Grande and then cut east across the Sandia-Manzano range to the pueblo of Galisteo. While the expedition rested there, it was joined by Captain Francisco de Valverde y Mercado and others who had left San Gabriel four days behind Oñate.[10] From Galisteo, the expedition marched eastward to the Pecos River and then to the Gallinas River. "From there on the plains became more extensive, with many arroyos, some larger than others, with permanent water and many trees, among them plums and wild grapevines."[11]

Though not stated in the expedition journal, possibly Oñate then followed the eastward-flowing, water-providing Conchas River in marching from the Gallinas to the bend of the Canadian River (called the "Madelena" by the expedition) where the Conchas Dam now exists northwest of present Tucumcari. There Vicente, who had remained at San Gabriel to manage affairs and recover from his wounds as much as possible, joined the expedition with twenty men.[12]

As they moved eastward down the Canadian from there, the expedition began to meet the nomadic Vaquero Apache tribespeople, who came to their camp with presents of fruit and buffalo tallow. Oñate responded with gifts of hardtack, tobacco, and trifles.[13]

The *entrada* reached the Canadian on July 2. We know this because we are told it was the day celebrated for the "Biblical Mary Magdalena," whose name the Spaniards gave the river.[14] From there the *entrada* moved on to the mouth of a tributary that flowed into the Canadian from the north, reaching the river on August 2, the day of the Feast of the Porciuncula. Oñate called the stream the "Rio de San Francisco." Two modern options exist for this stream: the Ute River that empties into the Canadian at Logan, New Mexico, or to the east the Rita Blanco that drains south into the Texas Panhandle. The month taken from July 2 to August 2 to march along the river indicates the latter, as does the Martínez map. At that point "most of the men in the army confessed and received communion."[15]

After several days' rest, Oñate took up his march again on August 10, "the day of the glorious Levite and martyr, San Lorenzo (St. Lawrence)." The *entrada* saw its first buffalo—herds so large that "it will be difficult for anyone who has not seen them to believe it."[16] Upon reaching a point "111 leagues" distant (from San Gabriel surely, this study contends, and not from where they joined the Canadian, as some scholars have reasoned), Oñate turned away from the river to the north, possibly in the area north of Borger, Texas.

This turn away from the Canadian provides a critical key to the route of Oñate's ensuing march. It may have been here that Oñate is said to have taken "Jusepe as guide and traveled north by east."[17] To reason that the turn was made at the Borger sand hills constitutes a major departure from other projections, which follow the thesis by Herbert Bolton and others that the *entrada* turned away from the Canadian River at the Antelope Hills. (See appendix C for further discussion.)

Oñate's report on the expedition, as testified to by many of his men, continued: "We spent a few days along two small streams, which flowed to the east like the preceding one."[18] This significant clue could well be, as Bolton has suggested, a reference to the Beaver (North Canadian) and the Cimarron River in the Oklahoma Panhandle's Beaver County. Though it may rightfully be questioned whether "small streams" is a correct description of the two, they are, in fact, the only side-by-side, easterly flowing

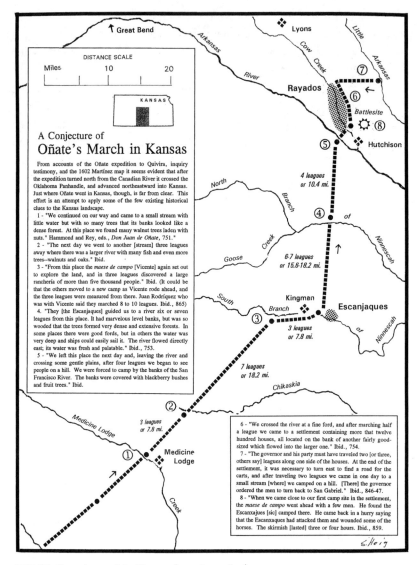

Great Bend

Lyons

Little Arkansas

Arkansas River

Cow Creek

⑦

Rayados

⑥ ←

Battlesite

☼ ⑧

⑤

Hutchison

DISTANCE SCALE

Miles 10 20

KANSAS

A Conjecture of
Oñate's March in Kansas

From accounts of the Oñate expedition to Quivira, inquiry testimony, and the 1602 Martínez map it seems evident that after the expedition turned north from the Canadian River it crossed the Oklahoma Panhandle, and advanced northeastward into Kansas. Just where Oñate went in Kansas, though, is far from clear. This effort is an attempt to apply some of the few existing historical clues to the Kansas landscape.

1 - "We continued on our way and came to a small stream with little water but with so many trees that its banks looked like a dense forest. At this place we found many walnut trees laden with nuts." Hammond and Rey, eds., *Don Juan de Oñate*, 751."

2 - "The next day we went to another [stream] three leagues away where there was a larger river with many fish and even more trees—walnuts and oaks." Ibid.

3 - "From this place the *maese de campo* [Vicente] again set out to explore the land, and in three leagues discovered a large ranchería of more than five thousand people." Ibid. (It could be that the others moved to new camp as Vicente rode ahead, and the three leagues were measured from there. Juan Rodríguez who was with Vicente said they marched 8 to 10 leagues. Ibid., 865)

4. "They [the Escanjaques] guided us to a river six or seven leagues from this place. It had marvelous level banks, but was so wooded that the trees formed very dense and extensive forests. In some places there were good fords, but in others the water was very deep and ships could easily sail it. The river flowed directly east; its water was fresh and palatable." Ibid., 753.

5 - "We left this place the next day and, leaving the river and crossing some gentle plains, after four leagues we began to see people on a hill. We were forced to camp by the banks of the San Francisco River. The banks were covered with blackberry bushes and fruit trees." Ibid.

North Branch

4 leagues or 10.4 mi.

④ of

6-7 leagues or 15.6-18.2 mi.

↑

Ninnescah

Goose Creek

South Branch

Kingman

Escanjaques

③

3 leagues or 7.8 mi.

of Ninnescah

7 leagues or 18.2 mi.

Chikaskia

②

Medicine Lodge

3 leagues or 7.8 mi.

Medicine Lodge

①

↗

Creek

6 - "We crossed the river at a fine ford, and after marching half a league we came to a settlement containing more that twelve hundred houses, all located on the bank of another fairly good-sized which flowed into the larger one." Ibid., 754.

7 - "The governor and his party must have traveled two [or three, others say] leagues along one side of the houses. At the end of the settlement, it was necessary to turn east to find a road for the carts, and after traveling two leagues we came in one day to a small stream [where] we camped on a hill. [There] the governor ordered the men to turn back to San Gabriel." Ibid., 846-47.

8 - "When we came close to our first camp site in the settlement, the *maese de campo* went ahead with a few men. He found the Escanxajues [sic] camped there. He came back in a hurry saying that the Escanxaques had attacked them and wounded some of the horses. The skirmish [lasted] three or four hours. Ibid., 859.

S. Hoig

FIGURE 20.2. *Oñate's march in Kansas (map by author)*

streams of any consequence in the entire region or eastward into present Oklahoma proper.

Unfortunately, little descriptive information is provided to define the route taken as the *entrada* advanced into Kansas (figure 20.2). Some intangible clues (figure 20.3) offered by the official report and participant

FIGURE 20.3. *Timeline and Projection of Oñate's March to Quivira—1601 (Sundays underlined)*

June 1601	
23	Expedition departs from San Gabriel
24	
25	
26	
27	Expedition reaches Galisteo,
28	assembles there
29	
30	

July 1601	
1	
2	
3	Expedition crosses mountains through Galisteo Pass
4	
5	
6	Pecos River reached
7	
8	Galinas River reached,
9	expedition rests one day,
10	then continues east
11	
12	Canadian River reached
13	and followed eastward
14	
15	
16	
17	
18	
19	
20	
21	

July 1601—*continued*	
22	
23	
24	
25	
26	
27	
28	
29	
30	
31	

August 1601	
1	
2	Ute River reached;
3	army confesses at mass,
4	then continues east along Canadian River
5	
6	
7	
8	
9	
10	First buffalo seen,
11	followed by sizable herds
12	
13	
14	
15	
16	
17	
18	Expedition turns north from Canadian River
19	

continued on next page

FIGURE 20.3.—*continued*

continued on next page

August 1601—*continued*		September 1601—*continued*	
20		20	Escanjaques lead expedition north
21	Expedition marches north,	21	
22	possibly along Palo Duro	22	Expedition meets Rayados
23	Creek to Beaver Creek, then	23	at largest river yet seen
24	turns east between Beaver	24	Oñate camps at Rayado village
25	and Cimarron for "several days"	25	Scouts are sent up Cow Creek
26		26	Expedition marches east to Little Arkansas
27		27	Officers ask Oñate to turn back
28		28	Escanjaques attack expedition
29		29	Return march resumed
30		30	
31			

September 1601		October 1601	
1		1	
2		2	
3		3	
4		4	
5		5	
6		6	
7		7	
8		8	Return made along
9		9	same route as coming,
10		10	using same campsites
11	During this segment	11	
12	of march, expedition	12	
13	crosses two rivers,	13	
14	possibly Medicine Lodge	14	
15	and the Chikaskia	15	
16		16	
17	Vicente scouts ahead;	17	
18	finds Escanjaque camp	18	
19	Expedition visits Escanjaque village	19	

FIGURE 20.3.—*continued*

October 1601—*continued*	November 1601—*continued*
20	6
21	7
22	8
23	9
24	10
25	11
26	12
27	13
28	14
29	15
30	16
31	17
	18
November 1601	19
1	20
2	21
3	22
4	24 San Gabriel reached in 59 days
5	

Of Oñate's march to Quivira, narrative accounts give the date of departure and return, but within that time frame the only dates provided are those on which the Canadian River and, it is thought, the Ute River (Rio de San Francisco) were reached. We are told that the expedition turned north away from the Canadian at 111 leagues, but from that uncertain point we are provided with only scattered references to distances traveled. The above assumes the turn north to have been at the Borger sand hills, and the distance thereafter is calculated according to a theorized route to the Escanjaque camp of the South Ninnescah and the Rayado village on Cow Creek tributary of the Arkansas River according to expedition narratives and the Martinez map.

testimonies include observations that the land was "so level" that *entrada* members occasionally became lost traveling over it, that it was "rich in pastures [grass]," and that there were "multitudes of cattle [buffalo]" in addition to "quail, turkeys, deer, and rabbits."[19]

Oñate's report states also that "occasionally, however, we came to some deep ravines and gorges, but, as for hills, we found none whatever, as the land over which the carts had to travel was level and easy to cross."[20] It is not clear, however, whether this statement refers to the march northward from the Canadian to the Cimarron only or if it also pertains to the countryside beyond. We are told as well that on occasion the expedition strayed somewhat as the *maestre de campo* explored ahead in search of water and camping sites.[21]

Eventually, the Spaniards reached a stream "with little water but with so many trees that its banks looked like a dense forest. At this place we found many walnut trees laden with nuts . . . The land was so thickly covered with grass that one could not see it." After spending the night there, they continued on to a larger stream three leagues distant where there were larger trees—walnuts, oaks, and others—and many fish, quail, turkeys, deer, and jackrabbits.[22]

Exploring on ahead, Vicente and a number of soldiers came onto a large ranchería of an Indian tribe that resided in tents rather than permanent dwellings.[23] At first sighting of the newcomers, the natives prepared to fight. Vicente managed to persuade them that he came in friendship; with Jusepe making use of sign language, the Indians were asked if they had seen any other Spaniards in their lands. They replied that they had and told of Spaniards who had been burned to death in a prairie fire set by Indians around a village eight or ten leagues away. One crippled survivor, they said, was still held prisoner by his captors.[24] Several Indians of the village returned with Vicente to the *entrada*, where they told Oñate the same story. Surely, it seemed, Humaña and Quivira were almost at hand.

At dawn on the day following Vicente's discovery of the Indian village, Oñate led his *entrada* there, "surrounded on all sides by refreshing rivers and delightful groves" as they went.[25] They reached the village at 3:00 that afternoon and went into camp nearby. The next morning Oñate took thirty armed horsemen and the two friars with him and rode into the encampment. They were greeted by an estimated 5,000 to 6,000 persons, young and old, who stood before their huts and raised the palms of their hands sunward. In greeting the Spaniards they placed their hands on their chests, loudly exclaiming what sounded like "Escanjaque." From this, the Spaniards gave them the name Escanjaques.[26]

At this time of year, the tall and well-proportioned (but to the Spaniards unclean) men of the village went entirely naked, while the women wore skins around their lower bodies or covered their privy parts with small pieces of soft skin. Some wore a sort of cloak made of buckskin or buffalo hide. The faces, breasts, and arms of both men and women were painted with stripes, giving them a fierce, warlike appearance.[27]

The Escanjaques, the Spaniards learned, did not plant or harvest crops and subsisted instead in part on roots and berries they gathered. Their main diet was buffalo, the meat of which they dried in the sun and ate uncooked and without salt. Unlike the Pueblo Indians, these tribespeople lived in circular huts made of branches, some standing ten feet tall. Many of the huts were covered with tanned skins "which made them look like tents,"[28] one of which measured ninety feet in diameter at the base. These were the first Plains Indian tepees the Spaniards had encountered.

Captain Juan Gutiérrez Bocanegra saw the Escanjaque homes as "small tents in the shape of pavilions . . . made of buffalo skins."[29] The Escanjaque warriors carried large buffalo-hide shields, bows, arrows, and war clubs that were held to their wrists by leather thongs so they would not lose them in battle. They were very skillful with their bows and arrows.[30]

The Spaniards were able to communicate with the Escanjaques both by sign and through Jusepe's ability to talk with two or three Vaquero Apache Indians in the encampment. Again, Oñate was told of an enemy tribe that resided in a large settlement a few days' travel away. The Escanjaques also repeated the story of the party of strangers that had been killed, saying that one member of the party had escaped the fire even though his feet had been badly burned. This survivor now lived among the other tribe and walked with a cane. The Escanjaques were at war with these people and were eager to join the Spaniards in fighting them.[31]

Oñate wasted little time, hurriedly marching toward the second village that same day, taking as guides two Escanjaques whom he had placed in chains to keep them from running away.[32] In ironing the pair, Don Juan apparently saw no breech of the friendship he professed, although the Escanjaques may have seen it differently. To the Spaniard's displeasure, nearly 100 painted, war-ready Escanjaque warriors trailed them on their march. The Indians indicated by aggressive signs that they wanted to help fight the enemies ahead. They followed the *entrada* to an arroyo three leagues away, camping there for the night. More Escanjaques had trailed behind and wanted to camp with the Spaniards, but Oñate would not allow them to do so.

Setting out again the next morning, the Spaniards traveled six or seven leagues to a river that "had marvelous level banks, but was so wooded that the trees formed very dense extensive forests . . . the river flowed directly east."[33] This easterly flowing, low-banked river is potentially the most specific clue offered as to their geographic position during this segment of the march (see appendix C). The Escanjaques soon arrived and erected a new encampment a short distance away.

From this place the Spaniards continued on, still trailed by the Escanjaques, until they came in view of a crowd of 300 to 400 Indians—all painted fiercely—gathered atop a hill on the opposite bank of a river. These Indians "advanced and challenged us to battle, shouting and throwing dirt into the air, which is the universal sign of war in this land."[34] Because their faces were decorated with stripes, Oñate's men called the Indians "Rayados." Their hostility was evidently directed at the Escanjaques, however, for after an exchange of signs, a few of them advanced in a friendly manner to talk with the Spaniards.[35]

Captain Juan Gutiérrez Bocanegra later testified: "The Governor explained to the [Rayado] Indians that he came to visit their land and that they should become Christians, but the Indians were annoyed because they saw that back of the Spaniards came the Indians we had met earlier at the rancherías who were their enemies."[36]

The Escanjaques continued to insist that the Rayados were the ones who had torched the Humaña party and that it was at their village nearby where the crippled man with burned feet was held.[37] Oñate managed to calm the two tribes to the point that some of them exchanged bows. Through signs, he was able to persuade the Rayados that he had come in peace, enough so that some of them came forth and placed small strings of beads around both his neck and the necks of others. The Indians invited the Spaniards to visit their houses, but the day was too far gone for Oñate to accept. Still, Rayados crossed the river bringing the *entrada* gifts of corn—the first the Spaniards had seen on the plains—and "round loaves of cornbread as big as shields and two or three inches thick."[38] The Spaniards responded with knives and other presents.

The Escanjaques' hostility toward the Rayados continued, however. They appeared the next morning and hurled more challenges against their enemies, again accusing them of having killed the party of Spaniards and of holding the one crippled survivor. Oñate felt he must act. He called a council of his men and discussed the problem. The Rayados' generosity and hospitality notwithstanding, Oñate decided he would seize a few more Indians and place them in chains. His purpose in doing so was not only to verify the Escanjaques' story of a captive Spaniard but also to secure guides who knew the region.[39]

The following morning a Rayado chief called Catarax (Coronado had known a Quivira chief "Tatarax," which scholars have taken as an indication that these were the same people the Spanish had met sixty years earlier; the name was likely a title indicating a head man) and five others crossed the river to visit the *entrada* camp, leaving their several hundred armed followers on the opposite shore.[40]

But instead of receiving the peace delegation in a friendly fashion, Oñate ordered that the Rayado leaders be taken captive and placed in chains. He told the chief he would release him and the others if his people would bring forth the crippled Spaniard. The captives insisted that they did not have the man, saying he was in another village farther on. They warned the Spaniards not to believe what the Escanjaques told them; they were, it was charged, mortal enemies who ate one another.[41] Oñate released one of the hostages with the idea that he would go to the village and bring back the Spaniard. If that was done, Oñate promised, he would release all the hostages, give them many gifts, and be their friend.[42]

As agreed, the Rayado leader was released, but the results were not what Oñate expected. Greatly alarmed by the Escanjaques' threatening posture and the capture of their chief and his men, the Rayados had made a mass exit from their village. When he learned this, Oñate gathered his *entrada* and crossed the river. A march of half a league brought them to the vacated Rayado settlement, which cluttered the banks of a tributary that flowed into the larger river for some distance.

Twelve hundred dome-roofed thatched huts stood silent and deserted amid stands of browned cornstalks (figure 20.4). Crops of beans and calabashes as well as new plantings of corn, uncultivated grape vines, and plum bushes were scattered between the huts, all giving testimony to an agrarian practice among the tribe. Oñate's official report on the expedition effectively described the Rayado village, providing a parallel view to the more limited accounts given by the Coronado Expedition:

> The houses were all round, made of forked wooden poles joined
> together by sticks and on the outside covered with straw. Inside they
> had some mats at the sides which they used as beds or cots on which
> to sleep. Most of the houses, which were two spears high, were so large
> that they could hold eight or ten persons. All had a flat roof or terrace
> [loft], about six feet high, with room for three or four persons, which
> they must have used in the summer, and which they entered through a
> suitable small straw door. To enjoy the fresh air they climbed to the top

FIGURE 20.4. *Early Indian homes in Texas*

by means of a portable wooden ladder; and there was no house which did not have a terrace.[43]

In his testimony, soldier Baltasar Martínez provided further description of the houses he witnessed on both banks of a small river that emptied into a larger one:

The houses, grouped in suburbs of thirty or forty houses each, are thirty or forty paces apart. From group to group there was a space of two or three hundred paces. The houses were built of small poles stuck in the ground close together, and brought together at the top in the shape of a pavilion. They were circular at the base and seventy or eighty feet in circumference. Their doors were so small that to enter one had to get to his knees. They closed them with mats made of twigs and straw. Inside they used one-half or one-third of the space for their beds, which they built of poles with sticks laid crosswise; they were about the size of the rope beds in Castile. About one-fourth of the distance from the top of the house they had a sort of terrace, to which they climbed on the outside by a wooden ladder . . . They covered the outside entirely with straw.[44]

Unfortunately, a witness claimed, all of the houses were so infested with fleas that going inside constituted dire punishment. One *entrada* member said the Rayados kept their corn in silos apart from the houses. Another Spaniard, however, described the corn as kept in small wooden terraces on the outside of the houses that were reached by ladders. Another said it was kept in the ear on the ground in the houses.[45]

One expedition member said he saw no metates for grinding the corn. He did witness, however, a small stone that may have been used for producing flour, such as that used in the cornbread the Indians had brought the *entrada*. Also found were ollas and clay jugs.[46] There was no evidence that the Rayados had experienced cloth, as had the Pueblo Indians of New Mexico, or metal in any form. Further, the Spaniards found no dogs, cats, or fowl—not even feathers—in the village.

More important, Oñate discovered, as had Coronado, that there was nothing that smacked of treasure in the Great Settlement—no golden vessels, golden dishes, golden earrings, or even pearls. Further, the primitive nature of the village and its inhabitants did nothing to validate the Quiviran myth or the glistening promises Oñate had managed to obtain from his original interview with Jusepe.

By his aggressive treatment of the Rayado chiefs, Oñate had denied himself the opportunity to make a thorough investigation regarding the Spanish prisoner they were said to hold. The man, as far as anyone knew, could have been Humaña. If a crippled survivor of the Humaña-Leyva party had still been alive in a Rayado village, he would likely have been killed as a result of Oñate's belligerent actions. Further, Oñate made no effort to learn more about the Rayados as a people. Nowhere in the literature of his march is there mention of the Spaniards having met a Rayado woman or family.[47]

Worse still, Don Juan had created fear and hostility among the Indians that presented a serious threat to his expedition. He had antagonized both the Escanjaques and the Rayados who, though enemies themselves, now saw the Spaniards as dangerous intruders. This, in turn, was destructive of his further search for the Golden City. As it had for Coronado, the threat of native hostility would force him to turn back without resolving conclusively whether such a city truly existed. Equally important to his overall mission, there is no indication that any time or effort was given to either pacify or Christianize the prairie Indians.

The Escanjaques followed the *entrada* into the village and immediately began sacking the houses of their corn supplies and setting fire to the structures. Oñate sent mounted soldiers to stop the burning, though he did permit the looters to take some corn before they left. Since it was late in the day, he ordered that four of the Rayado hostages and the two Escanjaques be released. It was hoped that the Rayados would encourage their fellow villagers to return to their homes. Oñate again pressed the two remaining Rayados for information on the Humaña party and the Spaniard with burned feet.

The two Rayado prisoners continued to insist that they knew nothing about such a prisoner. One, who appeared to be of higher rank because he persistently had the other speak for him, said Humaña and his men had been killed eighteen days' travel from where they now were. He said there were numerous other settlements and multitudes of people farther upstream and along another large river fed by six or seven branches. That night the two Rayados escaped from the soldier assigned to guard them.

Having released the two Escanjaques, Oñate was now without a resident guide. He dispatched a captain and several soldiers to go ahead and explore up the river "to see if they could discover a column of smoke in order to get an Indian guide."[48] The men returned that night to report that they had traveled three leagues and found settlements all along the way. Fearing to go farther, they returned to report to Oñate.[49] Still needing a guide, Oñate sent more soldiers out to capture such. The detail returned with four or five Escanjaques found still looting the village.

Oñate checked the Rayados' statements against those of the Escanjaques and found that the information substantially agreed. The Escanjaques said there was another stream to the east of the Rayados that was much inhabited and had larger villages. But they warned that because the Indians were so numerous, it would be very dangerous for the Spaniards to go there.[50] Oñate showed them some pins, some of gold and some of silver, but the Indians said they had never seen things made of such materials before.[51] This was discouraging because it indicated that metallic items had not surfaced even through Indian trade.

But Oñate, still nourishing hopes of making a worthy discovery, was not to be deterred. With the Escanjague prisoners as guides, he broke camp and set the *entrada* forth up the tributary alongside the Rayado village: "We traveled on one side of it with our carts for about two leagues and counted seventeen hundred houses . . . and saw many more in the distance."[52] With the end of the settlement still not in sight, the *entrada* turned eastward toward a tree line that indicated the parallel river the

Escanjaques had described. After traveling two leagues, they reached the stream.

There, Oñate faced a small insurrection. He was presented with a petition signed by nearly all of his officers and soldiers. The petition had been promoted by Captain Dionisio de Bañuelos (who was later found guilty for his role in the murders of Captains Pablo de Aguilar and Alonso de Sosa Albornoz) in the face of a growing concern among *entrada* members regarding the danger they faced. The petition stoutly requested that the *entrada* turn back for home.[53]

The main purpose of the *entrada*, it contended, had been accomplished merely in discovering the greatness of the country—even though nothing certain had been learned about the Humaña-Leyva party, no indication of great mineral wealth had been found or other great discovery made, and the priests had had no chance to convert any of the now-hostile natives. Yet the petition contended that great things could still be achieved:

> We pointed out that a greater service would be done his majesty by informing him of the high quality of the land, the many people, the wealth in cattle sufficient alone to enrich thousands of men with their tallow, fat, and hides, and the good places with the necessary materials for establishing important settlements; and above all the great importance that the king our lord should learn quickly about the discovery of what had been so eagerly sought throughout the world, in order that we might execute promptly what his majesty might command.[54]

It was further suggested that, in the governor's extended absence, the army (i.e., the colony) might become unruly and abandon San Gabriel. This, indeed, would prove to be very much the case. Oñate, very reluctantly some thought, consented to the petition and ordered the *entrada* to turn homeward.[55] Nothing more was said of the crippled Spaniard supposedly still held captive somewhere to the north.

The Spaniards were few in number, the petition argued, in a remote, heavily populated land with many warring enemies who were assembling to attack them. Winter was coming, they were short of arms, and the horses and mules were badly worn. When asked later if the expedition could have built a fort and spent the winter on the plains, expedition member Baltasar Martínez answered:

> It would have been extremely difficult, because the Indians were unfriendly and the army had already consumed two-thirds of the corn

flour and they would have been forced to eat only whole corn as there was no means for grinding it. Furthermore, the horses could not be let loose on the plains, but would have to be enclosed, in which case the corn would have to be saved for them. Therefore he doubts the men could have withstood the winter there and thinks the return was wise.[56]

Breaking camp the next morning, September 27 or 28, the *entrada* headed back over the route by which it had come from the Rayado village.[57] Vicente was riding ahead with twelve men in battle array to look for trouble as they approached their former campsite at around 2:00 in the afternoon. He found it soon enough when he saw that the Escanjaques were camped at the Rayado village with all their women and children and were still burning houses there. When he tried to intervene, the Indians began firing arrows at the soldiers, wounding some of them.[58]

Vicente fell back to the main column, then half a league behind, and organized his fighting force for what may have been the first white-Indian battle in the state of Kansas. Soldiers donned their armor, primed their harquebuses and artillery, and draped their horses with the thick cowhide shields. As they marched forward to meet the Indians, numbering in the hundreds and including women and children, the soldiers raised their palms to the sky as a sign of peace. But the Escanjaques were determined to fight and attacked with great fury. They formed a semicircle and attempted to surround the Spaniards, showering them with arrows and wounding several more. Juan Rodríguez, a soldier, described the action: "The Escanjaques attacked noisily and shot numerous arrows, while the Spaniards fired their harquebuses and an artillery piece; after the latter had knocked down and killed a few Indians, the natives retired behind some rocks where they entrenched themselves and came out from time to time to shoot many arrows and set fire to the plain. This skirmish lasted four or five hours, and thirty soldiers received light wounds."[59]

With their harquebuses and swords, the Spaniards drove the Escanjaques to cover, killing or wounding a number of them and capturing eight or ten of their women and boys. After a while Oñate ordered the women released and, with that, the fighting ceased. The Indian boys were held, however, and turned over to the friars. After camping that night under heavy guard, the *entrada* resumed its return trip home.

Soldier Juan de León later testified: "On the next day we continued our march toward San Gabriel over the same route and stopping at the same campsites as on the way out."[60]

ABBREVIATION KEY

H/R-*DJO* = Hammond and Rey, eds., *Don Juan de Oñate*
W-*CE* = Winship, *The Coronado Expedition, 1540–1542*

NOTES

1. "Merits and Services of Zaldívar," H/R-*DJO* 2: 890.
2. "Report of Loyal Colonists," H/R-*DJO* 2: 730–731.
3. "Expedition to Quivira," H/R-*DJO* 2: 746.
4. "Summary of the Five Discoveries," H/R-*DJO* 2: 901.
5. Bolton, *Spanish Exploration*, 253.
6. We are told that the *entrada* made its 220-league return march from the plains over the same route in fifty-nine days, thus averaging 3.73 leagues (±9.7 miles) per day. "Expedition to Quivira," H/R-*DJO* 2: 758; Bolton, *Spanish Exploration*, 265. Undoubtedly, hunting and rest stops figured into this calculation. Thus, it could be reasoned that a day's march, for both men and animals, was likely farther on the average.
7. Reinhartz and Saxon, *Mapping of the Entradas*, 77. The map is now held by the Archivo de Indies.
8. A league is equivalent to approximately 2.4 miles.
9. "Expedition to Quivira," H/R-*DJO* 2: 746–760.
10. "Valverde Inquiry," H/R-*DJO* 2: 839.
11. Ibid., 852.
12. Ibid., 839.
13. Ibid., 852.
14. "Expedition to Quivira," H/R-*DJO* 2: 747.
15. Ibid., 749.
16. Ibid.
17. "Valverde Inquiry," H/R-*DJO* 2: 839.
18. "Expedition to Quivira," H/R-*DJO* 2: 750; Bolton, *Spanish Exploration*, 255.
19. "Expedition to Quivira," H/R-*DJO* 2: 751. Bolton translates this as "partridges, turkeys, deer, and hares"; *Coronado*, 257. Several reports described the deer as astonishingly large. Likely, these were elk, which frequented the lower plains even into the nineteenth century.
20. "Expedition to Quivira," H/R-*DJO* 2: 750.
21. Ibid., 751.
22. Ibid.
23. Ibid.
24. "Merits and Services of Zaldívar," H/R-*DJO* 2: 890.
25. "Expedition to Quivira," H/R-*DJO* 2: 752.
26. "Valverde Inquiry," H/R-*DJO* 2: 865.

27. Ibid., 841, 854.

28. "Expedition to Quivira," H/R-*DJO* 2: 752. Rodríguez saw the Escanjaque houses as round huts "made of branches and straw, most of them covered with buffalo hides"; ibid., 865.

29. "Valverde Inquiry," H/R-*DJO* 2: 889.

30. "Expedition to Quivira," H/R-*DJO* 2: 752.

31. Ibid., 752, 754; "Zaldívar Inquiry," H/R-*DJO* 2: 806, 855, 865.

32. "Zaldívar Inquiry," H/R-*DJO* 2: 855.

33. "Expedition to Quivira," H/R-*DJO* 2: 753. Martínez described this stop beyond the Escanjaque village by saying that "the water was muddy but fresh. It was surrounded by good valleys and pleasing groves of trees"; ibid., 842. "Expedition to Quivira," H/R-*DJO* 2: 752n13, identifies this stream as the Arkansas, but it could have been the north branch of the Ninnescah, which has low, well-wooded banks and briefly runs due east below Hutchinson, Kansas. See appendix C for a discussion of Oñate's march from the Escanjaque village to the meeting with the Rayados.

34. "Expedition to Quivira," H/R-*DJO* 2: 753.

35. Ibid.

36. "Merits and Services of Zaldívar," H/R-*DJO* 2: 890.

37. "Valverde Inquiry," H/R-*DJO* 2: 843.

38. "Expedition to Quivira," H/R-*DJO* 2: 753.

39. Ibid., 754.

40. "Valverde Inquiry," H/R-*DJO* 2: 856.

41. Ibid., 843. The practice of cannibalism provides a distinct tribal trait that could help identify Escanjaque descendants who migrated southward on the Central Plains. French explorer Bernard de la Harpe met captive-eating Indians residing on the Arkansas River of northeastern Oklahoma in 1719; Lewis, "La Harpe's First Expedition in Oklahoma," 342. It is known that the Tonkawas of Texas practiced cannibalism well into the nineteenth century.

42. Ibid., 856.

43. "Expedition to Quivira," H/R-*DJO* 2: 754. This description compares to Castañeda's description in 1541: "The houses are round, without a wall, and they have one story like a loft, under the roof, where they sleep and keep their belongings. The roofs are of straw"; "Translation of Castañeda," W-*CE*, 280–283.

44. "Valverde Inquiry," H/R-*DJO* 2: 844–845.

45. Ibid., 845, 857.

46. Ibid., 845, 866.

47. "Expedition to Quivira," H/R-*DJO* 2: 755; "Valverde Inquiry," H/R-*DJO* 2: 844.

48. "Valverde Inquiry," H/R-*DJO* 2: 846.

49. "Merits and Services of Zaldívar," H/R-*DJO* 2: 890–891.

50. "Expedition to Quivira," H/R-*DJO* 2: 755–756.

51. "Valverde Inquiry," H/R-*DJO* 2: 844, 867.

52. Ibid., 867–868.

53. Ibid., 846, 858; "Oñate's Conviction," H/R-*DJO* 2: 1120–1121. Don Francisco de Valverde testified that he along with Vicente and five or six others refused to sign the petition because they thought the expedition should explore further and obtain more information.

54. "Expedition to Quivira," H/R-*DJO* 2: 756.

55. "Valverde Inquiry," H/R-*DJO* 2: 858.

56. Ibid., 847.

57. Ibid., 859.

58. "Merits and Services of Zaldívar," H/R-*DJO* 2: 891.

59. "Valverde Inquiry," H/R-*DJO* 2: 868.

60. Ibid., 859.

21

The Colonists Revolt

The natives had helped us during the four years that we have been here, hereby giving us all the provisions they had saved up for many years, and the situation has become so desperate that many of the natives are starving to death.

Gregorio Céssar[1]

When the Quivira expedition returned to San Gabriel, Oñate found to his great dismay that during his absence a sizable number of colonists, officers, soldiers, and churchmen had banded together and returned to Mexico. When he departed for the plains in June, he had left behind seventy people, including a number of families.[2] As they watched him march away with a large portion of his army, a majority of those remaining felt a great rush of freedom. They saw their chance to escape from the oppression and sordid conditions under which they had lived for many months.

Led by the friars and some army officers, many colonists began making plans to flee back to Mexico before the Quivira expedition returned and to report to the viceroy their "legitimate" reasons for abandoning the post.[3] They had many grievances, all of which were exacerbated, as Viceroy Monterrey informed King Philip, "by fear of the threats and punishments inflicted by Don Juan [de Oñate] until then to prevent their departure and to maintain the colony. This situation was intensified by their lack of freedom to send accounts to Mexico of their demands or complaints, which can easily be understood from the meagerness or lack of correspondence with them during the last five years."[4]

The rising mutiny among those at San Gabriel had come to the attention of Francisco de Sosa Peñalosa, whom Oñate had appointed lieutenant governor and captain general to command the post during his absence. Though Sosa Peñalosa empathized with the complainants, he had duly rejected requests of those seeking to leave. But the call to escape became so widespread among the Spaniards still at San Gabriel that the lieutenant governor called a general meeting of army officers, church officials, and others to discuss the matter.[5] Thus, on September 7, 1601, as Oñate's Quivira expedition marched across the buffalo prairies of western Kansas, the Spanish residents of San Gabriel pueblo gathered at their church to discuss and give testimony in support of abandoning Oñate's effort to colonize New Mexico.

After Fray Francisco de San Miguel (vice commissary of the province) and four other frays had conducted a high mass, Sosa Peñalosa recorded testimony from the friars and sympathetic army men as to why it was desirable to move to another place (safely out of Oñate's jurisdiction of New Mexico) from which the viceroy could be informed of their reasons for leaving San Gabriel. Fray San Miguel was the first to make his religious and legal oath and to testify. In his lengthy statement he observed, "From the time he came here to the moment of this statement, his conscience has ever been disturbed by the mistreatment of these natives."[6]

Fray San Miguel said that for some time he had been trying to hold back those who wanted to leave because he felt they would take the few horses still left in camp. In doing so, they would endanger those remaining at the hands of Indians who were waiting for an opportune moment to attack. But now, because of such great poverty and the absence of the rule of law in the land, he had concluded that people must be allowed to leave and report the true state of affairs to the viceroy.

Fray Francisco de Zamora concurred and spoke also regarding the treatment of natives: "They [Oñate's men] took away from them by force all the food that they had gathered for many years, without leaving them any for the support of themselves and their children."[7] He also swore to having seen Indians stabbed and knifed when goods were taken from them and complained of soldiers violating Indian women along the roads.

Fray Lope Izquierdo also testified concerning the injustices perpetrated upon pueblo natives, telling how "our men, with little consideration, took the blankets away from the Indian women, leaving them naked and shivering with cold. Finding themselves naked and miserable, they embraced their children tightly in their arms to warm and protect them, without making any resistance to the offense done them."[8] Frays Gastón de Peralta and Damián Escudero concurred fully with these testimonies.[9]

Army captains Alonso Sánchez, Alférez Bernabé de las Casas, Diego de Zubía, and Gregorio Céssar gave their depositions, telling of the contributions they had made to the colony, the services they had rendered, the hardships they and their families had endured, and the great financial losses they had suffered. They, too, spoke of the desperate conditions the Spaniards had inflicted upon the natives.

At the time of the meeting, the Quivira expedition had been gone two and a half months. No one knew when it might return, so the dissenters were aware that time was of the essence. They knew full well that when Don Juan returned, he would almost surely send troops after them. And everyone knew about his punishments. It was vital that they reach the Mexico haven of Santa Bárbara as quickly as possible, where they could place themselves under royal jurisdiction and make their pleas to the viceroy in Mexico City.

Viceroy Monterrey reported that first one group and then others began to arrive. "They took their departure from that post [San Gabriel]," he noted, "but messages kept coming, both from those who had remained behind (charging the others with being deserters), and from those who had fled, some bringing papers, others none."[10]

One of those arriving was Oñate supporter Captain Gerónimo Márquez. On October 2, even before Oñate returned, the loyalist "one-third or one-fourth" who had remained at San Gabriel met with Sosa Peñalosa. They nominated Márquez "to appear before his majesty or the viceroy of New Spain to inform him in our name of the present situation in this land, and also of our dire need for aid."[11] Twenty-three loyalist men who had remained at San Gabriel signed the petition requesting permission for Márquez to go to New Spain.

When he appeared before Sosa Peñalosa, Márquez testified to several facts, among them that many of those who had gone on the Quivira expedition had wives, children, and belongings in camp and expected to find them when they returned. He said "certain captains" had plotted the desertion and that the friars had supported them in sermons. He claimed also that there was presently an abundance of corn and wheat in the camp and that gardens were filled with fruits and vegetables. The captain further defended Vicente's attack on the Jumanos, who he said were the aggressors. Upon learning of the plan to desert, he said, many Indian slaves had run away for fear they would be taken from their native land or, if the Spaniards abandoned the land, that they would become infidels again.[12]

Loyalist Cristóbal Baca swore under oath that the native Indians were peaceful and virtuous, that they readily accepted the holy gospel, that the land of the interior was of very good quality and abounded in Cibola cattle, that those who deserted had taken property left with them by those who went on the Quivira expedition, that abandoning the land might cause serious harm to men on the expedition, and that there was plenty of wheat and cattle available at San Gabriel. He further supported everything Márquez had stated. Other loyalists testified similarly, insisting that the leaders of the mutineers had conducted a concerted but dishonest campaign to recruit members and get them to sign a petition to leave. They also blamed the priests, who they said made a sudden reversal in their sermons from encouraging everyone to support the colony and then abruptly telling them to do the opposite.

In response to this last charge, a board of the Order of St. Francis wrote the viceroy: "The best defense for the cause of the order consists in the fact that Governor Don Juan de Oñate is on bad terms with the friars of St. Francis. They will never enjoy peace while he is governor, because your lordship is perfectly aware of the just reasons which the friars have had on certain occasions to reprove him for the cruelties and killings inflicted on the poor Indians by his command."[13]

Monterrey was thoroughly conflicted by the opposing claims and countercharges. "With the arrival of the letters and reports upholding and denouncing those who are leaving New Mexico," he reported to the king, "the matter was greatly complicated."[14] He recommended that learned theologians and lawyers study the problem and offer their opinion. He referred the issue to priests in the Company of Jesus Ecclesiastical College at Mexico City for their consideration.[15]

Oñate arrived back from his Quivira quest to find his colony virtually deserted. Not only were most of the colonists gone, but others were on the verge of leaving. "We found that this treason had been carried out," Vicente de Zaldívar wrote, "all of which had been done on the order, advice, and machination of the friars."[16] Don Juan was furious to the extreme. He knew what to do about the captains and colonists, but the Franciscan priests were outside his authority. He immediately assumed his role as chief magistrate of the colony and decreed that the captains were traitors subject to beheading. He dispatched Vicente with a party to overtake and arrest the fleeing colonists. "The governor at once gave orders," Vicente wrote, "to proceed against these traitors, and, after having tried the case, he pronounced sentence as their crime deserved, and he ordered me to set out in pursuit of them and to execute the sentence . . . before they reached Santa Bárbara."[17]

But it was too late. The mutineers were already safely under arrest by royal officers at Santa Bárbara and busy issuing their long-pent-up complaints against Oñate. Though disheartened that he was unable to punish the "traitors," Vicente was determined that, should "justice be left unadministered" in Mexico, he would personally take the matter to Spain and bring it before the king. Eventually, he would do just that.[18]

In early January 1602, the theologians in Mexico City issued a studied reply to Monterrey regarding the San Gabriel colonists. They concluded that the colonists in New Mexico were not part of a formal army and could not be considered deserting soldiers. Nor could they "be forced to return to New Mexico," where they would "fall under the power of the one against whom they have formulated so many complaints." An opinion overriding all else was that there should be "free communication and circulation of letters, dispatches, and other matters between that province and this kingdom of Mexico."[19]

The theologians also concluded that apostolic preachers who had converted natives to the Christian faith and conducted baptisms had a divine obligation not to abandon them. As to the soldiers who had deserted, the theologians defied Oñate's contention that he was not under the authority of the viceroy, stating: "It [any decision regarding deserters] cannot and must not be entrusted to the governor of New Mexico or to any person dependent on him, as we may reasonably fear some excess if he were the judge in a case affecting himself."[20]

When he arrived in Mexico City, Vicente brought the Indian man called Miguel who had been captured in the battle with the Escanjaques. When questioned in the home of Captain Cristóbal Vaca at San Gabriel,

Miguel had said—or at least he had been understood to say—that two days from where he had been taken prisoner "there were ingots of gold which the natives traded for buffalo hides." He had indicated that the gold was found in a river, and the more water it carried, the more gold was obtained. He said he had witnessed the natives there pile it up on shore, then smelt it by fire and cast it into vases and one-to two-pound ingots for trade purposes. The king, who wore a blanket over his shoulder and before whom others bowed down, used cups made of gold.[21]

During April 1602, Miguel was interviewed for the Audiencia of Mexico before witnesses and with an interpreter in the home of the factor (chief officer) of the royal treasury. Some Mexican Indians were brought forth, along with a variety of wild animal skins, metallic trinkets, and other items assembled there to serve as objects of discussion. Miguel was described as "well built and had good features, somewhat darker than the Mexican Indians."[22]

First, he was asked to make marks on a sheet of paper, depicting the villages in his land. He did so, making "Os" of various sizes for village locations. The factor then ordered that the name of the town, as Miguel enunciated it, be written in each circle. Next Miguel drew lines, some straight and some snaking, to indicate rivers and roads. These, too, were given names. He then explained by signs at which point he had been born, where he had been captured as a boy about twelve years old, and where he had been taken prisoner by the Spaniards (figure 21.1).[23] (See appendix D for a discussion of Miguel's map.)

Next, Miguel was shown a group of flowers and asked if any like them were present in his land. He looked at them carefully, rejecting all but those he said were plentiful where he lived. The Mexican Indians were then brought forth, some well dressed in colorful blankets. Some were daubed with paint, while others were more ordinary but carried bows and arrows and other war gear. Miguel studied them before conveying that all people in his land were naked except for deerskins and the hides of native cattle.

Shown a turkey, he said they had them. Shown green turquoise, he said they had none. Shown a variety of bows and arrows, he pointed to the largest bows and arrows with long flint points. He indicated that in his native home they raised corn and made it into rolls. But where he had been held captive (at the Escanjaque camp), they had no corn and ate only deer and buffalo meat. He said that in his homeland there was

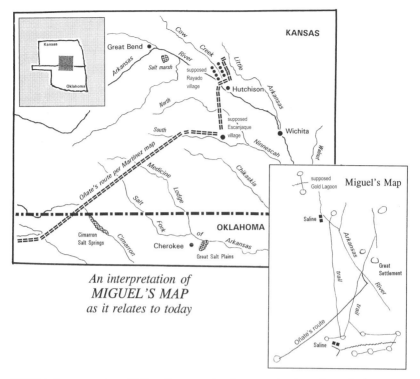

An interpretation of
MIGUEL'S MAP
as it relates to today

FIGURE 21.1. *Interpretation of Miguel's map as it relates to today (map by author)*

a king; at the Great Settlement there were a great chief and a lesser one, but where he was held captive among the Escanjaques there were several small lords.[24]

The factor then dismissed all of the Indians and most of the Spaniards from the room and displayed gold dust, a gold cup, gold and silver ingots, copper pieces, and some polished brass. The Indian looked the items over carefully before taking the largest gold ingot and placing it on the circle he had drawn for Encuche. Then he made signs that were "easily understood" to mean that such gold was used to purchase meat and hides from other places.

Asked if gold was obtained from the river at the place marked Encuche on his map, he answered that he heard it was obtained from a lake beyond Encuche that is about the depth of a man; they obtained it as dust and then took it to Encuche, where it was made into ingots. Asked if he knew or had seen how the gold ingots were made (see figure 21.2),

FIGURE 21.2. *How Indians could have smelted gold*

Miguel said that he twice saw them made at Tancoa, in his own land. They placed the gold dust in vases that had a hole in each of the four sides, and at each hole a man put in wood and fanned the fire with fans made of buffalo hide. They kept the vase covered for three or four days, then melted the gold and made ingots of the size stated. The captive Plains Indian said also that he had not only seen drinking cups made of gold but that he had drunk from them himself.[25]

The factor saw a contradiction in Miguel's answers, noting that he said he was a grown man when he saw ingots made at Encuche but also that he had never been back there after being taken captive as a boy. Communication was too difficult for the Spaniards to pursue the matter further, but Miguel had shown that the myth of Quivira was not yet dead and buried.

ABBREVIATION KEY

H/R-*DJO* = Hammond and Rey, eds., *Don Juan de Oñate*

NOTES

1. "Desertion of the Colony," H/R-*DJO* 2: 688.

2. "Monterrey to King, March 8, 1602," H/R-*DJO* 2: 770.

3. "Breaking Camp at San Gabriel," H/R-*DJO* 2: 672–673.

4. "Monterrey to King, March 8, 1602," H/R-*DJO* 2: 770–771.

5. "Breaking Camp at San Gabriel," H/R-*DJO* 2: 672.

6. Ibid., 673.

7. Ibid., 675.

8. Ibid., 680.

9. Ibid., 682–683.

10. "Viceroy to King, March 8, 1602," H/R-*DJO* 2: 771.

11. "Report of Loyal Colonists," H/R-*DJO* 2: 701. One soldier claimed he had been shown a paper by two deserting captains that contained fifty-seven signatures, then he signed but did not leave; ibid., 725.

12. Ibid., 705–706.

13. "Petition of the Franciscans," H/R-*DJO* 2: 982.

14. "Viceroy to King, March 8, 1602," H/R-*DJO* 2: 771.

15. "Reply of the Theologians," H/R-*DJO* 2: 775–781.

16. "Zaldívar to Oñate's Agents," H/R-*DJO* 2: 768.

17. Ibid., 768; Simmons, *Last Conquistador*, 109.

18. "Zaldívar to Oñate's Agents," H/R-*DJO* 2: 769.

19 "Reply of the Theologians," H/R-*DJO* 2: 778–780.

20. Ibid., 779.

21. "Valverde Inquiry," H/R-*DJO* 2: 860, 869.

22. Ibid., 872.

23. Miguel's map is presented here. Not surprisingly, the map is confusing to a viewer today. See appendix D for a discussion of the map.

24. "Valverde Inquiry," H/R-*DJO* 2: 873–874.

25. Ibid., 875–876.

22

Tales Too Tall

*From his signed report and from four witnesses who returned
with the friar I cannot help but inform your majesty that this
conquest is becoming a fairy tale.*

Marquis of Montesclaros[1]

At virtually the same time the Mexico City theologians were deciding
against him, Don Juan de Oñate's power was enhanced considerably when
King Philip appointed him *adelantado* of the provinces of New Mexico.
Philip declared: "You shall have the power to exercise this office in all the
cases and matters pertaining thereto, in the same manner as is done by my
adelantados in the kingdoms of Castile and in the Indies."[2]

This appointment came as a result of efforts by Don Juan's brother,
Don Alonso de Oñate, who had been in Spain since early 1600 bombarding the king with petitions in Don Juan's favor.[3] After making a presentation on Don Juan's behalf to the viceroy and Audiencia in Mexico City,
Vicente de Zaldívar also arrived in Spain during late 1602. He brought
glowing reports of the situation in New Mexico and pleas for financial
help to secure 300 fully equipped men so Don Juan could continue his
exploration and colonization efforts.[4]

At the same time, revelations of the conditions in New Mexico and of the numerous charges that had been launched against Don Juan, Vicente, and other officers reached the king. Principal among these reports was a lengthy discussion of Oñate's situation by Monterrey. The viceroy had made an exhaustive study of the discoveries by Cabeza de Vaca, Friar Marcos, Coronado, Chamuscado, Espejo, and others. While he accepted the loyalist argument that things in New Mexico were not as bad as the San Gabriel mutineers had said, he concluded: "From what I have learned here, I am not able to convince myself that this discovery by Don Juan has shed any valuable light on the information we already possessed about those plains."[5]

Monterrey was instructed to learn the truth about the accusations made against Oñate. "If he found Don Juan guilty and matters in such a state that it would be undesirable to leave him in charge, the viceroy should assume responsibility for the expedition in order to preserve what has been discovered and to continue the conversion of the Indians."[6]

In Spain, Don Alonso worked to secure royal assistance for a new expedition in his brother's continuing effort to discover the South Sea. Don Juan hoped to establish there a seaport from which his colony could be supplied rather than having to continue to use the long land route from Mexico City. The Council of the Indies, and thereupon the king, did agree to Don Alonso's request for supplying Don Juan with musketeers, shipwrights, and navigational pilots to explore for a supply port on the coast of the yet-undiscovered South Sea.[7]

Don Alonso learned, however, that he would have to pay for provisioning the ship's transportation from Spain to America.[8] The records do not indicate whether this hitch was overcome. But from Don Juan's letter of appreciation to the viceroy, it appears that this help did reach Oñate and that it provided support for a new South Sea venture.[9]

Grave doubts had been raised about the entire plan for New Mexico colonization. But even as the king and his high officials were debating New Mexico's fate, Don Juan was still engaged in the activities of discovery as he struggled to hold his disrupted colony together. The problems of conquest emerged once again with the pueblo of Taos, where the first of a long series of puebloan rebellions occurred (figure 22.1). The records speak only briefly of this event, but in 1603 Don Juan evidently conducted a punitive attack on the pueblo. We know this only because of accusations that he threw a young chief to his death from the roof of a Taos pueblo.[10]

PUEBLO OF TAOS—NORTH PUEBLO

FIGURE 22.1. *Pueblo of Taos*

During the spring of 1604, Oñate launched a peace mission to other pueblos through Frays Francisco de Velasco, Juan de Escalona, and Francisco de Escobar. Under the escort of Captain Gerónimo Márquez and a small group of soldiers, the friars went first to Acoma, where the natives—now subdued—had rebuilt their sky pueblo. Leaving his church companions there, Velasco accompanied Márquez and his men on to the Arizona homelands of the Zuni, Moqui, and Cruzado Indians, with whom friendly relations were reestablished.[11]

But otherwise the records are disturbingly silent concerning the post-Quivira period of Oñate's New Mexico colony. It appears that following the departure of the mutineering faction, even less was heard of events in Oñate's New Mexico colony than before. It is known that no quests of any significance were undertaken between 1602 and 1604. Oñate simply did not have the men or the resources for such. He had used up most of his personal fortune as well as the wealth of his family in Mexico; with questions concerning both his leadership and the worth of the New Mexico effort haunting Spanish officials, he received little additional help from the Crown.

His quests had been minimal at best. The discoveries he had made thus far had all failed to be of material value. He and his men had considered returning to Quivira and searching further on to discover a golden city. But it seems apparent that, much as it had been with Coronado and despite the stories of gold told by Miguel, neither he nor many of his men had much faith in the notion. Without a treasure trove, Quivira offered nothing more than great herds of buffalo and native souls to convert to Christianity. Marquis de Montesclaros, who replaced Monterrey as viceroy of Mexico in 1603, was even more skeptical: "The light that we have thus far gathered on this expedition reveals that the people [of Quivira] are rustic, wretched in clothes and spirit, that they do not possess silver or gold, [that they] dwell in straw and grass houses, and live on native fruits such as maize and vegetables, which they say are grown twice a year in places. Instead of cotton, I have been assured that they weave dog hair."[12]

Even the mines Marcos de los Farfán Godos had discovered in Arizona proved impotent. Hoping that they were rich in silver, Oñate sent samples of the ores to Mexico City to be assayed. Disappointingly, they were one-eighth copper without a trace of silver. Montesclaros expressed his dismay with this finding as well as with the glowing reports he had been receiving from Oñate. He told the king, "All these conjectures, Sir, are arguments that lead nowhere."[13]

In the fall of 1604, Oñate set out on his new search for the South Sea. During the journey he sought to establish relations with Indian tribes he encountered along the way and reaffirm Spanish conquest of their regions. Fray Francisco de Escobar, who kept a diary of the six-month march, told of Oñate's party leaving San Gabriel on October 7, 1604, with thirty mounted soldiers under Captain Márquez, accompanied by Escobar and lay brother Juan de San Buenaventura. The fifty people left behind at the capital reflect the reduced size of the New Mexico colony during this period.[14] Traveling directly west and retracing in reverse Coronado's original route, Oñate first visited the Zuni pueblos of northeastern Arizona and then the Hopi settlements, taking possession of the land in the name of King Philip III. Moving southwestward across the Little Colorado, the party reached Bill Williams Fork, the course of which led them to the mighty Colorado and on south to where the river empties into the Gulf of California.

During the expedition, Don Juan interrogated natives thoroughly regarding any metals they might know about, displaying gold objects and silver spoons to see if they were familiar to the tribesmen. But the yellow bracelets the Indians wore proved to be brass, and the likeness of the spoons was thought to be tin.[15] Escobar wrote: "They almost convinced me beyond all doubt that there were both yellow and white metals in the land, though there is no proof that the yellow metal is gold or that the white is silver, for of this my doubts are still very great."[16]

The expedition reached the Gulf of California in late January 1605. It was an exhilarating moment for them all, especially Oñate. Notwithstanding that Hernando de Alarcón had landed there in 1540, Don Juan strode into the lapping gulf tide and flailed it with his sword, declaring possession in the name of the Spanish king. Fray Juan de San Buenaventura followed suit, raising his crucifix to the heavens to proclaim the spiritual blessing of the church.[17]

Oñate may not have known about Alarcón's earlier visit, any more than he failed to realize that the waters he had found were not open sea but a gulf. What is now Lower California was then thought to be an island. The geographic misconception that it provided a direct sea link to China seriously debased the value of Onáte's discovery. While he had found a good potential port, it never served the cause of resupplying the New Mexico colony.

But the most harmful aspect of the expedition was caused by Father Escobar. The priest took great pride in his ability to master native tongues. He spent much time talking with Indian spokesmen, and from this flowed tales so fantastic they were hardly credible. One concerned a nation of people with ears so large and long that they dragged on the ground. The people of yet another tribe had only one foot. And there were people who lived on the shore of a lake during the day but slept beneath the water at night.[18]

One tribe of Indians habitually spent their nights in trees. Another did not partake of food because they had no way of discharging excrement. These anatomically challenged folks sustained their bodies simply through the smell of food. Yet another tribe never slept lying down but did so standing erect, with a burden of some sort on their heads. The most outlandish tale was the concoction regarding a nation "whose men had virile members so long that they wound them four times around the waist, and in the act of copulation the man and woman were far apart."[19] The inventive natives evidently had a great time with the gullible Escobar.

Oñate made matters worse by repeating these fantasies to help validate his expedition. He wrote the viceroy, "I discovered a great harbor on the South sea, and clarified the report of extraordinary riches and monstrosities never heard of before."[20] Thus it is little wonder that Viceroy Montesclaros wrote to King Philip to say, "I cannot help but inform your majesty that the conquest is becoming a fairy tale."[21]

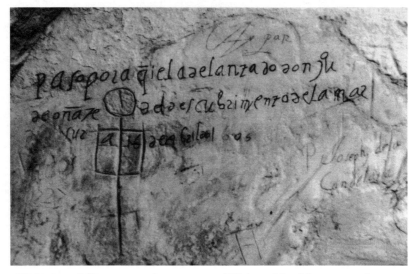

FIGURE 22.2. *Oñate's "Paso por aqui" inscription at El Morro, New Mexico, carved in 1605 on his return journey from the Gulf of California*

On its return home, nine days before reaching San Gabriel the expedition passed by El Morro, on the stone side of which Oñate left a message inscribed for the ages: "Paso por aqui el adelantado don juan de onate del descubrimiento de la mar del sur a 16 de April de 1605" (Passed by here the *adelantado* Don Juan de Oñate from the discovery of the South Sea on the 16 of April 1605) (figure 22.2).[22] The inscription would, in fact, serve as an epitaph for Oñate's effort to create a new empire in Mexico's north country. The South Sea expedition was his final attempt at a grand discovery. The idea of returning to Quivira with a larger expedition was not deemed a worthy financial venture. As with Coronado's expedition, few of those who had been there still had faith that somewhere was a treasure trove waiting to be discovered. Baltasar Martínez, a member of Oñate's Quivira expedition, testified that he had often heard the question of returning discussed by captains and soldiers who had gone with Oñate, but he had heard few express any hope of success. From what he had seen and heard, he did not think another expedition would be worthwhile for either him or the Crown, and he would not choose to return.[23]

The Crown agreed, especially when it involved approving Don Juan's plea for the support and aid of 300 men, paid and equipped, to revisit Quivira. Spanish officials were concerned as well by the letters from friars and laymen who reported "excesses, disturbances, and crimes that had been perpetrated by Don Juan de Oñate and some of his relatives."[24] In January 1606 the Council of the Indies recommended to the king that Don Juan be recalled on some pretext that would not excite a disturbance, that he be detained in Mexico, and that his army then be disbanded. This done, a "reliable, prudent, and God-fearing man" would be appointed in his place.[25]

Relying on the recommendations of Viceroy Montesclaros, the Council of the Indies saw little of material value in maintaining the New Mexico colony through the royal treasury. But it did express great concern that the Indians of the province be protected, befriended, and converted to Christianity. It recommended that friars, motivated by Christian zeal, should still be provided to teach them. King Philip endorsed the council's views.[26] In doing so, the king signaled the end to Oñate's dream of an empire in the north country. Spain would now have to decide if it wanted to continue the conquest he had begun.

ABBREVIATION KEY

H/R-*DJO* = Hammond and Rey, eds., *Don Juan de Oñate*

NOTES

1. "Montesclaros to King, October 28, 1605," H/R-*DJO* 2: 1009.

2. "Oñate Appointed Adelantado," H/R-*DJO* 2: 766–767.

3. "Introduction," H/R-*DJO* 1: 29.

4. "Council to King, April 33, 1603," H/R-*DJO* 2: 987.

5. "Discussion and Proposal," H/R-*DJO* 2: 918.

6. "Council to King, April 22, 1603," H/R-*DJO* 2: 988.

7. "Royal Cedula, June 23, 1603," H/R-*DJO* 2: 994–995.

8. Ibid.; "Council of the Indies to the King, May 19, 1603," H/R-*DJO* 2: 991; "Royal Cedula, January 21, 1604," H/R-*DJO* 2: 996; "Council of the Indies, February 23, 1604," H/R-*DJO* 2: 997; "Affidavit of Bond," H/R-*DJO* 2: 998–999; "Decree of the Council, July 19, 1604," H/R-*DJO* 2: 1000.

9. Oñate later wrote to the viceroy, thanking him for "showing me such mercy . . . when I found myself hard pressed for lack of soldiers and the necessary provisions, He [the Lord] made it possible for me to go to the South sea"; "Oñate to Viceroy, August 7, 1605," H/R-*DJO* 2: 1007.

10. "Oñate's Conviction," H/R-*DJO* 2: 1110.

11. Simmons, *Last Conquistador*, 172.

12. "Montesclaros to King, March 31, 1605," H/R-*DJO* 2: 1002.

13. Ibid.

14. "Father Escobar's Diary," H/R-*DJO* 2: 1012–1031.

15. Ibid., 1018–1019.

16. Ibid., 1019–1020.

17. Simmons, *Last Conquistador*, 173.

18. "Father Escobar's Diary," H/R-*DJO* 2: 1025.

19. Ibid.

20. "Oñate to Viceroy, August 7, 1805," H/R-*DJO* 2: 1007.

21. "Montesclaros to King, October 28, 1605," H/R-*DJO* 2: 1009.

22. Simmons, *Last Conquistador*, 175.

23. "Valverde Inquiry," H/R-*DJO* 2: 847, 849.

24. "Oñate's Excesses," H/R-*DJO* 2: 1032.

25. Ibid., 1034.

26. Ibid., 1032–1034; "Decree of the Council," H/R-*DJO* 2: 1035; "King to Montesclaros, June 17, 1606," H/R-*DJO* 2: 1036, 1038–1039.

23

The Discovery Ends

*Such distant discoveries, without gold or silver, will be expensive
and difficult to maintain, for no one comes to the Indies [America]
to plow and sow, but only to eat and loaf.*

Viceroy Velasco[1]

When all was said and done, Don Juan de Oñate had conducted the first
colonization of New Mexico, one of the earliest within the present United
States. He had done so at great personal and financial sacrifice, proffered
at the altar of conquistador glory. Like Coronado, he essentially failed in
his efforts, though he did leave behind the remnants of a Spanish settlement upon which others could build. He had also re-explored areas of
the North American Southwest and Central Plains, shedding new light
on those regions. The Spanish government had done very little to either
support or encourage him. Throughout Don Juan's reign in New Mexico,
Spanish officials had held back financial support and given him and his
men little encouragement or appreciation.

In addition, there was no state oversight. Don Juan had been allowed
to reign autocratically over the new province he so desperately hoped to
create for Spain. His methods, as much as anything else, did him in. But

now, everything had changed. His failure to make any discoveries of great material value, the depletion of his personal and family-related funds, and the revolt of his colonists and their charges against him demanded that the Spanish government face up to the question of continuing its New Mexico venture.

Viceroy Monterrey made a full review and discussion of Oñate's New Mexico discoveries as well as those that preceded him: Alvar Núñez Cabeza de Vaca, Fray Marcos de Niza, Francisco Vázquez de Coronado, Francisco Sánchez Chamuscado, and Antonio de Espejo. In addition, Monterrey had talked with Vicente de Zaldívar as he passed through Mexico City on his way to Spain as an emissary for Oñate. From this review and conversation, the viceroy concluded that the new country possessed no great lodes of gold or silver. He wrote the king advising him against giving any support for another expedition to Quivira by Oñate.

The Council of the Indies urged that a person be appointed to investigate the charges against Oñate and his captains. If the charges proved to be warranted, legal proceedings were to be started relative to punishing the guilty parties. On June 17, 1606, the king responded with a *cedula* ordering that the discovery be halted and that Oñate be tactfully recalled on some pretext.[2]

Once it had become the prevailing view that no Montezuma-like treasure troves were to be found there, Spain saw little tangible value in the new country. Neither the mining prospects discovered thus far nor the great herds of buffalo on the prairies offered enough incentive to encourage investment from the royal treasury. But the government of King Philip, tied closely to the church, did see a worthy purpose in the religious conversion of the Indians in New Mexico. On August 19, 1606, the king responded to Montesclaros's letter of October 28, 1605, and reissued specific orders for him to "take steps to halt the said conquest and discovery. You shall also preserve the Indians who have been converted to our holy Catholic faith, but at the least possible cost to my royal treasury; and, if possible, see to it that it be done by friars alone."[3]

The king's *cedula*, however, suffered from the limitations of ship communications of the day—actually, an entire fleet was required to cross the Atlantic in safety, since individual Spanish ships were at great risk of being attacked by English pirates. His edict did not reach Mexico City until early 1607. Once there, it was delayed even further in being executed. Montesclaros had been replaced by Don Luis de Velasco, who had returned from Peru to reassume his old office as viceroy of Mexico.[4] It appears that, for whatever reason, Oñate had not yet received notice of his dismissal when he penned a letter of resignation on August 24, 1607.[5]

We know very little of what took place with the Oñate discovery and colonization effort following the mutiny in 1601. Apparently, after that disastrous blow to his colonization efforts, Oñate placed a severe restriction on letters and reports to Mexico. Despite the call officials had made for open communication, the surviving records of that period are scant.

Most of what we do know, other than the peace missions Oñate sent to the western pueblos, involves his South Sea exploration in 1604–1605 and the vague charge issued against him for throwing an Indian chief to his death at Taos. Only there are we given a glimpse of the status of his colony and its relationship to the Indian population following the great mutiny.

It is surely true, as Don Juan stated in his letter of resignation in 1607, that the colony suffered greatly from receiving so little outside support.[6] Vicente de Zaldívar had recently returned to San Gabriel after a four-year absence to Spain. He brought only a few people with him, among them some new friars. When it was learned that the *maestre de campo* had failed to win any promise of future help during his visits to Mexico City and Madrid, the struggling colony's morale plunged even deeper. Apparently, even the loyalist officer corps and soldiers rebelled and threatened to desert. Oñate had managed to persuade them to remain until June 1608 to give the viceroy time to respond to the colony's crisis. He promised them that from that date on, they would be free to leave at will.[7] Oñate wrote to Velasco: "I do not tire of waiting or of enduring the hardships that one encounters here, [but] the soldiers are so worn out by seeing themselves put off for so long with mere hopes that they do not wish nor are they able to wait any longer. Nor do I find myself able to restrain them, for they are as exhausted, hard pressed, and in need of help as I am helpless to furnish it."[8]

Oñate also calculated that in conducting the expedition thus far he had expended from his estate, and from those of relatives and friends, the amount of 600,000 pesos. Though money values fluctuate over time, this was undoubtedly a sizable amount. Having failed to find the great mythical bonanza that had done so much to inspire and incite the expedition, Don Juan now pleaded the religious worth of his venture. He did not want eleven years of labor to be lost, he said, because "I am eager that our holy Catholic faith should be spread in these lands."[9]

A petition from Fray Francisco de Escobar, father commissary at San Gabriel, spoke to a serious problem with Christianizing the natives when the fate of the colony was so uncertain. The friars felt it would be a gross betrayal to persuade converts and then have to go away and leave them without the support of the church. Therefore, the friars were reluctant to conduct further baptisms of natives until "the affairs of this land are settled."[10]

Even then, if the land were abandoned, it would require taking along more than 600 Christian Indians. The result of doing so, it was thought, would mean that in the future holy baptism would be rejected by natives who feared their children and relatives might again be taken away.[11]

Oñate also restated the yet unsubstantiated claim that "the king our lord should increase his dominions by the addition of great and rich provinces, which, according to our information, are at our threshold." Without citing any specific instances, he issued the dubious assurance that "last year the reports of riches and greatness in the interior of the land were verified."[12]

At the same time, Oñate admitted, nothing except poverty had thus far been discovered, even though he had remained in the land solely to work for the cause of God and his majesty and "not for selfish interests."[13] His resources, however, were so depleted that he was unable to conduct any further explorations.

It disturbed Oñate greatly that the mutineers who had fled his camp had not been punished for their treason and "extensive testimonies and falsehoods."[14] They remained free, he complained, while his honor had been placed in doubt. But even as he sent Vicente to Mexico City with his letter of resignation and again to plead for financial help, the Spanish judiciary was moving very slowly but surely toward considering the charges levied against him by the former colonists. Still, much time would pass before Oñate's resignation became effective or he would leave New Mexico.

In early 1608, Frays Lázaro Ximénez and Escobar arrived in Mexico City bringing reports and messages for Viceroy Velasco from Don Juan. The communications pressed the matter of the potential abandonment of the New Mexico province and removal of the church by the end of the following June, unless otherwise instructed. Don Juan and the soldier residents at San Gabriel requested that the king either grant them permission to leave the colony or furnish them with sufficient clothing, horses, and cattle to enable them to remain.[15]

During March 1608, Velasco dispatched Fray Ximénez with eight soldiers and a gunsmith to New Mexico as reinforcements expressly to protect the Spaniards and peaceful Indians from harassment by Apache marauders. He also sent clothing and cattle as temporary relief until the king's decision was learned.[16] The king responded on September 13, again ordering that the discovery and exploration of New Mexico be suspended and, if the colonization were abandoned, to follow the advice of learned theologians, jurists, and other persons as to what to do with the Christian Indians there.[17]

The king's letter reached Velasco prior to December 17, when the viceroy answered to say that Father Ximénez had again returned from New Mexico. The priest said that 7,000 natives had been baptized, and many others were ready to accept baptism. Further, he brought new samples of ores to be assayed, and he conveyed an entirely new notion as to New Mexico's potential value—that, just perhaps, it might be suitable for farming. But the viceroy saw this idea as of little value without discoveries of gold or silver. "No one," he observed of the conquistador generation, "comes to the Indies to plow or sow, but only to loaf and eat."[18]

For the time being, Velasco said, he would hold the king's instructions in abeyance until the matter of the Christian Indians was resolved. During this same period, Philip ordered his fiscal, Don Francisco Leoz, to render a judgment regarding New Mexico that would be "most fitting for the service of God and the King."[19]

Writing to the king in February, Velasco weighed the communication timeline—he needed instructions from the king on the matter, and the first fleet from Spain was not due in Mexico until September. After that, he said, it would require three months more to get the word to New Mexico. Therefore, he reasoned, if the governor, friars, and others had not received word from the king by the end of December 1609, they would be free to leave New Mexico, taking with them the church and Christian Indians.[20]

On the same date he wrote to King Philip, Viceroy Velasco responded to Oñate's resignation, notifying him that the king had accepted the resignation and that he would be replaced by Captain Juan Martínez de Montoya of his colony. Very important, to prevent any abandonment of New Mexico before they heard from the king on that issue, Velasco ordered Oñate not to leave the New Mexico province or to abandon it without his express order. Should he do so, the governor would be charged with the crime of desertion.[21]

Despite the decisions of the viceroy, the royal Audiencia advisory, the Council of the Indies, and the king, Oñate had his own ideas regarding the transfer of his office. He passionately wanted the governorship passed to his son Don Cristóbal, as he felt his original contract for the expedition had authorized.[22] When Montoya presented himself to the San Gabriel governing body with his appointment, he was not admitted "for reasons which they considered sufficient."[23]

Clearly, this was done under Oñate's direction. The San Gabriel governing body proceeded to reelect Don Juan, who could not accept the position from which he had just been removed. Then, with the approval of the Franciscans, Don Cristóbal was elected governor. Historian Agapito Rey suggests that the boy may have held the post of governor of New Mexico province for the next year and a half, citing evidence that during that time he led an attack against the Apaches who had attacked San Gabriel.[24]

But Don Cristóbal's rule over New Mexico could not stand. On March 30, 1609, King Philip appointed Don Pedro de Peralta governor of New Mexico and commanded an orderly transfer of office. In his instructions, the king called attention to the plans of Spaniards and friars in New Mexico to establish, as they were encouraged to do, a new settlement for their operations.[25]

Velasco advanced the matter in his instructions to Peralta, ordering him "to found and settle the villa that has been ordered built, so that they [the residents] may begin to live with some order and decency."[26] From this instruction rose the city of Santa Fe, New Mexico.

The viceroy granted formal permission for Don Juan and his son to return to Mexico City, where he could press his claims for compensation for the services he had rendered to the Crown.[27] At the same time, the viceroy issued a decree continuing the New Mexico colony and supporting it with fifty soldiers plus ten more chosen from current residents, six friar priests, and two lay brothers—all at the expense of the royal treasury. The end purpose of continuing the colony was the conversion and preservation of the native Indians.[28]

During the spring of 1610, Don Juan de Oñate and his son Don Cristóbal left San Gabriel en route to Mexico. His grand *entrada* and colonization of New Mexico had come to its bitter end. Once a glorious dream and a momentous undertaking, it now lay floundering in a sea of unresolved ambitions. He had had negligible support from the Crown, as well as much misfortune. But in large part he and his followers had been betrayed by their own conquistador spirit, which, while brave to the utmost, was victimized by its cruel nature and exalted hopes.

Don Juan was done with New Mexico. But before him in Mexico was a judicial inquiry into his actions as governor and measurement of his historical role as a Spanish conquistador.

ABBREVIATION KEY

H/R-*DJO* = Hammond and Rey, eds., *Don Juan de Oñate*

NOTES

1. "Velasco to King, December 17, 1608," H/R-*DJO* 2: 1068.
2. "King to Montesclaros, August 19, 1606," H/R-*DJO* 2: 1036–1038.
3. Ibid., 1039.
4. Simmons, *Last Conquistador*, 178.
5. "Oñate to Viceroy, August 24, 1607," H/R-*DJO* 2: 1042–1045.
6. Ibid.
7. Ibid., 1043.
8. Ibid., 1042.
9. Ibid.
10. Ibid., 1044.
11. Ibid., 1042–1044.
12. Ibid., 1043.
13. Ibid.
14. "Velasco to King, March 7, 1608," H/R-*DJO* 2: 1056–1058.
15. Ibid.
16. "King to Velasco, September 13, 1608," H/R-*DJO* 2: 1065–1066.
17. Ibid.; "Velasco to King, December 17, 1608," H/R-*DJO* 2: 1067–1068.
18. "Oñate's Resignation Accepted," H/R-*DJO* 2: 1048–1049; "Royal Decree Forbidding Oñate to Leave New Mexico," H/R-*DJO* 2: 1050.
19. "Don Francisco de Leoz to the King," H/R-*DJO* 2: 1070.
20. "Viceroy to the King," H/R-*DJO* 2: 1046–1047.
21. "Don Francisco de Leoz to the King," H/R-*DJO* 2: 1070.
22. "Council of the Indies to the King," H/R-*DJO* 2: 1101.
23. "Velasco to King, February 13, 1609," H/R-*DJO* 2: 1081; Simmons, *Last Conquistador*, 181.

24. Rey, "Cristóbal de Oñate," 198.

25. "Peralta Appointed Governor," H/R-*DJO* 2: 1084–1086.

26. "Governor Peralta's Instructions," H/R-*DJO* 2: 1087.

27. "Oñate to Return," H/R-*DJO* 2: 1075.

28. "New Mexico to Be Maintained," H/R-*DJO* 2: 1076–1077.

24

Oñate's Reckoning

Messages kept coming, both from those who had remained behind (charging the others with being deserters), and from those who had fled.

Viceroy Monterrey[1]

On June 1, 1613, King Philip III, who had been kept advised of the charges against Oñate, wrote to Diego Fernández de Córdoba—the marquis of Guadalcázar and a relative of the king—explaining why an investigation of Don Juan de Oñate, his captains, and others had been delayed. Criminal judge Don Francisco Leoz, who had been commissioned to investigate and prosecute Oñate, had encountered social difficulties. "The accused," Leoz noted, "are among the most powerful and influential people in that kingdom [Mexico]."[2]

Leoz had requested that he be relieved of the potential task of sentencing the accused because of the embarrassment he would face while living among both those charged and their accusers. Accordingly, the king ordered Córdoba to undertake the role of prosecutor "in accordance with the law, and to pass sentence, imposing punishment in consultation with a legal adviser."[3]

No records of the trial itself, which took place prior to May 16, 1614, are known to have survived. But two sets of documents provide insight into the charges issued against Oñate, Vicente de Zaldívar, and others, as well as into Oñate's argument against them. The documents are "Conviction of Oñate and His Captains, 1614," and "Charges against Oñate, 1617."[4] The fiscal of the Audiencia of Mexico issued twenty-nine complaints against Oñate; he was exonerated on nineteen of them. But he was held to be guilty on ten of the charges.[5] Some were very serious charges, while others were insignificant.

The accusations that were dismissed included the charge that Oñate conducted his conquest and pacification in a way that caused the deaths of many natives; that he ill-treated the captains and soldiers of his army; that he belittled the clergy; that he permitted his soldiers to maltreat the natives, taking by force their corn and whatever else they had; that he ordered Vicente to murder and inflict punishment on the Jumanos; that he shoved a young Indian chief from a roof in Taos and caused his death; that he murdered a soldier in the Mexican town of Casco; and that he ordered the head of Captain Julián de Resa to be cut off.

Also, that he was responsible for frauds and shortages in the army's food supply; that, when he took possession of the land, he permitted the royal standard to be lowered before him; that he permitted his *maestre de campo* to address him as "majesty"; that he arranged for his son, rather than Captain Juan Martínez de Montoya, to replace him as governor; that he sent soldiers out at the risk of their lives to bring him wild fruits; that he permitted a man serving a sentence in the army to return to Mexico without finishing his term; that he sold the horses, arms, and clothing of soldiers killed at Acoma and gave the proceeds to Vicente without an accounting being made; that on one occasion he punished two Indians but let others go unpunished; that he once returned to New Spain, abandoning his New Mexico jurisdiction; and that he permitted Vicente and thirty soldiers to leave the province, taking men and women natives to be sold as slaves.[6] The former governor was determined to be not guilty on all of these charges.

He was found guilty, however, of the following charges: that he caused two Indians at Acoma to be hanged because he thought they had killed a Mexican in the army, but the man was later found alive; that he punished the Indians of Acoma—including those who had surrendered—with great severity, injuring many innocent people and killing others; and that while he was *adelantado* he lived "dishonorably and scandalously with women of the army, married and unmarried."[7]

Also, that he ordered that Captains Pablo de Aguilar and Alonso de Sosa Albornoz be put to death; that he ordered that two deserting soldiers be put to death; that he misrepresented the worth of the New Mexican land, causing many expenses and costs in maintaining the conquest; that he defied royal appointments to his expedition; that he publicly boasted that he was the mortal enemy of Viceroy Monterrey and spoke ill of him; that he participated in mocking inspector Juan de Frías while in camp on the San Pedro River; that he imprisoned his lieutenant governor, Francisco de Sosa Peñalosa, and would not release the man unless he would say the mutineers had forced him to let them leave; and that he allowed the people of his expedition to commit robberies and do much damage to the ranches, houses, and fields of Spaniards and natives between Zacatecas and Santa Bárbara; further, he would see that justice was done to those who complained against him.[8]

Guadalcázar issued his decision on May 13, 1614, declaring: "On the basis of these above charges, which have been proved against Don Juan de Oñate in this trial, I should condemn him and do condemn him to perpetual exile from the provinces of New Mexico, and from this court and five leagues around it, for exactly four years; furthermore, I condemn him to pay six thousand Castilian ducats."[9]

Vicente de Zaldívar was cleared of offenses against the Jumano Indians, of addressing Oñate as "majesty," of mistreating the auditor of the army, of asking for the heads of six army captains, of showing disrespect for Viceroy Monterrey, and of leaving the New Mexico province without authorization and taking Indian men and women whom he sold as slaves. The *maestre de campo*, however, was found guilty on a number of other charges: that he mistreated the captains and soldiers of the army to prevent them from speaking out about New Mexico's poverty and sterility; that he severely punished the natives of Acoma and killed many who were innocent; that he associated immorally with women of the army, causing a great scandal; that he ordered the killing of Captain Alonso de Sosa Albornoz; that he ordered three soldiers to be severely flayed; and that he ordered the killing of soldier Andrés Martín Palomo. For his excesses, Vicente was sentenced to be exiled from New Mexico for eight years and required to pay a fine of 2,000 ducats.[10]

Don Juan and Vicente were not the only victims of the court. Captains Alonso Núñez de Ynojosa, Dionisio de Bañuelos, Domingo de

Lizama and Juan de Salas were found guilty of having aided Oñate in the killing of Aguilar and the latter three also in the deaths of Alonso de Sosa and Captain Alonso Gómez. These men received punishments involving the loss of their office as captains, banishment of various lengths from the province of New Mexico, and fines of up to 500 ducats. Sentences of banishment from New Mexico and 200 lashes were issued to mestizo Francisco Vido, the mulatto slave called Juan, the Mexican Indian Agustín, and African Luis Bautista for their roles in the deaths of both Aguilar and de Sosa.[11]

Though we do not have the proceedings of the trial, it seems clear that the sentences imposed on these men and on Juan de Oñate and Vicente were considered to be for acts of murder and not legal executions, as the former *adelantado* sought to establish in his defense.[12] When a review of Oñate's case was held in 1617, he answered the charge of killing Pedro de Aguilar by contending that the event did not happen as stated.

What had happened, he said, was that Aguilar attempted to revolt two or three times, and Oñate sentenced him to death but relented. But even after a proclamation had been issued ordering that no one would be allowed to abandon the royal standard, Aguilar had tried again. He fled one night with five soldiers and a woman: "Then Don Juan sent someone after him, seized and sentenced him to death, accusing him also of the two previous charges, and he was beheaded, according to the practices of war ... Don Juan, however, took no other part in the affair than to seize an harquebus for his defense and to make sure that justice was carried out in proper manner."[13]

To answer the charge of ordering the killing of Alonso de Sosa, Oñate contended that the captain's death was proper punishment for deserting the army against orders. "This punishment was necessary," he said, "to avoid trouble, disturbances, and uprisings by his friends and relatives, who threatened very great harm."[14]

It could be counter-argued, of course, that executing the man might be the thing that would set off a potential uprising. Oñate's statement does explain perhaps why Sosa's body was covered with stones in a remote ravine to avoid discovery. Perhaps this was done with the thought that his relatives and friends would assume his absence meant he had escaped back to Mexico.

Oñate's claim that Sosa was fleeing with five soldiers and a "woman with whom he lived in concubinage" would mean that the officer was deserting not only his wife but also his several children and leaving them uncared for in New Mexico. Captain Velasco, contradicting Oñate, said Sosa had been stabbed to death by Vicente and others when they were sent out to round up the horses.[15]

The Crown reviewed several other charges as well in 1617. In the main, they were rebutted by the claim that they had been levied against Oñate by people who were his enemies and whom he had condemned to death for desertion and other crimes. While this may have been true in some instances, no records exist of Oñate having formally levied such sentences against Captain Velasco, who issued many of the charges in a letter to the viceroy, or against the deserting men and women colonists who escaped in 1601 and later testified against him. Though his assertion that they were accusing him in revenge holds possible merit, it is by no means a certainty that charges against him were leveled merely out of spite or for revenge.

There is reason to doubt as well that a number of colonists, officers, and priests conspired against him and fabricated like accounts of the events of their accusations. It is especially difficult to accept such a premise in the instances of the five friars—Francisco de San Miguel, Francisco de Zamora, Lope Izquierdo, Gastón de Peralta, and Damián Escudero—who issued strong indictments of Oñate in regard to his treatment of the New Mexico Indians.[16] To do so is to believe the priests joined together to falsely indict a person after having made a direct vow before their God to speak the truth.

Oñate would dedicate the rest of his life to clearing his name. While he eventually won the favor of the Council of the Indies, King Philip IV "would have nothing to do with such an ugly case, as he called it." In 1623, however, then in his mid-seventies, Don Juan won several personal victories. In a letter appointing him inspector of mines and lodes in Spain, the king addressed him by the title "*adelantado.*"[18] A Royal Order of that year, initiated by the Council of the Indies, awarded him 6,000 pesos as reimbursement for his investment in his New Mexico venture. Further, in 1625 he won an appointment as a caballero to the prestigious Military Order of Santiago in Spain.[18]

Despite his advanced age, Oñate actively pursued his role as mine inspector, traveling around to the mines of Spain. He fell seriously ill while on an inspection tour shortly before he died in Guadalcanal, Spain, on June 3, 1626.[19]

ABBREVIATION KEY

H/R-*DJO* = Hammond and Rey, eds., *Don Juan de Oñate*

NOTES

1. "Monterrey to King, March 8, 1602," H/R-*DJO* 2: 771.
2. "Royal Cedula to Viceroy, June 1, 1613," H/R-*DJO* 2: 1107.
3. Ibid., 1108.
4. "Oñate's Conviction," H/R-*DJO* 2: 1109–1124; "Oñate Charges Reviewed," H/R-*DJO* 2: 1125–1138.
5. "Oñate Charges Reviewed," H/R-*DJO* 2: 1125–1126. This does not square with the affidavit of the sentence pronounced by Guadalcázar, wherein seventeen charges are dismissed and Oñate is found guilty on twelve of them. Charges 4 and 28 are not mentioned in the review.
6. "Oñate's Conviction," H/R-*DJO* 2: 1109–1111; "Monterrey to King, March 8, 1602," H/R-*DJO* 2: 770–773.
7. "Oñate's Conviction," H/R-*DJO* 2: 1111.
8. Ibid., 1111–1113.
9. Ibid., 1113.
10. Ibid., 1114–1115.
11. Ibid., 1119–1124.
12. "Oñate Charges Reviewed," H/R-*DJO* 2: 1131–1132.
13. Ibid.
14. Ibid.
15. "Velasco to Viceroy, March 22, 1601," H/R-*DJO* 2: 613.
16. See "Desertion of the Colony," H/R-*DJO* 2: 672–689.
17. "Introduction," H/R-*DJO* 1: 37–38.
18. Beerman, "Death of an Old Conquistador," 306–307.
19. Ibid., 310–311.

25

The Conquistador Legacy

Truth is the only merit that gives dignity and worth to history.

Lord Acton[1]

Individuals who have been differently persuaded, as well as organized groups formed to honor Coronado and Oñate, will naturally resent any challenge to the idea that the two men were noble leaders who exercised benevolent oversight of those under their authority. Most of us have been trained early in our school years to see certain historical figures in a purified, heroic sense.

There is good in this, it can be argued, in shaping young minds to appreciate and accept moral values and honor their national heritage. But in adult life we must recognize the inherent danger of closing our minds to the full, sometimes ugly, truth of the past. History, unlike fiction, cannot be manipulated to reach a single, pleasing, but false conclusion.

The conquistadors saw themselves as Herbert Bolton described Coronado: each a virtuous knight in the service of his deified monarch, supported further by a contorted religious piety that justified virtually any

275

act of mayhem. These were men descended from the period of European history we know as the Inquisition, when barbarous behavior by those in power was, for both national and religious reasons, accepted practice. Virtually any action to quell dissenters or enemies of the state was justified by the "noble cause." Oñate's captain, Gaspar de Villagrá, proudly proclaimed the conquistador's virtue in his lyrical account of his New Mexico experiences:

> From a thousand chieftains he has slain.
> Castile, mother glorious
> Of warriors most victorious,
> Mirror of the moon and sun,
> Villagrá has come to lay
> On your altars here today
> A precious trophy he had won,
> His shining sword wiped clean
> Of its gory, bloody spleen.[2]

Bolton, whose outstanding scholarship on the conquistador is truly to be recognized, found merit in Coronado's actions by contrasting them with the horrific excesses of conquistadors Nuño de Guzmán in Mexico's Nueva Galicia province and Hernando de Soto in the American South. Relatively speaking, Bolton concluded, Coronado's treatment of the Indian natives he encountered was a "Sunday school picnic."[3]

In terms of the Quivira expeditions alone, Bolton's argument holds some validity; the atrocities of Guzmán and de Soto, after all, were gory to the extreme. During their expeditions to Quivira, Coronado and Oñate realized that their forces were severely extended on the far plains. The fates of Francisco Leyva de Bonilla, Antonio Gutiérrez de Humaña, and Friar Juan Padilla well illustrate the potential dangers the Spaniards faced there.

Other than dragging Indian guides about in iron collars and chains and the secretive garroting of the Turk, neither Coronado nor Oñate committed the types of serious infractions on the plains that they had employed among the generally compliant Pueblo Indians. But as Richard Flint points out, in regard to his overall performance with Indian natives otherwise, Coronado relied on torture and other horrific measures to establish dominance over the people he was sent to quell in Mexico and those he encountered during his two years in North America. Mass murders occurred when his men torched occupied pueblo settlements. Any

Indian even suspected of being resistant to Spanish overlording was often hanged, burned at the stake, or brutally maimed. Indian women were raped or forced into slave servitude.[4]

Clearly, Oñate was likewise guilty of horrific acts in maiming the Acoma prisoners by cutting off their noses, hands, or feet essentially to establish Spanish dominance over the New Mexico pueblos. Indian prisoners were burned at the stake under his command as well. It appears, too, that he brutalized and murdered his own officers and colony members when they sought to escape back to Mexico.

These revelations and introspection into Coronado's and Oñate's characters leave us with conflicted views as to their historical importance. Even as we recognize the inhumaneness of their acts, we must acknowledge the significance of their expeditions into the American Southwest and give credit to the courage, determination, and personal sacrifice required of their exploration efforts. For ensuing generations who must serve as juries on the conquistador period and its participants, such contradictions are difficult to consider.

Thus, we are left to accept the Spanish conquistadors as reflecting both worthy qualities and gross imperfections of our historical past and to measure ourselves against them. Even as we pay them tribute for their accomplishments, we are obliged to admit to the inhumane methods by which their historical legacy was too often achieved. It is a simple honesty that we owe to the record of humankind, as well as to our own character.

NOTES

1. John Bartlett, *Familiar Quotations: A Collection of Passages, Phrases and Proverbs Traced to Their Sources in Ancient and Modern Literature*, 14th ed., Emily Morison Beck, ed. (Boston: Little, Brown, 1968), 750.

2. Villagrá, *History of New Mexico*, 37.

3. Bolton, *Coronado*, 275.

4. Flint, *Great Cruelties*, xvii.

Appendix A

Coronado's March

As the Spaniards Tried to Tell Us

lpd = leagues per day
mpl = miles per league
2.6 miles per league (est.)[1]

In Flint and Flint's *The Coronado Expedition to Tierra Nueva*,[2] Professor Joseph P. Sánchez, University of New Mexico, provides a thorough examination of the various theories regarding the route of the Coronado Expedition to Quivira. These scholarly studies, however, have failed to resolve many of the questions concerning the 1541 expedition onto the mid-plains of North America. This book makes no pretense of doing so either. What it does offer is a new look at the clues in the existing Spanish documents to establish possible parameters of movement by the expedition.

The task requires consideration of data that range from the proven/certain to the unproven/uncertain, with various shades in between. Such an endeavor will hardly lead to definitive conclusions. Yet it is not too much to hope perhaps that within the Spanish accounts are revelations that could bring us closer to the historical truth of Coronado's march.

An important factor in understanding what the Spaniards of old are saying is that of "time": that is, when in terms of our calendar today did the Coronado Expedition reach a certain point, and how long did it take to get there? Coronado scholars Richard and Shirley Flint explain the discrepancies created by the adoption of the Gregorian calendar by Pope Gregory XIII in 1582, more than forty years after the Coronado Expedition to the plains but prior to Oñate's similar expedition. To better adapt the calendar to the forces of the planet and the universe, the pope took some of his dates out of the old Julian calendar. As a result, some dates given in record accounts of the Coronado Expedition are Julian calendar dates while other accounts, written retrospectively after the calendar alterations were made, contain Gregorian dates. The result is a confusion of time factors in the Coronado narratives that were written or copied before Pope Gregory's action and those written or copied after his action.

The Flints cite this calendar differential along with textual misreadings (such as misstating a penned "3" for a penned "5") by early scribes as creating two of the twelve days' variance between the May 5 (Gregorian calendar) starting date given by Pedro de Castañeda and April 23 (Julian calendar), as stated by Coronado. Accordingly, the Flints accept only the ten-day differential in concluding that May 3 (Gregorian) was the true date of Coronado's departure.[3]

Three significant calendar dates are provided in the Coronado Expedition literature:

April 23, Julian, or May 3, 1541, Gregorian,[4] the date the expedition departed from Tiguex[5]

Ascension of the Lord Day, which is forty days after Easter Sunday, May 27, Julian, or June 6, 1541, Gregorian. Whether this was the date of the hailstorm, the date they made the decision to divide, or both is unclear. Mota Padilla, who provided the date, wrote: "Afflicted with such disasters [the hailstorm], they determined on that day, which was that of the Ascension of the Lord, 1541, that the army would return to Tiguex to refit."[6]

Saint Peter and Saint Paul's Day, June 29, 1541, Julian, or July 9, 1541, Gregorian, when the advance party reached the Quivira River.[7]

A fourth day of significance can be computed from Castañeda's statement that it was during a rest period "of several days" in Canyon #2 when the expedition determined it had traveled 250 leagues in thirty-seven one-day marches. It was also in Canyon #2 that it was decided to send the main group back to New Mexico while Coronado led the advance party on to find Quivira.[8]

Thirty-seven days from the May 3 start would be June 8, which can be correlated with the Saint Peter and Saint Paul's Day date (July 9, Gregorian) to determine that it took thirty-one days (or less, depending on what day he actually started) for Coronado and the advance to reach the Quivira River. For clarification, see figure 7.1: Timeline projection of Coronado's march to Quivira.

We thus have four dates to work with:

	Julian	*Gregorian*
Departure date	April 23	May 3
Ascension of the Lord Day	May 27	June 6
Thirty-seventh day of march	May 29	June 8
Saint Peter/Paul's Day	June 29	July 9

These dates establish key time intervals of the journey to Quivira that essentially mark the expedition's start, midpoint, and reach of destination. It is within their general confines, therefore, that the cumbersome expedition marched from Tiguex onto the plains, divided, sent an advance party ahead to its final destination at Quivira, and returned to New Mexico.

OVERVIEW

The Spanish documents provide data in terms of leagues traveled or number of days marched. At times the data are contradictory or oblique. It is questionable, for instance, whether "days marched" is meant as "days actually marched" or "days on the trail." The latter appears to be the case when Castañeda states that, while at Canyon #2, they had made thirty-seven days' marches. It seems apparent, for example, that he meant the thirty-seven days on the trail to include the four days of bridge building.

Communication difficulty also arises when we are told the expedition moved in a particular direction. On occasion, direction *is indicated* as "due east." But it is often not clear whether the word *eastward* means "essentially

due east," "southeast," or "northeast." Juan Jaramillo wrote, "From the time
. . . we entered the plains and from this settlement of Querechos, he [the
Turk] led us off more to the east."[9] A logical interpretation of this statement would be "generally east," but it strains logic somewhat to accept it
as "east with a dominant bend southward," as the Blanco Canyon thesis
requires.

Likewise, Castañeda states that after meeting the Querechos, "For
two days . . . the army marched in the same direction as that in which
they had come from the settlements—that is, between north and east,
but more toward the north."[10] This clearly defies the idea of a drift to the
south.

The possibility remains that Coronado and his men were simply confused in their directions. Certainly, they would know east by the sunrise
each morning. But once the sun was in the dome of the sky, they could
easily become uncertain as to direction. Apparently, Coronado had a compass, but by his own statement he followed the Turk's guidance without question until he had become disoriented and lost on the prairie. He
wrote, "I traveled five days more as the guides wished to lead me until
I reached some plains, with no more landmarks than as if we had been
swallowed up in the sea."[11]

There are methods to determine direction while in the field, but we
do not know if the Spaniards employed them. The Teyas Indians who
were guiding the main expedition back would note the rising sun each
morning, then shoot arrows one over another in the direction they chose
to go until their destination for that day was reached.[12]

Another account states that Coronado and the advance party went
north "by the needle."[13] This implies the use of a compass. Still, it is very
doubtful that this was true north or that no directional deviation occurred
as the party moved overland. Early overland travel either by foot or by
horse was inevitably influenced by topographical features. On the open
plains, streams or tree lines that promised vital water sources could influence the course of a march. Rough terrain and impediments such as
buttes, canyons, lakes, or vegetation could do the same.

The *Relación del Suceso* tells how the buffalo herds were so thick at
times that "when we started to pass through the midst of them and wanted
to go through to the other side of them, we were not able to, because
the country was covered with them."[14] Once having deviated around or
through such a large natural barrier, it could be very difficult, even with a

compass, for the expedition to find the correct point from which to pick up the original line of the march.

Further, as with any such expedition, there were surely rest periods and delays because of travel weariness, camp making, food gathering and preparation, holding mass, and personal reasons such as toilet needs and bathing. We are required, therefore, to make reasoned judgments as to what message the Spanish words convey regarding the given time frames.

Some things are known with virtual certainty. One is that the Quivira expedition was launched from the Tiguex complex of pueblo settlements on the Rio Grande above Albuquerque. Because its ruins still exist, we know, too, that the expedition passed Pecos pueblo (Cicuye or Cicúique) northeast of Santa Fe four days later. Because of its close proximity to the pueblo, we can easily accept the Cicuye River as today's Pecos River.

TIGUEX TO THE PLAINS

Through examination of prehistoric trade routes and records of early-day expeditions that followed them, national park official Harry C. Myers delineates both Coronado's and Oñate's probable routes from their Rio Grande headquarters to the plains in his study, "The Mystery of Coronado's Route from the Pecos River to the Llano Estacado."[15]

Though the narrative evidence is faint, a consensus of opinion accepts that from Cicuye, the Coronado Expedition traced the west bank of the stream now known as the Pecos River southeastward to the site of present Anton Chico, New Mexico. It was there or below, it is believed, that the expedition constructed the bridge over which it crossed with its animals to reach the plains.[16]

Beyond the Pecos, Coronado's march becomes even more uncertain. Particularly difficult to assimilate are statements by both Castañeda and Jaramillo, who wrote the most comprehensive accounts of the expedition, that the march from Pecos to the canyons was principally north by east. These significant directional indicators seemingly contradict existing factual data, such as the large canyons of the Texas Panhandle and the ensuing movements of both the advance group and the main expedition. Bolton and other theorists have been forced to refute a northeasterly march from the Pecos to accommodate other conflicting clues.

Another factor that shapes general thinking and logical construction alike is the long-accepted belief (supported by archaeological and other less-substantive evidence) that Quivira was located in central Kansas. While this location may well be the case (and this book accepts it as correct), that assumption tends to overwhelm or shape any debatable or unproven clues to the contrary. If Castañeda and Jaramillo, for instance, were not "mis-remembering" with their explicit statements regarding turning northeast beyond the Pecos, then the Texas canyons and Quivira become far more difficult to accept on the basis of expedition literature.

ON THE PLAINS

Scholars have long disagreed as to the expedition's route beyond the Pecos River. By Coronado's admission, the expedition became hopelessly lost on the landmark-scarce plains. Myers traces the expedition eastward as far as Tucumcari Mountain, near the location where it encountered the first Querecho village. From there its route becomes obscure in leading to the first large canyon, where it encountered a Teyas Indian village before moving north for a few days to the second large canyon, where the expedition experienced a severe hailstorm. There, it reconsidered its situation and divided. The advance party under Coronado continued northward, while the main expedition turned back to Tiguex.

Several sizable canyons exist in the Texas Panhandle and West Texas. Bolton felt certain that Tule Canyon and Palo Duro Canyon below Amarillo were the ones the expedition visited. Archaeological finds of Spanish artifacts in Blanco Canyon northeast of Lubbock, Texas, however, have led scholars to consider it a Coronado site. In their detailed report on the archaeological work at Blanco Canyon, Donald J. Blakeslee and Jay C. Blaine express full confidence that the artifacts—in particular, Coronado-day crossbow bolt heads—found there firmly prove it was a Coronado campsite.[17] On his map in *Majestic Journey: Coronado's Inland Empire*, Stewart Udall depicts the possibility of the two canyons being even farther south, near San Angelo and Sweetwater, Texas.

Acceptance of the bridge location as Anton Chico, New Mexico, or slightly lower on the Pecos would establish the Palo Duro Canyon on an almost due easterly march from the river. Blanco Canyon would require a southeasterly movement in line with the Salt Fork of the Brazos, whose headwaters begin in eastern New Mexico. Palo Duro, Tule, and Blanco all appear to deny Castañeda's and Jaramillo's directional indications of a northeasterly march beyond the Pecos.

The results of the extensive archaeological work at Blanco Canyon, however, make the site difficult to ignore. Whether it was Canyon #1 or Canyon #2 remains undetermined. If Blanco were Canyon #1, then Tule Canyon, which is about forty-five to fifty miles north of Blanco, becomes a candidate as the second of the Coronado canyons. To date, however, no archaeological evidence has been found in support of Tule as Canyon #2.

Spanish accounts tell us that once across the Pecos River, the expedition marched along a small river eastward (or so its members thought). Significantly, nothing in the various accounts gives clear identity to the Canadian River, which traverses the Texas Panhandle west to east and served as a directional guide for many ensuing explorers. One would think the expedition chroniclers would have mentioned it, even if they simply crossed it on its easterly flow.

MARCH OF CORONADO'S ADVANCE PARTY TO QUIVIRA

Given that 250 of the said 330 total leagues to Quivira were traveled to Canyon #2, it can be reasoned that Coronado's advance party marched 80 leagues (208 miles) beyond that point. Though it is a generalized comparison at best, the airline (most direct) distance from Tule Canyon to Great Bend, Kansas, is about 300 miles.

The length of time for Coronado's march from Canyon #2 to Quivira has been given variously by the accounts as 30 days, as not more than 30 days, as 48 days, and by Coronado himself as 42 days. As deduced earlier, the time between Ascension of the Lord Day and Saint Peter and Saint Paul's Day provides only 30 days for Coronado and the advance party to have journeyed from Canyon #2 to the Quivira River.

Even accepting the captain general's own reckoning, it is necessary to consider that Jaramillo said the distance was covered "not by long marches" and that a delay was caused by the advance party having to send back for other Teyas Indian guides after the first group had deserted. Also, delays were surely caused by the need to hunt, kill, skin, and butcher buffalo, the meat of which was the only food available to the advance party. In addition, some members of the advance party—the foot soldiers, servants, Indian allies, and priests—were dismounted. It could also be the case that those who give the longer times for the march of the advance party from the canyons to Quivira (including Coronado himself) were speaking in terms of reaching the far end of Quivira rather than the first village.

LOCATION OF QUIVIRA

Just where was the Indian site known as Quivira? The *Relación del Suceso* says, "We found the river Quivira, which is 30 leagues below the settlement." Jaramillo states, "We crossed it [the Quivira River] there and went up the other side on the north, the direction turning toward the northeast, and after marching three days we found some Indians . . . [whose village] was about three or four days still farther ahead of us."[18]

Because of calculations of the expedition's movements as well as archaeological finds (see appendix E), the Arkansas River in Kansas is generally assumed to be the Quivira River. The *Relación del Suceso* states that Coronado went "25 leagues through these settlements, to where he obtained an account of what was beyond, and they [the Indians] said that the plains come to an end."[19]

It is apparent from these statements that Quivira was not just one Indian settlement but instead a complex of villages spread along the course of several streams from the Arkansas River northeastward. The village of the Indian hunters, said to be three or four days ahead on the river (the Arkansas or perhaps a tributary of it) from where the expedition met the hunters, was only the first of several Quiviran settlements Coronado visited. We are told that the advance party continued on for several days through settlements to a larger river, which the Indians said marked the end of Quivira. The Smoky Hill River has been considered a good possibility for this larger river.

RETURN OF THE MAIN EXPEDITION

Two other time-frame data are worthy of consideration: (1) the return march of the main expedition from Canyon #2 to Tiguex and (2) the return march of Coronado's advance party from Quivira to Tiguex.

Castañeda states that with the help of Teyas guides on its return, the returning expedition party covered in 25 days what had taken 37 days going. Marching westward from Canyon #2, the expedition struck the Pecos River 30 leagues below the bridge.[20] This could be about 78 miles south of Santa Rosa, New Mexico.

This information provides insight as to just how far the expedition advanced onto the plains during its wandering route to Canyon #2. A 6.75-lpd average daily march for that segment of the journey can be obtained by dividing 250 by 37. Thus the 25-day return march would be

168.75 leagues (25 days at 6.75 lpd), or 438.75 miles (168.75 leagues × 2.6 mpl), from Canyon #2 to Tiguex.

The trip from the bridge to Tiguex, which took 8 days, can be calculated at 53.6 leagues (8 days at 6.7 lpd). Adding to this the 30 leagues the expedition marched upriver to reach the bridge on its return, we get a total of 83.6 leagues (217.36 miles). Deducting that amount (83.6 leagues) from the expedition's 168.75-league return march (Canyon #2 to Tiguex), we get a distance of 85.15 leagues from Canyon #2 to the point where the return march struck the Pecos River. This translates to 221.39 miles (85.15 leagues × 2.6 mpl).

In brief, the calculation for the main expedition would be:

Total return march = 438.75 miles (168.75 leagues)
Pecos River point to Tiguex = 217.36 miles (83.6 leagues)
Canyon #2 to Pecos River = 221.39 miles (85.15 leagues)

This last figure compares with an approximate airline distance of an estimated ±230 miles from Blanco Canyon to the place where the expedition reached the Pecos River and about ±200 airline miles from Tule Canyon.

RETURN OF THE ADVANCE PARTY

Coronado is said to have returned to Tiguex in 40 days. The distance from Quivira (or the Quivira River) to Tiguex was 200 leagues (an average of 5 leagues, or 13 miles, per day).[21] This distance of 200 leagues, or 520 miles, compares to the 450+-mile airline distance from the Great Bend area of Kansas to the site of Tiguex on the Rio Grande above Albuquerque.

On May 27 the expedition was resting in a second large canyon encountered somewhere on the prairie where it was struck by a fierce hailstorm. At that time, reportedly, the expedition had been on the march for 37 days. Through the counting of steps by a member, the expedition deduced that it had traveled 6 or 7 leagues a day—a total of 250 leagues, or about 650 miles, to that point.

These generalized deductions based on uncertain data hardly provide sure answers to the route of the Coronado Expedition and the location of Quivira. Others considering this matter may well use different distances and reach different conclusions than the ones cited here. But still, the time and distance indicators embedded in the various Spanish accounts offer our most tangible clues, short of further archaeological disclosures that may someday tell us more.

ABBREVIATION KEY

W-*CE* = Winship, *The Coronado Expedition, 1540–1542*

NOTES

1. The relationship of a Spanish league to a current mile is variable, but it has been equated as approximately 2.6 to 2.65 miles. Others use 2.5 miles per league. Vehick,"Oñate's Expedition," 14, uses a 2.6-mile equivalent. This study will use the 2.6-mile equivalent, but obviously uncertainty is involved. Time and date factors, however, are indicated more specifically through the observance of Franciscan religious anniversaries. From these, certain facets of the march can be firmly established and others can be deduced.

2. Flint and Flint, *Coronado Expedition to Tierra Nueva*, 281–302.

3. Richard Flint, "Reconciling the Calendars of the Coronado Expedition," in Flint and Flint, eds., *Coronado Expedition to Tierra Nueva*, 153–155.

4. Castañeda gives May 5 as the expedition's starting date. Richard Flint explains this conflict in starting times as caused largely by the adoption of the Gregorian calendar by Pope Gregory XIII. By his act in 1582, the pope superceded the old Julian calendar and dropped ten days' time from that year. Flint ascribes this calendar differential, plus textual alterations by early scribes, as creating the twelve-day variance between the May 5 (Gregorian calendar) given by Castañeda and the April 23 (Julian calendar) given by Coronado; Flint and Flint, *Coronado Expedition to Tierra Nueva*, 151–163. The matter of starting dates can be further tested against the given date of Saint Peter and Saint Paul's Day, June 29 (Gregorian calendar), provided by Jaramillo, on which the expedition reached the Quivira River. Following that date, Jaramillo tells us that the expedition marched 6 or 7 days to Quivira. Thus Coronado arrived at Quivira on July 5 or 6. Coronado tells us further that it took 77 days total to reach Quivira. Counting 77 days backward from July 6 produces the date of April 22, making the starting date of April 23 much more agreeable than May 5.

5. W-*CE*, 364.

6. Day, "Mota Padilla," 105.

7. "Jaramillo's Narrative," W-*CE*, 379.

8. "Castañeda's Narrative," W-*CE*, 237–238.

9. "Jaramillo's Narrative," W-*CE*, 376.

10. "Castañeda's Narrative," W-*CE*, 232.

11. "Coronado to King, October 20, 1541," W-*CE*, 367.

12. "Salazar Inspection," W-*CE*, 241–242.

13. *Relación del Suceso*, W-*CE*, 359.

14. Ibid., 356.

15. In Flint and Flint, *Coronado Expedition to Tierra Nueva*, 140–150.

16. Castañeda hints at this, saying: "It is 30 from Cicuye to where the plains begin. It may be we went across in an indirect or roundabout way, which would make it seem as if there was more country than if it had been crossed in a direct line, and it may be more difficult and rougher. This cannot be known certainly, because the mountains change their direction above the bay at the mouth of the Firebrand (Tizon) river"; "Translation of Castañeda," W-*CE*, 276.

17. Blakeslee and Blaine, "The Jimmy Owens Site," in Flint and Flint, eds., *Coronado Expedition to Tierra Nueva*, 203–218. See also Gagné, "Spanish Crossbow Boltheads of Sixteenth-Century North America," in ibid.

18. *Relación del Suceso*, W-*CE*, 359; "Jaramillo's Narrative," W-*CE*, 379.

19. *Relación del Suceso*, W-*CE*, 359. George A. Root's 1904 map depicting Coronado's route to Quivira (see appendix D) establishes the high hills near Lindsborg, Kansas, as the end point of Coronado's march and the place where he turned around. Supported by Spanish chain mail found at an excavation site nearby, the site later became known as Coronado Heights and developed as a tourist site.

20. "Salazar Inspection," W-*CE*, 241–242.

21. Though this seems like a slow pace for the return, the calculated September 20 arrival back at Tiguex compares well to the October 20 date when Coronado wrote to the king to report on the expedition; "Coronado to King, October 20, 1541," W-*CE*, 364–369.

Appendix B
Oñate's Family

Considerable mystery surrounds the family of Don Juan de Oñate y Salazar: his wife, Isabel de Tolosa Cortés Montezuma, and their two children. Oñate's biographer Marc Simmons states that "about 1619 or 1620, Oñate's wife of thirty years, Doña Isabel, died at their home in Pánuco and was buried there."[1] Simmons does not give the source of his information, but it is contradicted by Oñate's statement in vouching for a bond on January 27, 1598: "Whereas I, Governor Juan de Oñate, in what concerns me as the legitimate father and administrator of the person and estate of Don Cristóbal de Oñate, my legitimate son, and of Doña Isabel Cortés, my legitimate wife, now deceased."[2]

Oñate's statement establishes certain facts concerning his family. Since Doña Isabel was deceased when Don Juan left on his expedition to New Mexico in 1598, both their son, Cristóbal, and daughter, María, were born prior to that date. The precise years of their births, however, are not altogether clear. It is possible that Doña Isabel died while giving birth to María.

Simmons states that Don Cristóbal died in 1612 at age twenty-two, dating his birth to 1590.[3] From this, Simmons reasons that Don Cristóbal was only eight years old when he was taken north as a lieutenant by his father in 1598. When Don Juan attempted to have the boy succeed him as governor of New Mexico, an official described Don Cristóbal as "a youth lacking in age and experience and of whom it is said that he hardly knows how to read and write."[4] On another occasion he was designated as a "mere youth, with little wealth and less experience."[5]

During an inquiry in 1602, Vicente de Zaldívar, under whom young Cristóbal served during the New Mexico venture, made a statement regarding the young man: "Don Juan de Oñate took along a son of about sixteen years" on his expedition.[6] Juan Rodríguez, testifying in regard to Zaldívar's service, stated that "Don Juan de Oñate took along his son, Don Cristóbal, 14 years of age."[7] The latter statement, which is the more specific, would make the boy's date of birth 1584.

Before he died, Don Cristóbal married and sired a son. Despite the criticisms of Don Cristóbal as a youth, he was respected enough by the time of his death that a prominent Spanish poet composed a poem in tribute to him.[8]

Oñate's statement regarding his wife's death prior to January 1598 renders impossible the birth of daughter Mariá de Oñate y Cortés Montezuma in late 1598 or 1599, as given by Simmons.[9] Further evidence lies in Oñate's request on March 2, 1599, that his daughter be sent to him in New Mexico. Surely, to be sent off into what was still a wilderness, she would have had to have been more than merely one or two years old at the time. Nothing in available Spanish records, however, tells us her age. We do know that upon returning to Mexico with her father in 1610, she married Vicente de Zaldívar—within two years, according to Simmons—and soon produced a son.[10]

One of the more puzzling items concerning Don Juan's family appears in the list of goods made by the Gordejuela inspection of the relief expedition sent to the New Mexico colony in 1600. Within the lengthy itemization of goods and equipment compiled on August 23, 1600, was this notation:

Four carts, covered with canvas, bought at Peñol Blanco, together with thirty-two oxen to transport these goods to New Mexico . . . 130 pesos for each cart with eight oxen [520 pesos].

Further, there are in these wagons six boxes of gifts which Doña Maria de Galarza is sending *to the wife of the adelantado [governor], Don Juan de Oñate.*[11]

This statement is particularly curious, since the goods in the four carts were sent under the auspices of Don Juan Guerra de Resa, Oñate's in-law and principal financial backer who likely knew Oñate quite well. Almost certainly, Doña Isabel was deceased at this time, and it is clear that Don Juan took no other legal marital partner thereafter. In 1623 he swore in a legal statement that he had married "Doña Isabel Cortés Tolosa, daughter of Juanes de Tolosa and Doña Leonor Cortés, natural daughter of the marquis, Hernando Cortés,"[12] with the implication that she was his only legitimate wife.

Among the charges lodged against Don Juan after he returned to Mexico was this one: "And charge that, while the *adelantado* was in charge of the said enterprise and government, he lived dishonorably and scandalously with women of the army, married and unmarried."[13] He was acquitted of this charge, yet the possibility lingers that he may have conducted communal relations with one or more women during his stay in Mexico. To date, these riddles of Don Juan's family life remain unsolved.

ABBREVIATION KEY

H/R-*DJO* = Hammond and Rey, eds., *Don Juan de Oñate*

NOTES

1. Simmons, *Last Conquistador*, 190.
2. "Juan Guerra de Resa's Bond," H/R-*DJO* 1: 378–379.
3. Simmons, *Last Conquistador*, 188.
4. "Don de Loez to King," H/R-*DJO* 2: 1073–1074.
5. "Council of the Indies to the King," H/R-*DJO* 2: 1101.
6. "Merits and Services of Zaldívar," H/R-*DJO* 2: 879.
7. Ibid., 883.
8. Simmons, *Last Conquistador*, 188.
9. Ibid., 45.
10. "Services of Don Juan de Oñate," H/R-*DJO* 2: 1148; Simmons, *Last Conquistador*, 188.
11. "Gordejuela Inspection," H/R-*DJO* 1: 529–530 (emphasis added).
12. H/R-*DJO* 2: 1146.
13. H/R-*DJO* 2: 1111; "Oñate's Conviction," H/R-*DJO* 2: 1109–1124.

Appendix C

A New Look at Oñate's Route

SAN GABRIEL TO THE CANADIAN RIVER TURNOFF

There is good reason to believe Spanish scholar Herbert E. Bolton erred in saying that the Oñate Expedition may have turned away from the Canadian River at the Antelope Hills.[1] Accounts tell us that the expedition marched up the Canadian to a point "one hundred and eleven leagues beyond ... [where] it became necessary to leave the river, as we encountered some sand dunes."[2] This seems clear enough, except that to calculate where this took place, it is critical to know from what starting point the 111 leagues are measured.

Oñate departed from San Gabriel at the mouth of the Chama River near present Española, New Mexico, on or about June 23, 1601. He traveled four days south to the pueblo post of Galisteo, where he spent five or six days organizing his expedition. That done, the expedition crossed the Sangre de Cristo Mountain range through Galisteo Pass and marched due east for five days to the Pecos River, dubbed the San Buenaventura by Oñate.[3]

One day more took them to the Gallinas River, which the Spaniards called the River of Bagres. After resting the horses there for a day or so, Oñate marched on for three days to a river he named the Magdalena, arriving there on July 22, the day celebrated for the biblical Mary Magdalena.[4]

This last stream, as George P. Hammond and Agapito Rey state, was obviously the Canadian River.[5] Oñate struck it at the point where it bends from south to east in eastern New Mexico. On August 2 the expedition arrived at a tributary the Spaniards called the Rio de San Francisco.[6] There "most of the men in the army confessed and took communion." After resting for several days, Oñate took up his march again on August 10, "the day of the glorious Levite and martyr, San Lorenzo (Saint Lawrence)."[7] From that point he marched down the Canadian to the spot where he turned away from the river to the north at some sand dunes.

While Bolton and others have surmised that the expedition's departure from the Canadian River occurred at the Antelope Hills in present Oklahoma, it appears far more likely that it was at the northeastward bend of the Canadian River north of Borger, Texas.

NORTHWARD TURN FROM THE CANADIAN

The meaning of words is often flexible, particularly when they involve language translation. Further, there are distinct variations in the translation of Spanish documents regarding this facet of the march. One English translation is provided in Bolton's *Spanish Exploration in the Southwest* and another by Hammond and Rey in *Don Juan de Oñate, Colonizer of New Mexico*. The two translations vary significantly in places.

The turn away from the Canadian is especially crucial as to Oñate's route. Bolton translated the "True Report of the Expedition to the North (Quivira), 1601" to say: "Having traveled to reach this place one hundred and eleven leagues, it became necessary to leave the river, as there appeared ahead some sand dunes, and turning from the east to the north, we traveled up a small stream."[8] To this, Bolton added a footnote with the tentative suggestion that "the place where the turn was made seems to have been the Antelope Hills, just east of the Texas Panhandle."[9] Some scholars have taken this aside by Bolton as virtually a conclusion of researched fact.

It is important to observe, however, that Bolton's choice of the Antelope Hills was anything but definite, offered as little more than an off-hand assumption. Evidently, the location was chosen largely because of the prominence of the hills as a landmark along the river. The 1602 Martínez map (figure 20.1) depicts the expedition as swinging north at a bend of the river at a place strikingly similar to its course north of Borger today.

The eastward extension of the river, as depicted by the map, is not particularly true, but no one with Oñate's expedition, if it turned away to the north at the Borger sand hills, would have experienced that part of the river. The river's extension beyond the bend would simply have to be an imaginary concept by Juan Rodríguez, who supplied cartographer Martínez with all of the data for the map (see appendix D).

In accepting the Antelope Hills as the turnoff place, W. W. Newcomb and T. N. Campbell measure the point of departure from the head of the Canadian.[10] Susan Vehick takes it to mean 111 leagues from the spot where, at 60 leagues, they saw the first buffalo.[11] In doing so, she opens the potential for extending the departure from the Canadian even farther to the east beyond the Antelope Hills.

In *Don Juan de Oñate, Colonizer of New Mexico*, Hammond and Rey translate Oñate's "Faithful and True Report" differently, saying: "After traveling one hundred and eleven leagues beyond this place ["this place" seeming to imply where they had just seen the first buffalo] it became necessary to leave the river, as we encountered some sand dunes, so we turned from east to north."[12] The important difference in the wording of this interpretation lends credence to Bolton's theory more than does his own translation; in a footnote, Hammond and Rey give further support to the Antelope Hills as the point of turnoff.[13]

But is it so? The distance from the Rio Grande to the Borger sand hills is somewhere around 295 overland miles. Following the looping course of the Canadian River, the Antelope Hills are another 100 miles distant. One hundred and eleven Spanish leagues (at 2.6 miles per league) equates to approximately 288.6 miles. Thus, in accepting San Gabriel on the Rio Grande as the starting point for the 111-league march prior to turning, the sand hills on the Canadian River above Borger, Texas, appear a far more reasonable possibility.

THE ANTELOPE HILLS

A strong argument can be made against accepting the Antelope Hills as "sand dunes" or even "sand hills." Again, the interpretation of words matters: pure sand dunes glisten under the sun; plant-covered sand hills do not. Actually, the Antelope Hills are neither. They are a group of separated plateaus or tablelands, sand-drifted at the base with flat tops. They are clustered well off the river's south bank on the inside of a wide northwardly loop of the river. Though surrounded aslant at the base by sandy, vegetated soil long drifted there, they are hardly discernible as sand dunes, even from a distance.

On its march westward along the Canadian River in 1853, the Whipple Railroad Survey described the Antelope Hills as "composed of sandstones cemented with lime, and . . . of the mesa form."[14] From a distance they are clearly seen as plateaus, and there is no reason to think they would impede Oñate's march. It is on record that California Gold Rush caravans in 1848–1849 traveled through the Antelope Hills without particular difficulty, as did many other trade and exploratory groups.

It was much different with the sand dunes at Borger. In 1845, a US Army expedition under Lieutenant James W. Abert marched from Bent's Fort west to east along this same stretch near present Borger. An 1867 US Department of War map designates a "White Sandy Creek" joining the Canadian from the south at the river's bend. The September 14, 1845, entry in Abert's journal describes the travel difficulty encountered there: "Our way now lay along the lowlands on the riverside, where the grass grew tall and the sand was deep. We were so much delayed by various difficulties that our whole day's march did not exceed 8 miles."[15] Coming from a different direction, Whipple likewise witnessed a line of "drifted sand hills" while marching westward along the Canadian near Borger, Texas.[16] Approaching this wide bend in the river, he was warned by a Kiowa tribesman that ahead were "a long succession of sand-hills [that] for two days' journey would compel us to cross the river at this place."[17]

Though these visitations took place nearly a century and a half after Oñate's visit, this was still long before any effects of civilization had touched the then-remote area of the Texas Panhandle. It can thus be argued that the Borger-area site far better matches the True Report's description of a turning point than do the Antelope Hills. Further, the sweep of the river's bend to the northeast at Borger would seem to have impelled Oñate to follow it northeastward after his lengthy eastward march. He was guided by Jusepe; and the expedition's destination was, as the True Report clearly states, to visit the native settlements "by a northern route and direction."[18] Accordingly, it would seem reasonable that both Oñate and Jusepe, after having traveled east for some distance, would have felt it was time to turn north.

BEYOND THE CANADIAN RIVER

The question of where the turn from the Canadian was made is further impacted by ensuing information. After leaving the river, the *entrada* traveled up a "small arroyo," as Hammond and Rey interpreted the Spanish account. Bolton read it as "up a small stream."[19] Hammond and Rey's translation reads: "We turned from east to north and ascended a small arroyo until we came to extensive plains teeming with innumerable cattle [buffalo]. We traveled on, continually finding the land and the road better, so that the carts moved along without any difficulty."[20]

Bolton calculated the watercourse to be Commission Creek in western Oklahoma. But Commission Creek, slanting down to the Canadian from the northwest as it does, is simply not a good candidate. If the turn was made at the Borger-area sand dunes, the stream the expedition followed could have been today's northeasterly Palo Duro Creek (known variously on early maps as Blackwood, Hickory, or Scalped Skull Creek).

Beaver County in the Oklahoma Panhandle is much more of a flat plain than Ellis County, Oklahoma, which lies directly north of the Antelope Hills. Ellis is cut west to east by the valley of Wolf Creek and features low, rolling sagebrush hills with considerable loose, sandy soil in the southern portion of the county that would be uninviting to carts.

The True Report continues with another important clue: "We spent a few days along two small streams, which flowed to the east like the preceding one [the Canadian]."[21] As Bolton himself observed, the only two streams in the entire area that flow to the east and that parallel each other for a time are the Beaver (upper North Canadian) and the Cimarron through the northern portion of Beaver County in the Oklahoma Panhandle.

Had the expedition turned directly north at the Antelope Hills, as Bolton theorized, it would have encountered the two streams as well, but only after they had both turned to the southeast in the Harper County, Oklahoma, area. Only by turning north from the Canadian at the Borger sand hills would Oñate's *entrada* have reached the more westward Beaver County, Oklahoma, and traveled due east between the two streams for a time, as the True Report describes.

From the Martínez map and narrative accounts, it appears almost certain that the expedition turned northeasterly from the Canadian River across the Oklahoma Panhandle into Kansas. Had the group turned away at the Antelope Hills or farther east, it would have possibly encountered the extensive salt beds of the Cimarron River in northern Woodward County, Oklahoma; the Waynoka, Oklahoma, "Little Sahara" sand dunes; or the Glass Mountains (stratified buttes, actually) of Major County, Oklahoma. If so, the Spaniards may have made note of them: they are all striking contrasts to their surrounding landscape.

Salines in that day were highly prized items, and Oñate was seeking anything of value to report to the Spanish king. Portuguese navigator Juan Rodríguez, the expedition member who supplied information for the Martínez map of Oñate's route, testified that the Apache Indians had told them that farther on there were many "salines with salt." Rodríguez made no mention, however, of encountering any salines on the march; he said only that he had seen salt in one Rayado thatched hut. He thought it looked like salt from the sea, but the Indians told him the salt came from salines in the region.[22]

Also implausible would have been a course from the Canadian, such as Hammond and Rey present with their map "Oñate's Route to the Kingdom of Quivira." In that map the authors show Oñate's march turning from the Canadian at the Antelope Hills and heading virtually due north Coronado-like, striking the Arkansas River near Ford, Kansas. From there, the Hammond and Rey route follows up the right bank of the Great Bend of the Arkansas northward and down its eastward arc to a projected Rayado village above Arkansas City.

Though witnesses stated that the *entrada* moved north from the Canadian, an "essentially north" concept is highly doubtful and contrary to the Martínez map. Soldier Diego de Ayarde said the *entrada* was "moving always to the north," but that does not deny an easterly drift as well.[23] Rodríguez testified more specifically that the movement of the expedition was "always east by a quarter northeast."[24] He had to mean, of course, that such movement occurred after leaving the Canadian.

Had the expedition later marched along the Arkansas River, as Hammond and Rey's map indicates, Oñate and others would almost certainly have indicated its size and character in their descriptions of the region traveled. Also, it is doubtful that the Indian guide Jusepe would have taken such a looping course to reach the Indian village above Arkansas

City, Kansas, as the Hammond and Rey map depicts. Having traveled over the country before, Jusepe would likely have known the region well enough to avoid such a severe detour.

OÑATE'S MARCH THROUGH KANSAS (FIGURE 20.2)

From all evidence, it appears fairly certain that Oñate turned northeast-ward from the Canadian River, crossed the Oklahoma Panhandle, and continued in the same direction into Kansas. But precisely where he marched has never been resolved. Seemingly, the best clues we have are the streams he crossed, as designated in the literature of the expedition, and the distances he marched from one camp to the other. In support of that information are limited descriptions of the flora and other aspects of the various watercourses.

Beyond the two easterly flowing streams, the True Report mentions six rivers the Spaniards encountered. The expedition camped first at a small river with little water and thick woods; second, the Spaniards marched three leagues to a river with more water, many fish, and nut and oak trees. Third, they marched three more leagues to the river on which the Escanjacque village was found. Fourth, they marched three leagues plus six or seven more (total of nine or ten leagues) to a river that ran due east and possessed level banks and dense woods. Fifth, they marched four leagues-plus to a larger river and tributary with the Rayado village; and sixth, they marched through the settlement to its end two or three leagues and turned east two leagues to a small stream before turning back.[25]

This book projects these streams/rivers as the (1) Medicine Lodge, (2) the Chikaskia, (3) the South Ninnescah, (4) the North Ninnescah, (5) the Arkansas, and (6) the Little Arkansas. Nothing in the Oñate narratives gives any hint of the expedition crossing, as it would have had to do, the headwaters of the North Canadian (the Beaver), the Cimarron, or the Salt Fork of the Arkansas. Ensuing distances between streams and other clues cause this projection to choose Medicine Lodge Creek as the first stream mentioned beyond the Canadian River. Obviously, this conclusion is arguable.

Stream #1, Medicine Lodge Creek

After camping here for one night, the expedition moved 3 leagues (7.6 miles) to Stream #2. This is the approximate distance from a point just west of the town of Medicine Lodge NNE to the Chikaskia River.

Stream #2, the Chikaskia

After camping here for one night, the expedition marched to Stream #3. Juan Rodríguez stated that Vicente went "eight or ten leagues" [20.8/26 miles] before reaching the settlement.[26] Expedition member Juan de León, however, testified that Vicente explored "about twenty leagues [52 miles] before reaching the settlement."[27]

This conflict in the distances marched (which undoubtedly are estimations) can perhaps be resolved by considering that Vicente's advance party likely broke camp on the Chikaskia ahead of the main expedition to scour the countryside. The main expedition, meanwhile, would have marched directly to the South Fork of the Ninnescah, where it went into camp.

From the bend of the Chikaskia north of Medicine Lodge, the direct distance to the South Fork of the Ninnescah is about 25–26 miles at a point near Celista (west of Kingman). It is doubtful that Vicente's scouting march was a straight line, as would have been the case with the main expedition, or that it was a factual measurement.

Stream #3, the South Ninnescah

After camping for one night on the South Ninnescah, Vicente scouted downriver 3 leagues and discovered the Escanjaque village. At daybreak the next morning the expedition followed Vicente, "surrounded on all sides by refreshing rivers and delightful groves," arriving at 3:00 in the afternoon and camping near some swamps.[28]

After a brief visit, Oñate moved on 3 leagues northward to make evening camp. The following day the expedition, trailed by Escanjaques, continued north 6 or 7 leagues to Stream #4. This total march of 9–10 leagues (23.4–26 miles) compares favorably with the ±25-mile distance on a northeasterly slant from the South Ninnescah west of Kingman to the North Ninnescah west of Castleton.

Steam #4, the North Ninnescah

This stream is described as having "marvelous level banks, but [it] was so wooded that the trees formed very dense extensive forests . . . the river flowed directly east."[29] This appears to be a central clue in the march. It requires a stream that not only runs due east (at the point where it was seen by the expedition) but that has prefatory and succeeding attributes—

namely, a stream such as the South Ninnescah below and a large river at the correct distance above.

Few Kansas streams below the Arkansas River flow directly east for any distance. The North Ninnescah does so for 8 or 10 miles below Hutchinson before dipping southeastward toward Wichita. But it also qualifies as the "easterly flowing stream" by having the South Ninnescah below and a large river—the Arkansas with its parallel tributary, Cow Creek—located due north at an appropriate distance.

Stream #5, the Arkansas

The True Report states that after the expedition left the "due easterly" stream (marching north according to Diego de Ayarde[30] and the Martínez map), it encountered the Rayados massed on a hill. Later that day the Spaniards camped on the banks of the "San Francisco River," which they crossed the next morning. After marching half a league, they came onto the Rayado village located on both sides of another good-sized stream (a tributary of the larger one).[31]

Oñate's "True Report" of the Quivira expedition places the hills where the Rayados were first seen at 4 leagues (±10 miles) beyond the easterly flowing river.[32] Evidently, the hills were not far from the large river.

Captain Juan Gutiérrez Bocanegra described the Rayado village as located "between two rivers, one large and one small."[33] Cow Creek closely parallels the southeasterly flow of the Arkansas for a distance before emptying into it at Hutchinson 15 miles north of Castleton. This distance seems to correspond well with the True Report and Bocanegra's account.

Stream #6, the Little Arkansas

After visiting the deserted Rayado village, the expedition marched 2 or 3 leagues along the side of the river (apparently up the tributary) before abruptly turning east and marching 2 more leagues to another heavily populated stream where Oñate turned back. The relationship of Cow Creek and the Little Arkansas matches this configuration.

At the Rayado village, Oñate learned of another large, easterly flowing river to the north that divided into six or seven branches. Bolton believed this must have been the Kansas River, which is fed by its Delaware, Big Blue, Republican, Solomon, Saline, and Smoky Hill tributaries.[34] Oñate did not visit these rivers, however.

THE QUIVIRA OÑATE FOUND

It is entirely possible that the location where Coronado found Quivira in 1541 was not the same place Oñate visited in 1601. Kansas historian W. E. Richey, in an address to the Kansas Historical Society well before Bolton, concluded that when Coronado arrived, "the hills of the Smoky Hill river near Lindsborg located the first settlements and marked the beginning of the land of Quivira."[35] During the sixty-year interim, the Quiviran Indians could have moved south to the Arkansas because of pressure from other tribes.

This discussion by no means resolves the question of Oñate's march through Kansas. At best, it offers an approach to further consideration by which others can make decisions relative to stream descriptions and distances marched between them. This author can argue with confidence only that the expedition did enter Kansas and that it marched on a general northeasterly course.

ABBREVIATION KEY

H/R-*DJO* = Hammond and Rey, eds., *Don Juan de Oñate*

NOTES

1. Bolton, *Spanish Exploration*, 255n2.
2. "Expedition to Quivira," H/R-*DJO* 2: 750.
3. Ibid., 747.
4. Ibid.
5. Ibid., 749.
6. Ibid.
7. Ibid.
8. Bolton, *Spanish Exploration*, 255.
9. Ibid., n. 2.
10. Newcomb and Campbell, "Southern Plains Ethnohistory," 30.
11. Vehick, "Oñate's Expedition," 15.
12. "Expedition to Quivira," H/R-*DJO* 2: 750.
13. Ibid., n. 9.
14. Whipple, "Reports of Explorations," 29.
15. Abert, *Report of an Expedition Led by Lieutenant Abert*, 41.
16. Whipple, "Reports of Explorations," 31.
17. Ibid.
18. Bolton, *Spanish Exploration*, 250.

19. Ibid., 255.

20. "Expedition to Quivira," H/R-*DJO* 2: 750.

21. Ibid.

22. "Valverde Inquiry," H/R-*DJO* 2: 864.

23. Ibid., 884.

24. Ibid., 871.

25. Ibid., 846.

26. Ibid., 865.

27. Ibid., 854.

28. "Expedition to Quivira," H/R-*DJO* 2: 751–752. While the "True Report" does not say that the Escanjaque village was on a river (as it logically would be), Juan de León does. He states that Vicente "went ahead with twelve men to explore and came to a large river" in reaching the village campsite. This indicates that he had reached a different stream than the one on which the expedition had previously camped.

29. "Expedition to Quivira," H/R-*DJO* 2: 753.

30. "Merits and Services of Zaldívar," H/R-*DJO* 2: 884.

31. "Expedition to Quivira," H/R-*DJO* 2: 753.

32. Ibid.

33. "Merits and Services of Zaldívar," H/R-*DJO* 2: 890.

34. Bolton, *Spanish Exploration*, 261n2.

35. W. E. Richey, "Early Spanish Exploration," 157.

Appendix D
The Oñate Maps

THE 1602 MARTÍNEZ MAP (FIGURE 20.1)

Juan Rodríguez,[1] a native of Chutuma, Spain, enlisted with Oñate at age forty. He served as a commander in the company of Captain Francisco de Zúñiga and took part in all of the discoveries conducted by Oñate and his *maestre de campo* (second in command). He was back in Mexico City in April 1602, where he testified on behalf of Vicente de Zaldívar and gave the Valverde Inquiry a lengthy report regarding the Quivira expediton.[2]

He is also the Juan Rodríguez who provided cartographer Enrico Martínez with the very creditable details for preparing a map depicting Oñate's New Mexico province in 1602 and his expedition's march to Quivira.[3] Martínez was an experienced navigator who had sailed up the California coast and later visited the Philippine Islands. One would suspect, however, that Rodríguez must have helped with the actual drawing of the map or that he had detailed notes and sketches for reference.

The Martínez map is lacking identifiable landmarks, particularly streams, that would help viewers today better understand precisely where beyond the Canadian River the expedition went. Still, it remarkably reflects many aspects of the march and the topography of southwestern America that are recognizable four centuries later through narrative accounts, archaeological study, and known landmarks.

Among these are certain identifiable rivers, particularly the Rio Grande and Canadian; the locations of important ancient pueblos such as San Gabriel, Galisteo, and Pecos; the expedition's crossing of the Manzano Mountains through Galisteo Pass; the march eastward to the New Mexico bend of the Canadian; the march down that watercourse passing the two tributaries that could be today's Ute and the Rita Blanco; the critical-to-course swing northeastward at another bend in the river, possibly near Borger, Texas; and the march's abrupt turn north again at the Escanjaque village (also shown on the map drawn by Miguel, discussed in the next section). It is significant that these aspects are one and all supported in the various narrative accounts.

We do not know with such certainty that it was a tributary of the Arkansas River on which Quivira—the "*Pueblo del nuevo descubrir*," or "Village of New Discovery"—was found. But today many scholars believe the river shown at the upper right of the map, on whose tributary the Indian settlement is depicted, was indeed the Arkansas between Wichita and Great Bend. Also, the theory that the big river's tributary was Cow Creek is supported (though not proven) by archaeological evidence that has been found there.

This study differs from others on a crucial point, making the argument that the turn from the Canadian occurred at a series of sand hills on the Canadian River above Borger, Texas, rather than at the Antelope Hills (see appendix C). Whether the turn was at the Antelope Hills or at the Borger point, however, the map clearly shows the line of the march to be north by east, which would take it directly into present Kansas.

Beyond the Canadian River, the Martínez map leaves us uncertain regarding what streams are designated. But though the map does not tell us everything we wish to know, we should be grateful that it does tell us a great deal.

In accepting that Oñate turned from the Canadian into Kansas, theorists are presented with three prominent options as to the tributary of the Arkansas River on which he found the Rayado village: Cow Creek, the

Little Arkansas, and Walnut Creek (feeding south into Arkansas City). The northeasterly line of the march indicated on the Martínez map and the predominant flow of the streams to the east at the Rayado site seem to make Cow Creek the most likely candidate of the three.

MIGUEL'S MAP, 1602 (SEE FIGURE 21.1)

Miguel, an Indian slave whose original home was at the site he designated as Tancoa on a map, had originally been taken prisoner by the Escanjaques. Recaptured by Juan de Oñate's men during their clash with that tribe in 1601, he was taken first to Oñate's headquarters at San Gabriel, New Mexico, and then to Mexico City by Oñate's *maestre de campo*, Vicente de Zaldívar. There, in the spring of 1602, he was brought to the home of Don Francisco de Valverde y Mercado, royal factor of Spain, who had been sent to Mexico to conduct an inquiry of Oñate's expedition.

Miguel was asked to draw a map of the land where he had been held captive. The Indian was provided with a pen and ink and told to indicate the pueblos of his land on a sheet of paper that was on a table, and he proceeded to mark on the paper some circles resembling the letter O.[4] After Miguel had done this, Spanish official Ambrosia de Rueda (apparently) wrote in the circles what each represented, as Miguel was interpreted to say. Also, he was shown flowers and other plants, as well as costumes and weaponry of Mexican Indians, and asked to compare them with those of his country. "Then he [Miguel] drew lines, some snakelike and some straight, and indicated by signs that they were rivers and roads; they were also given names, according to his explanation."[5] Miguel explained by signs where he had been born, how he was captured, how he was taken to the place where he grew up, and where he was made a prisoner by the Spaniards.

It should not be surprising that Miguel's map is confusing and often contradictory to the modern viewer. The inherent problems of communication through hand signs, and the scarcity of identifiable locations on the prairie that were known to everyone, would impair even schooled cartographers. By any consideration, Miguel's map apparently requires some rationalization, but it is possibly best understood in relation to the Cow Creek concept.

Francisco de Valverde y Mercado conducted Miguel's interview in the presence of a physician called Doctor Contreras, interpreter Juan Grande, official Antonio de Ronda, governor of Santiago Don Juan Bautista, and a Mexican Indian interpreter. The fact that none of the men had been with Oñate's Quivira expedition could have led them to accept Miguel's map with the attitude (assumption) that the position of the writing (which was added by the Spaniards) on it indicates that the top of the page was north. Compass directions were not given, and this has a great impact on understanding the map.

The most tangible clues Miguel's map offers as to location are the site of San Gabriel and the route of Oñate's expedition from there to the Escanjaque camp (indicated only by a sharp turn of the march). In this context, the map depicts the Rayado's Great Settlement, a few river lines, and two salines. The salines are significant in that they are identifiable geologic sites that span the time period between 1601 and the present.

The Map's Directions

The common assumption is that the top of any map above the written material is north. But this is apparently not so with Miguel's map. The known direction of Oñate's march is the most substantial clue. It is established fact that Oñate's march was to the northeast of San Gabriel. The map as prepared shows the march leading to the northwest. What is perhaps the true direction of the march can be achieved by turning the map sideways (with the writing facing left), as Susan Velick wisely saw.[6]

This produces some corrections but still leaves many questions in relation to other known facts. Here, the identification of lines made for rivers and routes on Miguel's map follows designations made by William Wilmon Newcomb and Thomas Nolan Campbell.[7]

The Line of March

Oñate's line of march as indicated on the map has the interesting aspect of changing direction abruptly at the far end. This produces a right angle and then extends for a short distance to a line designated as a river. This surely indicates Oñate's march northeastward to the Escanjaque camp, where it turned sharply due north to the Rayado village. This line is similar to the route shown for Oñate on the Martínez map and concurs with expedition narratives.

River Lines

Though poorly distinguished, there are apparently three streams depicted on Miguel's map. There is the wiggly line at the bottom (with the map turned sideways), the longer line that runs through the indicated junction and is forked at the top end, and the one that joins the latter at the junction.

On the assumption that the map applies to the general region of south-central Kansas, the longer line becomes suspect as representing the Arkansas River. With the map turned sideways, this longer line could possibly be the downward swing of the Arkansas northwest of present Wichita.

It perhaps requires some imagination to say that the line coming down to the juncture represents the Little Arkansas and that one branch of the fork is today's Cow Creek, but these are possibilities to be considered. As Vehick points out, this was enemy territory to the Escanjaques who held Miguel captive; thus, he would not have known the area well.[8]

With the map turned, the wiggly line extending from Yahuicacha to Equacapac would become an east-west stream. The possibility that this is the Cimarron River of Oklahoma is discussed in the next section.

Two Salines

Turning the map sideways also gives some logic to the position of the saline on the wiggly line near Equacapac. This could have been either the saline (functioning today as a commercial salt producer) on the Cimarron River in northern Woodward County, Oklahoma, or the Great Salt Plains on the Salt Fork of the Arkansas east of Cherokee, Oklahoma. These were large, highly visible surface salines, and both were well known and much used by local latter-day tribes, as well as the distant Apaches of Texas and Osages of Missouri. In 1811 Osage factor George C. Sibley accompanied a party of Osage Indians to the Cimarron salt beds and provided a definitive account of them.[9]

Thus, the salines should have been commonly known to earlier occupants and hunters in the region, such as the two tribes identified as Escanjaques and Rayados. Either would fit well into the configuration established by the line of Oñate's march. Miguel could have been taken there by the Escanjaques on a salt-gathering venture.

Vehick appropriately observes, however, that there are no known Indian settlements such as Miguel indicates (Equacapac and Aguacane) along the Cimarron or the Salt Fork. Also, because of the briny water around salines, Indians did not prefer to live close to them. The saline Miguel shows near Tancoa could relate to a known saline marsh located just south of the Arkansas River in the general area of Cow Creek.[10]

If the Arkansas River were, as Vehick has suggested is possible, the long line with a fork at the end, then the saline indicated on the map near Tancoa would be along that river. While there are large salt works in Reno (e.g., the Hutchinson Salt Company), Rice, and Ellsworth Counties of Kansas, they are predominantly subsurface operations. There is no indication that Indians in 1601 used subsurface salines in that area; further, the records of the Coronado and Oñate Expeditions do not indicate that the Spaniards witnessed such.

Four Town Circles

The town locations most pertinent to the Oñate Expedition are San Gabriel and the Great Settlement. It is difficult to conjecture where the other Indian settlements represented by Miguel's circles were located. An argument could possibly be made that the two circles on the line below Etzanoa (Elzanoa) signify the Great Settlement, which the Oñate Expedition narratives and the Martínez map indicate was on both sides of a tributary of a larger stream.

Gold Lagoon

The map depicts Miguel's (mythical) gold lagoon near Encuche, and with the map turned, the lagoon becomes located to the north. This fits with the Martínez map, which depicts a stream to the north as *rio del oro*, or river of gold. Narratives of the Oñate Expedition indicate that the Indians told of a city of gold to the north.

By what we know today, Miguel's tale of gold on the plains was pure fantasy. The closest gold- and silver-producing area to the plains is the Colorado Rockies. It is possible, of course, that Miguel actually saw gold brought from that area, and the location of Encuche (with the map sideways) hints to that direction. But while there is evidence of Indian tribes finding gold dust in the rivers of present Colorado, no indication had surfaced that any Indian tribe collected or processed it as Miguel described. The Spaniards interviewing him in Mexico City saw a contradiction in his testimony that caused them to be suspicious of his story.[11]

Still, Spanish officials surely must have been amazed, even as we are today, with the ability of Miguel—an untutored inhabitant of the wilderness—to describe a native smelting procedure in detail as he did. He told the Spaniards that he had twice seen Indians of his homeland put "gold dust in some vases that had a hole in each of the four sides and that at each hole a man put in wood and fanned the fire with fans made of buffalo hide. Keeping the vase covered three or four days, they melted the gold and made ingots of the size stated."[12]

Space and Distance

When viewing an early Indian-drawn map such as Miguel's, a person today should be aware that space and distance were conceptualized much differently four centuries ago. The Spaniard tried to establish an understanding of distance, and thus space, by asking Miguel how long it took him to travel by foot from one point to another. The distances and directions appear to be valid only in a general sense.

CONCLUSION

Thus far, Miguel's map has been of limited value in telling us much about the plains region of his time. He had, after all, been captured as a boy and thereafter held captive by the Escanjaques. His freedom to hunt and roam was limited, and his knowledge of the world around him was more limited than that of the normal tribesman. That reality, compounded by communication barriers and exacerbated by the Spanish desire to hear tales of golden wonders, may have impaired his capacity to produce a more revealing account of his early-seventeenth-century world.

ABBREVIATION KEY

H/R-*DJO* = Hammond and Rey, eds., *Don Juan de Oñate*

NOTES

1. There were two men named Juan Rodríguez with the Oñate Expedition. Another is listed in the Ulloa Inspection as a native of Manzanilla, Spain. Perhaps this second man was one of the two colony deserters whose life Gaspar de Villagrá spared; "The Ulloa Inspection," H/R-*DJO* 1: 164.

2. "Valverde Inquiry," H/R-*DJO* 2: 862–871, 883.

3. Reinhartz and Saxon, *Mapping of the Entradas*, 77.

4. "Valverde Inquiry," H/R-*DJO* 2: 872–873.

5. Ibid., 873.

6. Vehick, "Oñate's Expedition," 22.

7. Newcomb and Campbell, "Southern Plains Ethnohistory," 31.

8. Vehick, "Oñate's Expedition," 23.

9. Major John Sibley, "Extracts from the Diary of Major Sibley." See also "Sibley and the Salt Mountain," in Hoig, *Beyond the Frontier*, 82–90.

10. Vehick, "Oñate's Expedition," 22–23, figure 6.

11. "Valverde Inquiry," H/R-*DJO* 2: 876.

12. Ibid.

Appendix E
The Sword and the Stone
Conquistador Artifacts?

By any measure, the passage of the Spanish conquistadors across the American Southwest was a colorful and exciting adventure of discovering worlds yet unknown to literate man. Yet beyond even that, the expeditions of Coronado in 1541 and Oñate in 1601 left behind intriguing mysteries and buried clues as to precisely where the Spanish conquistadors marched over a landscape now dotted with cities and crossed by fenced roadways.

The tracks of the conquistadors across Texas, Oklahoma, and Kansas have long since been covered over by the sands of time. But it was inevitable that the two expeditions of discovery would leave behind lasting evidence of their presence: a spur, a piece of mail, some discarded or lost weapon, a crossbow point, the charred remnants of a campsite or its accouterments, perhaps even a legend chiseled in stone with a message to the ages. Few things are more fascinating than unsolved mysteries of the past.

Archaeological crews work long, hard, and patiently in the heat and dust to search for historical evidence, and their work is both essential and admirable. Still, many important artifact remnants have been discovered happenstance by early residents of the plains. Some of these finds are clearly authentic relics (Spanish mail, for instance), while others have proven to be frauds. It is crucial that artifacts be verified as the real thing; it is equally crucial that items not be discarded until their historical value is determined with absolute certainty.

In 1885, a wrought-iron bit thought to be of Spanish origin was found in western Kansas and eventually turned over to the Kansas Historical Museum.[1] The bit is still held by the museum and is accepted as evidence of conquistador presence in Kansas. Other Spanish items include chain mail found on the Smoky Hill River, a piece of chain armor uncovered near Lindsborg, and a lead bar carrying a Spanish brand discovered in McPherson County.[2]

In 1886, an especially intriguing artifact was discovered in western Kansas. An early-day Kansan, John T. Clark, came upon a double-edged sword blade, minus its hilt nomenclature, protruding from a clump of buffalo grass thirty miles northwest of Cimarron, Kansas. When the disfigured blade was scoured with brick dust, the commonly inscribed legend could be read as "No Me Saques Sin Razon; No Me Embaines Sin Honor" (Draw me not without reason, sheath me not without honor). Another inscription, it was first believed, spelled out the name "Gallego."[3]

The discovery site on the headwaters of Pawnee Fork lies west and north of where Coronado is believed to have struck the Arkansas on his march from the Texas Panhandle to Quivira and which he passed by again on his return to New Mexico. This location fostered the theory that perhaps Captain Juan Gallego of the Coronado Expedition lost the sword during a buffalo hunt to secure meat for the advance party. The muster roll for Coronado's expedition identifies Gallego's equipment simply as "a coat of mail, breeches of mail, buckskin jacket, crossbow, other arms of Castile and of the country, and seven horses."[4]

In 1902, the blade was sent to ethnologist F. W. Hodge at the Bureau of Ethnology in Washington, DC, to examine. Hodge expressed his opinion that it was a significant relic that deserved institutional supervision.[5] Eventually, the sword found its way to the Kansas Historical Society, where it was acclaimed to be true evidence of Coronado's expedition in present Kansas.

During the 1980s, however, new questions about the sword emerged. Upon careful examination, the difficult-to-read inscription, thought originally to be "Gallego," was determined to be "Solingen"—the name of a highly reputed sword maker in Germany whose wares were vended throughout Europe.[6]

Double-edged swords, designed to cut armor, had fallen out of military favor during the first half of the sixteenth century when defensive armor became obsolete; their manufacture had been largely discontinued. Still, modern-day sword experts proclaimed that the blade was an eighteenth- rather than a sixteenth-century weapon. Because the sword had no hilt, some concluded that perhaps it was a trade item lost from a Santa Fe Trail caravan. But questions arise. Were swords not sold fully manufactured? If that was so with this blade, then what became of the pommel, grip, and crossguard? Could they have been lost to the passing of time and elements of nature? Imagination can lead us to a Spanish conquistador who dropped his weapon during a buffalo chase, to a wayward Spaniard soldier who became lost from his companions on the buffalo prairies and perished, or perhaps to Major Scott Anthony's 1864 clash with the Cheyennes at this place on Pawnee Fork[7] where an officer may have carried his personal antique sword into battle. Most likely, we will never know the true story of how the weapon ended up in a clump of grass along Pawnee Fork.

An inscription reading "Fran. Vásquez de Coronado" was reportedly found on a rock ledge near Elkhart, Kansas, at Point of Rocks in extreme southwestern Kansas in 1941. At the time, Elkhart was preparing to hold a grand fourth-century celebration of Coronado's 1541 expedition. A citizen of the region with some artifact experience declared that the engraving had been made "in the correct script used by the Spanish at that period."[8] It was also observed that Coronado may well have passed this way on his return from Quivira to New Mexico.

But others pointed to the spelling "Vásquez" rather than "Vázquez" and challenged its authenticity. Neither Elkhart nor the Kansas Historical Society makes claim for the rock message today. Thus, unless evidence to the contrary surfaces, it must be assumed that the discovery was a publicity ruse.

Over the years, archaeological digs have uncovered items thought to be revealing of the two expeditions, each exciting our curiosity about the story behind it. Crossbow bolt heads, iron points, chain mail, glassware shards, and other artifacts have been found at Blanco Canyon near Lubbock, Texas. Similar bolt heads and copper points have also been uncovered at Hawikuh pueblo in Arizona, and other artifacts have been unearthed at known conquistador sites in New Mexico.

In a professional paper, archaeologist William B. Lees lists a variety of European-produced items that have been uncovered from Wichita Indian excavations in Rice, McPherson, and Marion Counties in Kansas. They include chain mail, iron awls, iron knife blade fragments, iron ax blades, glass beads, copper-alloy tinklers, copper-alloy beads, and necklaces composed of glass, turquoise, and bone beads.[9]

After he departed from Quivira, Coronado stopped at an Indian village, possibly along the Arkansas River or a tributary, to obtain "picked fruit and dried corn" as well as guides to lead the way back to New Mexico.[10] Expedition member Juan Jaramillo left a valuable historical clue in telling that Coronado "raised a cross at this place, at the foot of which he made some letters with a chisel, which said that Francisco Vázquez de Coronado, general of that army, had arrived here."[11]

Unfortunately, Jaramillo did not state whether this message was cut into wood or stone. But Coronado was surely aware that a message in stone would last for the ages while wood would eventually rot away. Historians have long hoped that perhaps someday evidence of this notable event would emerge.

For a time in 1937, the world had reason to believe that event had occurred. Kansas newspapers reported the startling discovery of a sandstone slab engraved with an inscription indicating it was left by Coronado. If valid, it stood to be the most significant conquistador artifact yet uncovered on the plains and undeniable proof of Coronado's presence.

The story of its discovery, as told, was intriguing in itself.

Kansan Ralph Steele was a part-time journalist with a wife and three young children to support. In 1937 the country was still seeking to recover from the Great Depression and the Dust Bowl onslaught of the Central Plains. Money was scarce. Steele had worked for newspapers in Glasco and La Crosse, Kansas, and written features for the *Kansas City Star*. For a time he held the position of state editor for the *Wichita Eagle*, sending local news to the paper from his home in Effington.

Because the pay for "stringing" was small and so was his income from work as a seed-and-feed loan man, Steele took a side job with the government's Works Progress Administration's writer's project. Under the proj-

FIGURE A.1. *The Coronado Stone*

ect, Kansas editors were compiling a state guidebook, and they assigned Steele to find a genuine Indian burial mound for them.[12]

Steele claimed that while hiking one day along the west bank of the Missouri River south of Atchison between rail locations known as Oak Mills and Dalby, he discovered a broken, triangular slab of yellowish-brown limestone half-buried in the Kansas soil (figure A.1). When the slab had been cleaned, its inscription read:

> *AGOSTO EL TRE*
> *1541*
> *TOMO*
> *POR ESPAÑA*
> *QUIVER . . .*
> *. . . RANCISCO . . .*[13]

This was interpreted to read: "August 3, 1541. I take for Spain, Quiver[a]. [F]rancisco [de Vázquez Coronado]."[14]

Steele's discovery created considerable excitement, particularly among Kansas newspaper editors. Almost immediately, questions arose as to whether the relic was the real thing. Stories about the discovery ran in the *Kansas City Star, Wichita Eagle*, and other regional newspapers—several of which strongly challenged the stone's authenticity.

Finding scant support for the stone and disturbed at being accused of planting it, Steele accepted the purchase offer of four dollars made by Kansas City insurance salesman and history buff Lyle Stephenson. In 1937, when it was impossible to prove the stone's authenticity, four dollars was four dollars.

The Associated Press spread word of Steele's find nationally, and the Smithsonian Institution in Washington, DC, became very interested. Officials there secured the stone from Stephenson and asked a number of highly respected and qualified persons in various scientific fields to evaluate it independently.

All of these professionals argued against the stone's authenticity. Spanish linguists observed that the "TRE" in the stone's date was missing the "S" required for the Spanish "TRES," meaning three. Historians pointed to the fact that "Quiver" was a misspelling of "Quivira." Geologists said the stone itself was common to the Atchison area and not the Arkansas River area near Lyons, where many believe Coronado's cross and marker were left.

Eventually, the sandstone slab was declared a worthless fabrication. Interest in it waned, and the Coronado Stone faded from public attention. Then, on November 30, 1941, Stephenson died, leaving behind a new mystery: no one knew what had become of the forsaken Coronado Stone.

Still, questions as to the stone's legitimacy remained. The place it had been found in far northeastern Kansas near the Missouri River was contrary to accounts of Coronado's march. And the August 3, 1541, date was especially troublesome. Prior to Steele's "discovery," no Coronado authorities had ever cited that date in their writings, yet it could be proven correct by calculating the time the expedition marched before leaving Quivira after its date of departure from Tiquex. It appeared that whoever had chiseled the stone had been uniquely informed.

Further, the misspelling of the name Quivira could have occurred in 1541 as easily as in 1937. Significantly, there was no approved dictionary spelling of the word in August 1541. Nor was there any evidence that the name, which the Spanish took from the spoken language of an Indian slave, had even been put into writing prior to Coronado's letter to the king on October 20, 1541, after the expedition had returned to Tiguex. To counter the errant location of Steele's find, it was not at all unreasonable to argue that a curious Indian could have discovered the strangely marked stone and carried it back to his home camp to show to others.

In 1989, Kansan John M. Peterson brought the matter back to life with an article in the *Kansas Anthropologist*.[15] In preparing the piece, he had conducted a thorough but futile search to find the stone. Abandoned by academia and the press, it had disappeared even from record.

In his article, Peterson summarized the professional doubts regarding the Coronado Stone. He explored the discovery of the stone as best he could and traced its history. When Peterson found that Lyle Stephenson had died, he traced the stone's 1938 return from the Smithsonian to author Paul Wellman at the *Kansas City Star* and, Peterson surmised, on to Stephenson. Peterson could learn nothing about what Stephenson or his heirs had done with the stone. He did, however, find the description of a very similar stone in artist Margaret Whitemore's book *Historic Kansas, a Centenary Sketchbook*, published in 1954. Eventually, Steele's Coronado Stone was rediscovered in Rice County's Coronado-Quivira Museum.[16]

Eventually, too, the truth came to light: the Coronado Stone was indeed a fraud. Steele had confessed as much in a story that ran in the Atchison *Globe* on November 16, 1966. He had also told of his deception in an article he wrote for the St. Joseph *Gazette*.[17]

Before he died in 1986, Steele described how, in jesting with another journalist, he had engraved the stone with a chisel and hammer, sandpapered the lettering, and dipped the stone in mud to "age" it. The "Agosto el tre" date had resulted when he tried to carve, incorrectly, "Agosto el Treinta"—meaning August 30—but ran out of room.[18]

Steele's bogus find was a bad joke at best. Still, the thought still lives on. Could there be a true Coronado Stone buried somewhere in the Kansas soil awaiting discovery? And surely there is evidence somewhere of Oñate's clash with the Escanjaques, of Humaña's death by fire at the hands of the Rayados, or of other instances where the Spanish conquistadors—intentionally or by happenstance—left tangible evidence of their presence on the buffalo plains of America.

Perhaps one day these historical mysteries will be solved by professional archaeological teams or even by some curious citizen who turns over, as Steele so wrongly claimed he did, an innocent-looking slab of sandstone and discovers Coronado's proclamation to the ages.

ABBREVIATION KEY

F/F-*DOCS* = Flint and Flint, eds., trans., annots., *Documents of the Coronado Expedition, 1539–1542*

W-*CE* = Winship, *The Coronado Expedition, 1540–1542*

NOTES

1. *Kansas Historical Quarterly* 4 (February 1935): 78.

2. Richey, "Early Spanish Exploration," 160–162.

3. Ibid.

4. "Muster Roll of the Expedition," F/F-*DOCS*, 139.

5. Richey, "Early Spanish Exploration," 160–162.

6. Ibid.

7. Grinnell, *Fighting Cheyennes*, 161–162; Hoig, *Sand Creek Massacre*, 107–109.

8. *Wichita Evening Eagle*, April 11, 1941.

9. Lees, "Evidence for Early European Contact," 3.

10. Ibid.

11. "Jaramillo's Narrative," W-*CE*, 381.

12. *Kansas City Star*, July 11, 1957.

13. Clippings, Wichita Public Library: *Kansas City Star*, July 11, 1937; *Wichita Eagle*, July 11, 1937.

14. Clippings, Wichita Public Library: *Wichita Eagle*, July 11, 1937.

15. Peterson, "Coronado Stone."

16. Ibid., 8; Lees, "New Light on the 'Coronado Stone,'" 28.

17. Lees, "New Light on the 'Coronado Stone,'" 28–29.

18. Ibid., 30.

Bibliography

ARCHIVES

- Kansas State Historical Society, Research Division, Topeka
- Oklahoma Historical Society, Archives and Research Division, Oklahoma City
- University of Central Oklahoma, Special Collections, Edmond
- University of New Mexico, Center for Southwest Research, Albuquerque
- University of Oklahoma, Western History Collection, Norman
- Wichita Public Library, Local History Department, Wichita, KS

NEWSPAPERS

Clippings from *Kansas City Star, Topeka Capital, Wichita Eagle*, and *Wichita Evening Eagle*. Local History Department, Wichita Public Library.

BOOKS, ARTICLES, AND OTHER SOURCES

Abert, James. W. "Notes of Lt. J. W. Abert," 30th Cong., 1st sess., 1847–1848. *Sen. Exec. Doc 7.*

Abert, James W. *Report of an Expedition Led by Lieutenant Abert on the Upper Arkansas and through the Country of the Comanche Indians in the Fall of the Year 1845, Journal of Lieutenant J. W. Abert, from Bent's Fort to St. Louis in 1845.* Senate Document No. 438, 29th Cong., 1st sess. Washington, DC: Government Printing Office, 1846.

Ahern, Maureen. "Mapping, Measuring, and Naming Cultural Spaces in Castañeda's Relación de la jornada de Cibola." In *The Coronado Expedition, from the Distance of 460 Years*, ed. Richard Flint and Shirley Cushing Flint, 265–89. Albuquerque: University of New Mexico Press, 2003.

Bancroft, Hubert Howe. *History of Mexico, 1521–1600.* Vol. I: History of Mexico, 1516–1521; vol. 2: The Works of Hubert Howe Bancroft. San Francisco: The History Company, Publishers, 1886.

Bandelier, A. F., ed. *The Journey of Alvar Nuñez Cabeza de Vaca and His Companions from Florida to the Pacific, 1528–1536.* Trans. Fanny Bandelier. New York: A. S. Barnes & Company, 1925.

Bannon, John Francis, ed. *Bolton and the Spanish Borderlands.* Norman: University of Oklahoma Press, 1964.

Bartlett, Katharine. "Notes upon the Routes of Espejo and Farfán to the Mines in the Sixteenth Century." *New Mexico Historical Review* 17 (January 1942): 21–36.

Beerman, Eric. "The Death of an Old Conquistador: New Light on Juan de Oñate." *New Mexico Historical Review* 54 (October 1979): 305–19.

Blakeslee, Donald J., and Jay C. Blaine. "The Jimmy Owens Site." In *The Coronado Expedition from the Distance of 460 Years*, ed. Richard Flint and Shirley Cushing Flint, 203–18. Albuquerque: University of New Mexico Press, 2003.

Blakeslee, Donald J., Richard Flint, and Jack T. Hughes. "Una Barranca Grande: Evidence and Discussion of Its Place in the Coronado Route." In *The Coronado Expedition to Tierra Nueva*, ed. Richard Flint and Shirley Flint, 165–76. Niwot: University Press of Colorado, 1997.

Bloom, Lansing B. "Oñate's Exoneration." *New Mexico Historical Review* 12 (April 1937): 175–92.

Bloom, Lansing B. "When Was Santa Fe Founded?" *New Mexico Historical Review* 4 (April 1929): 188–94.

Bolton, Herbert E. *Coronado, Knight of Pueblos and Plains.* New York and Albuquerque: Whittlesey House and University of New Mexico Press, 1949.

Bolton, Herbert E. "Father Escobar's Relation of the Oñate Expedition to California." *Catholic Historical Review* 5 (April 1919): 19–41.

Bolton, Herbert E., ed. *Spanish Exploration in the Southwest, 1542–1706*. New York: Barnes & Noble, 1946.

Brandon, William. *Quivira, Europeans in the Region of the Santa Fe Trail, 1540–1820*. Athens: Ohio University Press, 1990.

Brasher, Nugent. "The Chichilticale Camp of Francisco Vázquez de Coronado: The Search for the Red House." *New Mexico Historical Review* 82 (February 1, 2007): 433–68.

Brink, James Eastgate. "The Function of Myth in the Discovery of the New World." *Coronado and the Myth of Quivira*, ed. Dianna Everett, 11–17. Canyon, TX: Panhandle-Plains Historical Society, 1985.

Cannon, Cornelia James. *The Fight for the Pueblo: The Story of Oñate's Expedition and the Founding of Santa Fe, 1598–1609*. Boston: Houghton Mifflin Company, 1934.

Carvajal, Gaspar de. *The Discovery of America According to the Account of Friar Gaspar de Carvajal*. New York: American Geographical Society, 1934.

Chapman, Walker. *The Golden Dream: Seekers of El Dorado*. Indianapolis: Bobbs Merrill, 1967.

Chávez, Thomas E. *Quest for Quivira: Spanish Explorers of the Great Plains, 1540–1821*. Tucson: Southwest Parks and Monuments Association, 1992.

Chevalier, François. *Land and Society in Colonial Mexico*. Berkeley: University of California Press, 1992.

Chipman, Donald E. *Nuño de Guzmán and the Province of Pánuco in New Spain, 1518–1533*. Glendale, CA: Arthur H. Clark, 1967.

Chipman, Donald. "The Oñate-Moctezuma-Zaldivar Families of Northern New Spain." *New Mexico Historical Review* 52 (October 1977): 297–310.

Columbus, Christopher. *Journal of First Voyage to America*. New York: Albert and Charles Boni, 1924.

Cuebas, Juan de, trans. "The Muster Roll and Equipment of the Expedition of Francisco Vazquez de Coronado." *Bulletin No. XXX*, the William Clements Library, Ann Arbor, Michigan, 1939.

Day, A. Grove. *Coronado and the Discovery of the Southwest*. New York: Meredith Press, 1967.

Day, A. Grove. *Coronado's Quest: The Discovery of the Southwestern States*. Berkeley: University of California Press, 1940.

Day, A. Grove. "Gómara on the Coronado Expedition." *Southwestern Historical Quarterly* 43 (January 1940): 348–55.

Day, A. Grove. "Mota Padilla on the Coronado Expedition." *Hispanic American Historical Review* 20, no. 1 (February 1940): 88–110. http://dx.doi.org/10.2307/2507482.

Descola, Jean. *Les Conquistadors*. Paris: A. Fayard, 1954.

Donoghue, David. "Coronado, Oñate, and Quivira." *Mid-America* 18 (April 1936): 88–95.

Dunn, Oliver, and James E. Kelley Jr. *The Diario of Christopher Columbus's First Voyage to America, 1492–1493*, abstracted by Bartolomé de las Casas. Norman: University of Oklahoma Press, 1989.

Edwards, Mike. "Wonders and Whoppers." *Smithsonian Magazine* (July 2008): 82–88.

Everett, Dianna, ed. *Coronado and the Myth of Quivira*. Canyon, TX: Panhandle-Plains Historical Society, 1985.

Flint, Richard. *Great Cruelties Have Been Reported: The 1544 Investigation of the Coronado Expedition*. Dallas: Southern Methodist University, 2002.

Flint, Richard. *No Settlement, No Conquest: A History of the Coronado Expedition*. Albuquerque: University of New Mexico Press, 2008.

Flint, Richard. "Reconciling the Calendars of the Coronado Expedition, Tiguex to the Second Barranca, April and May 1541." In *The Coronado Expedition from the Distance of 460 Years*, ed. Richard Flint and Shirley Cushing Flint, 151–63. Albuquerque: University of New Mexico Press, 2003.

Flint, Richard. "What's Missing from This Picture? The *Alarde*, or Muster Roll, of the Coronado Expedition." In *The Coronado Expedition from the Distance of 460 Years*, ed. Richard Flint and Shirley Flint, 57–80. Albuquerque: University of New Mexico Press, 2003.

Flint, Richard, and Shirley Cushing Flint, eds. *The Coronado Expedition from the Distance of 460 Years*. Albuquerque: University of New Mexico Press, 2003.

Flint, Richard, and Shirley Cushing Flint, eds. *The Coronado Expedition to Tierra Nueva: the 1540–1542 Route Across the Southwest*. With an introduction by Carroll L. Riley and historiographical chapters by Joseph P. Sánchez. Niwot: University Press of Colorado, 1997.

Flint, Richard, and Shirley Cushing Flint, eds., trans., annots. *Documents of the Coronado Expedition, 1539–1542: They Were Not Familiar with His Majesty nor Did They Wish to Be His Subjects*. Dallas: Southern Methodist University Press, 2005.

Flint, Richard, and Shirley Cushing Flint. "New Vantages on the Coronado Expedition." In *The Coronado Expedition from the Distance of 460 Years*, ed. Richard Flint and Shirley Flint, 1–10. Albuquerque: University of New Mexico Press, 2003.

Flint, Shirley Cushing. "The Financing and Provisioning of the Coronado Expedition." In *The Coronado Expedition from the Distance of 460 Years*, ed. Richard Flint and Shirley Flint, 42–56. Albuquerque: University of New Mexico Press, 2003.

Forbes, Jack D. *Apache, Navajo, and Spaniard*. Norman: University of Oklahoma Press, 1960.

Forrest, Earle R. *Missions and Pueblos of the Old Southwest*. Chicago: The Rio Grande Press, 1965 [1929].

Gagné, Frank R. "Spanish Crossbow Boltheads of Sixteenth-Century North America: A Comparative Analysis." In *The Coronado Expedition from the Distance of 460 Years*, ed. Richard Flint and Shirley Flint, 240–52. Albuquerque: University of New Mexico Press, 2003.

Grinnell, George Bird. *The Fighting Cheyennes*. Norman: University of Oklahoma Press, 1956.

Hackett, Charles Wilson. *Historical Documents Relating to New Mexico, Nueva Vizcaya, and Approaches Thereto, to 1773*. 3 vols. Washington, DC: Carnegie Institution, 1923–1937.

Hammond, George P., ed. "The Conviction of Don Juan de Oñate, New Mexico's First Governor." In *New Spain and the Anglo-American West*, 1: 67–69. N.p., 1932.

Hammond, George P. *New Mexico in 1602*. Albuquerque: The Quivira Society, 1938.

Hammond, George P. "Oñate a Marauder?" *New Mexico Historical Review* 10 (October 1935): 249–70.

Hammond, George P., ed. *The Rediscovery of New Mexico: The Exploration of Chamuscado, Espejo, Castaño de Sosa, Morlete, and Leyva de Bonilla and Humaña*. Coronado Cuarto Centennial Publications, 1540–1940, vol. 3. Albuquerque: University of New Mexico Press, 1966.

Hammond, George P., and Edgar F. Goad. *The Adventure of Don Francisco Vásquez de Coronado*. Albuquerque: University of New Mexico Press, 1938.

Hammond, George P., and Agapito Rey, eds. *Don Juan de Oñate, Colonizer of New Mexico, 1595–1608*. Coronado Cuarto Centennial Publications, 1540–1940, vols. 5, 6. Albuquerque: University of New Mexico Press, 1953.

Hammond, George P., and Agapito Rey, eds. and trans. *Narratives of the Coronado Expedition, 1540–1542*. Albuquerque: University of New Mexico Press, 1940.

Hammond, George P., and Agapito Rey, eds. and trans. *Obregon's History of 16th Century Explorations in Western America entitled Chronicle, Commentary, or Relation of the Ancient and Modern Discoveries in New Spain and New Mexico, Mexico, 1584*. Los Angeles: Wetzel, 1928. MF Reel 396, No. 3977, Western Americana, Research Publications, 1975.

Hanke, Lewis. *The Spanish Struggle for Justice in the Conquest of America*. Philadelphia: University of Pennsylvania Press, 1949.

Hemming, John. *The Search for El Dorado*. New York: E. P. Dutton, 1978.

Hoig, Stan. *Beyond the Frontier: Exploring the Indian Country*. Norman: University of Oklahoma Press, 1998.

Hoig, Stan. *Indian Wars of the Southern Plains*. Norman: University of Oklahoma Press, 1993.

Hoig, Stan. *Jesse Chisholm, Ambassador of the Plains*. Niwot: University Press of Colorado, 1991.

Hoig, Stan. *The Sand Creek Massacre*. Norman: University of Oklahoma Press, 1961.

Hoig, Stan. *Tribal Wars of the Southern Plains*. Norman: University of Oklahoma Press, 1993.

Illustrated History of New Mexico. Chicago: Lewis, 1895.

Isley, Bliss. "The Grass Wigwam of Wichita." *Kansas Historical Quarterly* 2 (February 1933): 66–71.

Jaderborg, Elizabeth. *Why Lindsborg?* Lindsborg, KS: Lindsborg News-Record, 1976.

Jaramillo, Nash. *The Conquest of New Mexico, Don Juan de Oñate, 1595–1608*. Santa Fe, NM: La Villa Real Southwest, 1976.

Jones, Horace. *The Story of Early Rice County*. Lyons, KS: Lyon's Daily News Plant, 1959.

Jones, Horace. *Up from the Sod: The Life Story of a Kansas Prairie County*. Lyons, KS: Coronado Publishers, 1968.

Jones, Paul A. *Coronado and Quivira*. Lyons, KS: Lyons Publishing Company, 1937.

Jones, Paul A. *Quivira*. Wichita, KS: McCormick Armstrong Company, 1929.

Kansas Historical Collections 8: 152–68.

Kappler, Charles J., comp. and ed. *Indian Treaties*. New York: Interland, 1972.

Kiessel, John L. "To See Such Marvels with My Own Eyes: Spanish Exploration in the Western Borderlands." In *The Coronado Expedition from the Distance of 460 Years*, ed. Richard Flint and Shirley Flint, 11–19. Albuquerque: University of New Mexico Press, 2003.

Las Casas, Bartolomé de, *The Devastation of the Indies: A Brief Account*. Translated by Herma Briffault; introduction by Hans Magnus Enzenberger; dosier by Michel von Nieuwstadt. New York: A Continuum Book, Seabury, 1974.

Lees, William B. "Evidence for Early European Contact with the Wichita Indians in Kansas." Presented at the Conference on Historical and Underwater Archaeology Society for Historical Archaeology, Tucson, 1990. http://uwf.edu/wlees/SHA1990.pdf.

Lees, William B. "New Light on the 'Coronado Stone.'" *Kansas Anthropologist* 11 (1990): 28–30.

Leonard, Irving Albert. *Books of the Brave: Being an Account of Books and of Men in the Spanish Conquest and Settlement of the Sixteenth-Century New World*. Cambridge, MA: Harvard University Press, 1949.

Lewis, Anna. "La Harpe's First Expedition in Oklahoma, 1718–1719." *Chronicles of Oklahoma* 2 (December 1924): 331–49.

Lumis, Charles F. *The Spanish Pioneers*. Chicago: Rio Grande Press, 1893.

Meyer, Michael C., and William T. Sherman. *The Course of Mexican History*. New York: Oxford University Press, 1979.

Mooney, James. "Quivira and the Wichitas." *Harper's New Monthly Magazine* 49 (June 1899): 126–35.

Mota Padilla, Matías Angel de la. *Historia de la Conquista de la Provincia de la Nueva-Galicía*. México: Impr. del Gobierno á cargode J. M. Sandoval, 1870.

Myers, Harry C. "The Mystery of Coronado's Route from the Pecos River to the Llano Estacado." In *The Coronado Expedition from the Distance of 460 Years*, ed. Richard Flint and Shirley Flint, 140–50. Albuquerque: University of New Mexico Press, 2003.

Newcomb, William Wilmon, and Thomas Nolan Campbell. "Southern Plains Ethnohistory: A Re-examination of the Escanjaques, Ahijados, and Cuitoas." In *Pathways to Plains Prehistory: Anthropological Perspectives of Plains Natives and Their Pasts*, ed. Don G. Wyckoff and Jack L. Hoffman. Oklahoma Anthropological Society Memoir 3. Duncan, OK: Cross Timbers, 1982.

Obregón, Baltasar de. *Historia de los descubrimientos antiguos y modernos de la Nueva España*. Mexico: Departamento editorial de las Sria, de edvcacion pvblica, 1924. MF Reel 396, No. 3976, Western Americana, Research Publications, 1975.

Peñalosa, Don Diego de. *Su Descubrimento del Reino de Quivira*. Madrid: Imprinta y Fundición de Manuel Tello, 1822.

Peterson, John M. "The Coronado Stone from Oak Mills, Kansas." *Kansas Anthropologist* 10 (1989): 1–10.

Poole, Stafford. *Juan de Ovando Governing the Spanish Empire in the Reign of Philip II*. Norman: University of Oklahoma Press, 2004.

Powell, Philip Wayne. *Soldiers, Indians and Silver*. Berkeley: University of California Press, 1952.

Price, H. Byron. "Bolton, Coronado, and the Texas Panhandle." In *Coronado and the Myth of Quivira*, ed. Diana Everett. Canyon, TX: Panhandle-Plains Historical Society, 1985.

Reinhartz, Dennis, and Gerald D. Saxon, eds. *The Mapping of the Entradas into the Greater Southwest*. Norman: University of Oklahoma Press, 1998.

Restall, Matthew. *Seven Myths of the Spanish Conquest*. New York: Oxford University Press, 2003.

Rey, Agapito. "Cristóbal de Oñate." *New Mexico Historical Review* 26 (July 1951): 197–203.

Reynolds, John D., and William B. Lees. *The Archeological Heritage of Kansas: A Synopsis of the Kansas Preservation Plan*. Ed. Marilyn Holt, Robert J. Hoard, and Virginia Wulfkuhle. Topeka: Cultural Resources Division, Kansas State Historical Society, 2004.

Richardson, Rupert Norval. *The Comanche Barrier to the South Plains Settlement*. Glendale, CA: Arthur H. Clark Co., 1933.

Richey, W. E. "Early Spanish Exploration and Indian Implements." *Kansas Historical Collections* 8 (1904): 152–68.

Root, George A. "Map Showing Coronado's Route to Quivira in the Year 1541." *Kansas Historical Collections* 8 (1904).

Sánchez, Joseph P. "A Historiography of the Route of the Expedition of Francisco Vázquez de Coronado: Rio de Cicúye to Quivira." In *The Coronado Expedition to Tierra Nueva*, ed. Richard Flint and Shirley Flint, 25–29. Niwot: University Press of Colorado, 1997.

Sauer, Carl Ortwin. *Sixteenth-Century North America*. Berkeley: University of California Press, 1971.

Schroeder, Albert H. "A Re-Analysis of the Routes of Coronado and Oñate into the Plains in 1541 and 1601." *Plains Anthropologist* 7 (February 1972): 2–23.

Sibley, Major John. "Extracts from the Diary of Major Sibley." *Chronicles of Oklahoma* 5 (June 1927).

Simmons, Marc. *The Last Conquistador: Juan de Oñate and the Settling of the Far Southwest*. Norman: University of Oklahoma Press, 1991.

Snow, David H. *New Mexico's First Colonists*. Albuquerque: Hispanic Genealogical Research Center of New Mexico, 1998.

Thomas, Alfred Barnaby. *Coronado: Spanish Exploration Northeast of New Mexico, 1696–1723*. Norman: University of Oklahoma Press, 1935.

Thomas, Hugh. *Rivers of Gold: The Rise of the Spanish Empire, from Columbus to Magellan*. New York: Random House, 2003.

Tichy, Marjorie F. "New Mexico's First Capital." *New Mexico Historical Review* 21 (April 1946): 140–44.

Udall, Stewart L. *Majestic Journey: Coronado's Inland Empire*. Photos by Jerry Jaska. Santa Fe: Museum of New Mexico Press, 1987.

Vehick, Susan C. "Oñate's Expedition to the Southern Plains." *Plains Anthropologist* 31 (1986): 13–33.

Villagrá, Gaspar Pérez de. *A History of New Mexico*, vol. 4. Trans. Gilberto Espinosa; introduction and notes by F. W. Hodge. Los Angeles: Quivira Society, 1933.

Weber, David J. *Bárbaros, Spaniards and Their Savages in the Age of Enlightenment*. New Haven, CT: Yale University Press, 005.

Weber, David J. "Reflections on Coronado and the Myth of Quivira." In *Coronado and the Myth of Quivira*, ed. Diana Everett, 1–17. Canyon, TX: Panhandle-Plains Historical Society, 1985.

Weber, David J. *The Spanish Frontier in North America*. New Haven, CT: Yale University Press, 1992.

Wellman, Paul I. *Glory, God, and Gold: A Narrative History of the Southwest*. New York: Doubleday, 1954.

Whipple, Amiel W. "Reports of Explorations and Surveys to Ascertain the Most Practicable and Economical Route for a Railroad from the Mississippi River to the Pacific Ocean." 3rd Cong. 2 sess. 1854–1855, *Sen. Exec. Doc. 78*.

Williams, Samuel C. "Tatham's Characters among the North American Indians." *Tennessee Historical Magazine* 7 (October 1921): 154–79.

Winship, George Parker. *The Coronado Expedition, 1540–1542*. Chicago: The Rio Grande Press, 1964.

Winship, George Parker. *The Journey of Coronado, 1540–1542, from the City of Mexico to the Grand Canon of the Colorado and the Buffalo Plains of Texas, Kansas, and Nebraska*. New York: Greenwood Press, 1969.

Index

Page numbers in italics indicate illustrations.